Shakespeare Jungle Fever

T0385575

Shakespeare Jungle Fever

Shakespeare Jungle Fever

National-Imperial
Re-Visions of Race, Rape,
and Sacrifice

Arthur L. Little Jr.

Stanford University Press
Stanford, California

Stanford University Press
Stanford, California

© 2000 by the Board of Trustees of the
Leland Stanford Junior University

Printed in the United States of America
On acid-free, archival-quality paper
Library of Congress Cataloging-in-Publication Data

Little, Arthur L.
   Shakespeare jungle fever : national-imperial re-visions of race, rape, and sacrifice /
Arthur L. Little, Jr.
      p.   cm.
   Includes bibliographical references and index.
   ISBN 0-8047-4024-0 (cloth : alk. paper) : ISBN 0-8047-4633-8 (pbk. alk. paper)
      1. Shakespeare, William, 1564–1616—Views on race.   2. Shakespeare, William,
   1564–1616—Characters—Blacks.   3. Shakespeare, William, 1564–1616. Antony and
   Cleopatra.   4. Shakespeare, William, 1564–1616. Titus Andronicus.   5. Shakespeare,
   Willliam, 1564–1616. Othello.   6. Imperialism in literature.   7. Nationalism in
   literature.   8. Sacrifice in literature.   9. Blacks in literature.   10. Race in
   literature.   11. Rape in literature.   I. Title.
   PR3069.R33 L58   2000
   822.3′3—dc21   00-056357

Designed by Janet Wood
Typeset by TypeWorks in 10.5/13 Bembo

Original Printing 2000

Last figure below indicates year of this printing:
09   08   07   06   05   04   03   02

To the loving memory of my grandmother

Contents

Illustrations

Acknowledgments

Looking back over the tremendous amount of gains, losses, and growth that have accompanied this project, I find the composing of this page perhaps the most daunting task of all. Who in my ambit hasn't been a part of this book? This question signifies much more than a rhetorical gesture. Nonetheless, there are a few persons who have made an indelible imprint on this book and whose visions and generosity of spirit have made possible the conquering of whatever silences this book has been able to accomplish or at least adumbrate. I wish to thank first and foremost those early modern scholars who have encouraged me to say *something* and whose own intellectual ventures have given credence to my own: Janet Adelman, Gary Cestaro, Heather Dubrow, Lowell Gallagher, Kim F. Hall, Margo Hendricks, Stephanie Jed (whom I have never met), David Kastan, Harry Keyishian, Ania Loomba, Michael Neill, Martin Orkin, Avraham Oz, Patricia Parker (a very special thanks), Jyotsna Singh, Bruce Smith (also a very special thanks), and Nancy Vickers. Because this is my first book, I also add to this list Lawrence Evans, Marjorie Garber, and Barbara Johnson, whose intellectual care, guidance, and example first allowed me to discover myself as a serious reader.

I also owe a great deal of gratitude to those UCLA colleagues who have supported me and who have provided through their own work examples of what it means to have visions that dig deep and are responsibly democratic: Dan G. Calder (in memory), King-Kok Cheung, Helen Deutsch, Lowell Gallagher (again), V. A. Kolve, Chris Littleton, Anne Mellor, Harriet Mullen, Felicity Nussbaum, Judith Rosen, Karen Rowe, Jenny Sharpe, Valerie Smith, and Richard Yarborough. I would be much remiss if I did not thank those who have contributed to many of the labor-intensive aspects of this book and have worked with me, as this project moved through various stages (not without a certain amount of panic on my part). I extend to them a most wholehearted thanks: Daphne Brooks, Dwight McBride, Connie Razza,

J. C. Stirm, Julian Yates, and especially Norman W. Jones, whose friendship and assistance during the final months of this project have proven nothing short of a gift. I would be extremely grateful if any of them were to think that my work has in any way contributed to the promising careers they are in the process of making for themselves. I would also like to thank the department's Joan Aberbach, Jeanette Gilkison, and department librarian Lynda Tolly for their invaluable assistance and their even more invaluable conversations.

In addition to these, I wish to thank those who have given me a chance to test this project through publishing and speaking opportunities and also those who listened and responded. I would like to thank first and foremost Stanford University Press, especially Helen Tartar, who has shown enthusiasm and encouragement from the moment my initial proposal landed on her desk, and Mary Severance, Matt Stevens, and Joe Abbott for truly transforming the manuscript into a book. I also wish to express my gratitude to the *Shakespeare Quarterly* for publishing my work on *Othello* and for giving me a chance to further think through that work here; and Michael Bristol, who invited me to the Shakespeare Division of the 1995 Modern Language Association to formulate for myself, really for the first time, many of the ideas at the basis of this book's introduction. Here I wish once again to acknowledge Martin Orkin, who invited me to participate in the 1996 Post-Colonial Shakespeare conference in Johannesburg, where in addition to the very rewarding experience of the conference, I watched South Africans outside the conference move me from one primary identity location to another. At one moment I was simply black, at another American (almost white even with my dark skin), and at still another a black American or black South African. That experience has made possible my grasping, my getting, some of the groundwork of this project.

I must of course also thank UCLA for its generous and continuous funding during the writing and completion of this project, as well as the community at the Bread Loaf School of English in New Mexico for its very meaningful contribution to my intellectual, professional, and personal life during a very important final phase of this book's completion.

This book owes its existence especially to those who have kept me centered and who have listened to me even when I had stopped knowing how to listen to myself or to them. They are my moral family: Norman Aguon, Gary Cestaro (again), and James Hardeman—and, of course, there are my San Francisco cohorts. I wish to thank, too, some other truly invaluable friends: Erica Hagen, Michelle Harding, and Liz Harvey.

And because I'm submitting this book as I look out over the beautiful city of Los Angeles—yes, I did say "beautiful"—I should thank my former therapist, Scott Sherman, who worked miracles; my first realtor, Bob Zay, who worked magic; and my car, my little Miata that makes getting around L.A. a truly transporting experience.

To all these and many more, thanks for all their invaluable contributions to this project. Its fissures and oversights remain my own. I do hope whatever investments readers make will prove the investments of those named here to have been worthy ones.

A. L. J.

A RAPIST IS ALWAYS TO BE A STRANGER

TO BE LEGITIMATE

SOMEONE YOU NEVER SAW

A MAN WIT OBVIOUS PROBLEMS

—Ntozake Shange, *For Colored Girls Who Have*
Considered Suicide When the Rainbow Is Enuf

Introduction: Altars of Alterity

Every culture is a wound culture, repeatedly and simultaneously manifesting itself through a highly stage-managed process of wounding and healing. I wish to locate this double act of wounding (cutting)—of cultural fissure—and healing (signing)—of cultural cohesion—in the racial, gender, and sexual discourses and productions of early modern England's national-imperial culture. (Cutting and signing share an etymological history.) Focusing on Shakespeare's three main plays featuring black bodies—*Titus Andronicus*, *Othello*, and *Antony and Cleopatra*—this book maps, geographically and otherwise, how gender, race, and sexuality shape early modern England's national-imperial vision, its wound culture, and how that vision, in turn, shapes England's notion of gender, race, and sexuality. It is worth noting from the outset that "race" in the early modern era, perhaps this book's most conspicuous topic, works less as a stable identity category than as a semiotic field, one as infinitely varying as the cultural discourses constituting what we have come to identify as the early modern era or the Renaissance. Even in a single text, depictions of race can draw from mythology, the Bible, the voices of classical authorities, the humors, the physiognomy, and one's cultural location and habits. None of this, however, should be taken to argue that race in Shakespeare's day is less stable or real, that is, any less a discursive device, than it is in our own cultural moment. We come up short, I would argue, when we fantasize that our contemporary constructions of race—through our well-honed technologies of racism—offer us proof of a real racial ontology more truly embedded in individual subjects than arbitrarily embodied in and across an infinite number of our cultural discourses. Race, then and now, is not a discrete subject, and I follow through my discussion of it by focusing most particularly on the narrative and theatrical spaces and entanglements it shares with rape and sacrifice, a triad I offer as one of early modern England's most imaginative models for defining and negotiating its national and imperial self. In paradigmatic form, the previously chaste white woman kills herself in the name of national and imperial purity after she has been tainted by a rape that violates her not only sexually but racially. Her self-sacrifice, sustaining the fiction that it is simply *taking back* her virginity and whiteness, also manages to imbue that same virginity and whiteness with national and imperial definition, significance, and purpose.

I began this project as a study of gender and sacrifice in early modern drama, beginning with such tenets as the one of Leonard Tennenhouse, who has shown that "Jacobean tragedies offer up their scenes of excessive punishment as if mutilating the female could somehow correct political corruption. The female in question may be completely innocent, her torture gratuitous, yet in play after play she demands her own death or else claims responsibility for her murder."[1] What better evidence of patriarchy's health than its prized female subject's getting rid of herself so that the patriarchy may have its enclosure, its symbolic self? Of course not all women in tragedy die, but almost without notice a discussion of women in tragedy slips into a discussion of women in sacrifice. Woman seems to be the natural subject of early modern tragedy. As if to make this point emphatic and unequivocal, almost all translations of Greek tragedy (into Latin or into a vernacular language) printed before 1560 focus on female sacrifice: Euripides' *Hecuba* (1506), *Iphigenia in Aulis* (1506), *Alcestis* (1554), and *Phoenissae* (1560) and Sophocles' *Antigone* (1533).[2] These translations would have left the distinct impression that in origin and essence there is a natural bond among tragedy, sacrifice, and woman.[3] Nonetheless, it is important to point out that tragedy's ascription of a natural place to women in the sacrificial narrative is not particular to classical or early modern drama but is part of a broader ideological construction of woman. Woman doesn't just have a prominent place in sacrificial narratives but is herself read as naturally sacrificeable.

Rene Girard's study of the sacred and profane, one of my initial exploratory texts for this book, is relatively silent about and dismissive of the cultural and sacrificial importance of women. Still he admits, "Like the animal and the infant, but to a lesser degree, the woman qualifies for sacrificial status by reason of her weakness and relatively marginal social status. That is why she can be viewed as a quasi-sacred figure, both desired and disdained, alternately elevated and abused."[4] Girard understates the case. Patriarchal culture *strives* for a logical bond between sacrifice and gender: however much the woman wishes to die, her death consecrates and gives iconicity to the laws, customs, and beliefs of the men around her. As Mieke Bal has argued in her reading of the Book of Judges, the daughter as sacrificial victim is seen by its hero (and has been seen by its patristic readers) as a natural victim as opposed to an accidental one. We are supposed to believe that the sacrificial woman's death is as natural as the patriarchy for which she dies. Nancy Jay may seem to overstate the issue when she insists throughout her cross-cultural work on religion, sacrifice, and paternity that "a study of sacrifices focusing on gender leads to a new understanding: sacrifice as remedy for having been born a woman."[5]

However so, on more than a few occasions women would be read not only as a natural part of some sacrificial narrative but as having sacrifice inscribed in their very bodies. Susan Griffin has argued in her study of twentieth-century pornography: "For above all, pornography is ritual. It is an enacted drama which is laden with meaning, which imparts a vision of the world. The altar for the ritual is the woman's body. And the ritual which is carried out on this altar is the desecration of flesh. Here, what is sacred within the body is degraded."[6] Woman's body as natural ritualistic object has a long history, especially the woman's bleeding body: it serves as a vital instrument in shaping the woman's and the community's health. As the classicist Helen King argues in her essay on Hippocratic texts, "Although sacrificial blood may appear to be an obvious empirical source of analogies with *any* bleeding from the human body, it is highly significant that comparisons [between these medical texts and sacrificial ones] are restricted to the gynecological treatises"; she concludes, "Health for a woman is to bleed like a sacrificial victim."[7] In an early modern example that draws, like so many early modern texts, on a more classical model for representing and understanding the female body and self, Helkiah Crooke (1616) describes menstruation "as an excrement vomited out by Nature offended with an vnprofitable burden. . . . This blood therefore is laudable and Alimentary, and as Hippocrates writeth in his first Booke *de morbis mulierum*, floweth out red like the bloud of a sacrifice."[8] Woman bleeds and becomes chastised again, although she is seen as having to expiate her "bad" blood repeatedly as her chasteness wanes. Sacrifice is a "corrective." And, as Nicole Loraux argues throughout *Tragic Ways of Killing a Woman*, tragedy (and the culture that informs it) demands the woman's blood and, in fact, will do whatever it must to bring the woman to her moment of bleeding. Following through on this idea throughout this study, and most explicitly in the first chapter, I am particularly interested in stressing how a play's sacrificial demands, its carefully plotted "sacrificial preparations" (to lift a phrase from Girard), seem almost to happen by chance; indeed, it is almost as if these preparations situate the narrative's masterful sacrificial drive as an afterthought. Sacrifice enters cultural play very much as a trick, as a hoax.[9] And rape, sometimes even in-distinguishable from sacrifice, acts most expediently as a way of getting us to sacrifice.[10] Sacrifice corrects rape.

And just as rape so frequently tends the narrative of sacrifice, the issue of race finds itself frequently coupled with the issue of rape, which, even when committed by someone from within the community, is often ascribed to a racial Other—a stranger, someone from outside the community. In early modern drama the black man frequently stands in this place, at least the *symbolic* place, of the rapist. Western imperialism has forged and continues to forge a natural racial and gender bond between the black male and rape. Griffin articulates this argument in words far from anachronistic to the cultural and racial dramas of the late sixteenth and early seventeenth centuries: "At the heart of the racist imagination we discover a pornographic fantasy: the specter of miscegenation. The image of a dark man raping a fair woman embodies all that the racist fears. This fantasy preoccupies his mind."[11] Concurring with this view, Ania Loomba has argued that racist common sense knows that black men and women are innately animalistic, and sexism has long promoted rape as "an inevitable expression of frustrated male desire."[12] Since at least the sixteenth century, the West (especially England and later the United States) has fairly consistently pictured the black man as a rapacious menace to the sexual sanctity of white women.[13] (The racism here is enfolded in a sexism that suspects that the white woman subconsciously wishes to be raped.) I will argue in Chapter 1 that the rape and sacrifice of Lucrece are inscribed in a racial narrative that should not escape critical attention, especially because it works, that is, *produces cultural meaning*, even if we leave it undiscussed and untheorized.

The classical Lucrece, a template for representing and narratively situating the early modern raped woman, participates in an "ethnographic allegory," the scrutinizing and allegorizing of Other cultures as a way of writing about one's own; in addition to being a writing about cultural Others, ethnography is also, as James Clifford defines it, an "inscription or textualization [that] enacts a redemptive Western allegory."[14] Simply put, ethnographic allegory represents the culture of an Other as a way of redeeming or chastising the self. When the Other is imported into Western mythologies, it functions primarily as a way of *visualizing* the chastity of Western imperialism. Furthermore, this visualizing through the racial Other or through the racializing of the Other is one of the mainstays of the chastising visions of Lucrece's Rome. Lucrece becomes Rome's well-guarded, humanist *topos*.[15] She is Rome's humanist allegory, its allegorization of itself. As Clifford says,

"Culturalist and humanist allegories stand behind the controlled fictions of difference and similitude that we call ethnographic accounts."[16] And what is the sacrificial narrative if it is not a "controlled fiction," indeed, if it is not a narrative about such control, a control made especially emphatic through the visualizing and chastising of the racial Other?

Race presumably does what it needs to do in these narratives, even though it escapes any sustained analytical attention. When I write in this book about the idea of miscegenational rape, I mean to insist on a critical foregrounding of the textualizing, and, indeed, the fleshy—fetishistic, scopic, imaginary[17]—incorporation of blackness into the white rape narrative. What is it/he doing there? To be sure, interracialness works in such narratives as a device, an ideology, rather than as an actual occurrence. The black male enables and completes the white rape narrative even as he gets trapped at its borders and disappears from it. Early modern dramatic rape narratives frequently and prominently feature black men. In fact, the vast majority of black men appearing in early modern tragedy find themselves directly or indirectly implicated in a rape scene, making it all the more likely that an early modern audience would see—would have a history of seeing—black men as natural rapists.[18] As I argue in Chapter 2, this history includes Othello, whose relationship to Desdemona cannot be separated from a discourse of rape. Images of Othello's violent and violable relationship to Desdemona are seen or implied throughout the play and, especially, in many later sensational pictorial representations. More complicated still is the fracturing of a rape discourse in and across the gender and racial narratives of both Antony and Cleopatra.

New historicism, the most influential of recent strategies for reading early modern texts and cultures, has freed us from many of the rules of convention, made chic the defamiliarizing of the familiar and vice versa; it has expanded our sense of the kinds of texts that we may ponder in our efforts to elucidate or at least engage early modern culture. Some theorists, notwithstanding their own agendas, may invite that new historicism has done this to a fault. New historicism has put some in the habit of thinking that the more archivally or otherwise remote the nonliterary text, the more profound and authentic the critical exercise. Nonetheless, new historicism, making use as well of a number of other poststructuralist methods, has been instrumental in bringing to the early modern table previously marginalized or effectively nonexistent voices and bodies. Although studies of gender, race, sexuality, and nonaristocratic classes have benefited from this move, I join those early modern scholars who have criticized new historicism for its more stubborn undertheorization of race and racial discourse in early modern England.[19] To the extent that new historicism has attended to these issues, it has been more interested in the New World than in Africa or Ireland, two of the main geographies of this study. None of this is to single out new historicism as *the* culprit or even as *a* culprit. New historicism, literary analysis in general, and, above all here, race are subjects and issues far too complex and unwieldy for any easy responses.

Admittedly, new historicism has played a significant role for almost two full decades in shaping our early modern critical discourse and has rightly insisted that we are only capable of reading from our own vantage. In practice, however, new historicism has offered a barrage of cogent and provocative narratives about how early modern culture is discrete, how it is not us, not our culture. Such a specious position, shot through with a conservative (and virginal) aesthetics and politics, however much unstated or unexamined, does finally rest on untenable and not-too-easily dismissible grounds (as theoretically attractive to some as they may be). As Neil L. Whitehead has put it,

> [A]n unrealizable historicist ambition . . . drives this type of analysis—that is the illusion that the past and others might be understood "in their own terms." The simple fallacy of logic that this illusion involves is shown by the fact that if historicism indeed achieved the aim of understanding a past culture "in its own terms," the result of course would be totally unintelligible, except to that culture and at that moment. Nothing would have been explained, and rather than the past being made "present" it would have been rendered *impenetrable*.[20]

It is as though there remains still locked in the assumptions of new historicism a Renaissance culture, a *virginal* Renaissance culture (a Renaissance or Shakespeare of transcendent signification), outside the fictions through which we engage it. But, using Stephanie H. Jed as one of my models, I propose that we take a more cautious view of the cultures we study and of ourselves, of our own chastising habits. It is only symptomatic of the fact that dominant ideologies dominate our critical discussions that the burden of proof for those who wish to locate Other subjects in the early modern era, say, racial or sexual ones, is not shared by those who wish not to see such subjects in or even around early modern studies and culture. To whatever extent blacks or gays as we know them may or may not have existed in the Renaissance, such theoretical erasures leave in place an assumed and affective whiteness and straightness (however much our culture often equates these latter identities with a deracialized or desexualized subject position). Perhaps our efforts to frame discourses of race around issues of racial *difference* do little more than validate further our long-held convictions that "they" create and have race and "we" do not, then or now. But I insist here and throughout this study that we do not, nor do we know how, to speak outside such constitutive "realities." There comes a profound and disconcerting disconnection between us now and them then, even though our culture at the same time prides itself on the argument that they, those early moderns (those Renaissance folk and especially Shakespeare), pervade our society, ourselves, with the cadences and forms that give "cultural capital" its perceived beauty and grace, indeed, its very foundation.[21] Our resistance especially to reading early modern race speaks less, I think, to the early modern era's capitalization on race than to our refusal to make significant our place, our white place, in the tribal and historical trajectories of race and racism.

Some parts of my argument rely on what Samuel Johnson has so infamously called the Shakespeare quibble, a kind of ineffective and mere ostentatious playing with words. New historicism, in its overly determined and self-proclaimed "turn away from the formal, decontextualized analysis that dominate[d] new criticism,"[22] has effectively shied away from offering extended close readings of its literary examples. Especially from the point of view of studying race and racial alterity in early modern culture, this move has been to its profound detriment. Like Patricia Parker's most recent book (1996), my study resists "the trivialization of language and wordplay as secondary or accessory, in the recognition that this very reduction to the ornamental was itself a historical process, one frequently associated with the relegating of women and other marginal subjects to the status of the secondary or accessory."[23] More often than not, Others assume a place in dominant discourse less through any kind of positivist model and more through associative thinking—and dissociative place. Although I do at times flaunt my propensity to play, to accessorize, I do so always with the conviction that these readings are begged and made available by the material and ideological realities of early modern culture. These readings are finally only as suggestive as they may be found resonant with the realities of early modern culture. The anthropologist James Clifford's argument remains a mantra for this study: "But whereas the free play of readings may in theory be infinite, there are, at any historical moment, a limited range of canonical and emergent allegories available to the competent reader (the reader whose interpretation will be deemed plausible by a specific community). These structures of meaning are historically bounded and coercive. There is, in practice, no 'free play.'"[24] Or, coming at this from a different place, Louis Althusser claims that there are no "free" subjects:"The category of the subject is only constitutive of all ideology insofar as all ideology has the function (which defines it) of 'constituting' concrete individuals as subjects."[25] Such points of view undergird this project.

I imagine this book as an ongoing conversation, however implicit, with Jed, Parker, and Hall, who are part of an emerging cultural philology that seeks to understand the way culture (in all its ideological messiness) plays with the aesthetics of language. Rather than fantasizing about Shakespeare's texts as sites and sights of infinite play, I am insisting that I remain open to the polymorphous possibilities, the crossings and contradictions, made available by a whole complex of early modern (as well as contemporary) discourses. To quibble is also in part to "let go" of the text, to accept that moments of textual comprehension and absorption are never as predictable or schematically fixed as we or those early moderns may have desired. The real stuff of culture may be gotten at by massaging the ongoing interchange between seemingly more objective, public, and empirical signifying processes and those more insular and metonymically driven—"what you know you know"—quibblings. In the end efforts to get at Shakespeare's quibbling are less about toying with language than about trying to grasp some of the particulars of how Shakespeare pressed words or critiqued his culture's pressing of words into a more full cultural service.

The real work of culture happens not only when we read myopically or even between the lines but when we employ such knowledge to assist us in reading the line's very linearity, what fashions it, anchors it, as logic, as cultural articulation—as silencing, chastising device. I have grown to distrust greatly the critical and theoretical positioning and posturing of cultural critiques that seem to work as a matter of course against such close textual scrutiny, not only because such scrutiny is vital to any real effort to understand the creation and uses of whiteness, one of our culture's most sustained and pervasive fictions, but because without such an interrogation there is only an abject me—a *not*-white me, a *not*-straight me. Whether academics are willing to admit as much, our books *are* always personal.

This study adopts as one of its guides Jed's *Chaste Thinking: The Rape of Lucretia and the Birth of Humanism* (1989), not only because of its obvious subject matter but because of its aim at least to adumbrate what she sees as "chaste thinking," that is, a too-easy cutting off of one's own discourses from the complexities and messiness of the discourses one seeks to investigate and clarify.[26] In reading her own first encounter with a manuscript copy of Coluccio Salutati's *Declamatio Lucretiae* as a way of understanding the birth of humanism (in fifteenth-century Florence), Jed brilliantly manipulates the legend of Lucrece (whose story I take up in the first chapter of this book) to interrogate that space between the putatively private rape of Lucrece by Tarquin and the public uses and abuses of her consequent putatively self-determined sacrifice. What comes most to disturb Jed's feminist philology is the fact that Lucrece's rape, the violation of Lucrece's body, seems to have only a feeble, if not a remote, connection finally to the uses to which her body is put.

Jed's sacrificial-rape paradigm has an extensive history: as Nancy Sorkin Rabinowitz argues in reading Euripides' sacrificial Iphigenia, "The glorification of Iphigenia takes her as a fetishized commodity, exalting her self-sacrifice by ignoring the attendant condition of its production: that is, the exchange of women."[27] (Lucrece's narrative seems to work as a later and more visual and expedient consolidation of Helen's and Iphigenia's stories—Helen's abduction leading to Iphigenia's sacrifice.) Or, evoking a present-day example, we ignore the relationship between acts of rape perpetrated by men and our masculinist training of boys to be boys, our acculturating them to be men. Although Lucrece and rape remain important topics here, I wish to broaden Jed's notion of chaste thinking and to posit as one of the working premises of this book that the *institutional* and *official* foundations of culture are essentially chastised ones. In other words, culture (so defined) becomes legible when read with, through, and against those moments it chooses to forget. If culture names itself through anything, it is through the moment it obliterates, the histories it erases, the institutional hands it does not admit or does not know it owns, the bodies it pretends not to see or doesn't. Those "isms" with which we are so familiar in our contemporary culture are no less a part of such chastising strategies. The pathologies that come to shape our individual selves, our individual bodies, depend on culture's forgetting its role, what often amounts to its founding contributions to the same.

With my eyes toward a textual and metatextual reading of Shakespeare and early modern England, I study here how Shakespeare alters this self-fashioning narrative through his critique of early modern England's growing attention to issues of alterity, that is, of racial Others, and how early modern drama and culture deploy race in rendering aesthetic—classical and poetic—its national and imperial ambitions and visions. In arguing for Shakespeare's interrogation of early modern practices of chaste thinking, this book tries to resist any neat either-or oppositions, for example, whether blackness *really* signals a religious difference instead of a racial one. I would argue that such discretions belong more to our present-day chaste critical practices than to the narrative and ideological density of early modern culture. This book, however, does have its particular investments, and its four main chapters do insist on foregrounding and reading the cultural and racial significance of white female, black male, white male, and black female bodies, respectively. And by evoking a range of literary and nonliterary texts showing the deeply embedded and not-so-deeply embedded racial materials of Shakespeare and his England, this study betrays something more substantial than a "trace of alterity" coursing through early modern England's imperial fantasies and policies. I propose as my book's most committed premise that Shakespeare positions himself as an "alternative" reader of his culture's reading of alterity;[28] that identifying Shakespeare as an "alternative" reader does not automatically or even necessarily give us a Shakespeare who speaks from the margins or for the marginalized; and that against a very long tradition of discrete and conservative arrogations of Shakespeare as a certain kind of cultural capital, Shakespeare emerges as one of early modern England's most careful and provocative readers of alterity, of early modern England's evocations and chastisements of it. However successfully Western cultures may have fixated on Shakespeare as "the quintessence of Englishness and [as] a measure of humanity itself"[29] (a kind of imperial, universal, and nonethnocentric Englishness and humanity), such readings do not often square well with the unpredictable erotics and the altered spaces—the danger zones, the "jungle" preoccupations, of Shakespeare's plays.

Among a host of other reasons for doing this book, I write it as a response to what I have increasingly chosen (or what has increasingly chosen me) as my "first" professional encounter with Shakespeare studies: my being made an unprepared witness to a professor claiming to a group of eager and culturally starved undergraduates that Shakespeare is not about gays and lesbians (and their sexual issues), blacks, women, or the downtrodden. Shakespeare is not about "them." No, he professed, Shakespeare is and has always been about "all humanity." In the anti-Other legislation being quickly amassed in the United States and especially here in California, this Shakespeare is indeed "*our* contemporary." But given my own identification as an African American and as a gay man, it is perhaps only in my own best interest that I choose to engage a different Shakespeare. Part of what I want to press in this study is the significance of doing Shakespeare and early modern criticism as an African American. The realities of our cultural moment, of our American cultural history, predict the impossibility that an African-American Shakespeare scholar interested in pursuing critical questions of race could do so without his or her racial identity being suspiciously or at least cautiously present as part of the reading experience. I may be understood to bring or accused of bringing "a special attitude" to Shakespeare, not unlike what the black gay writer James Baldwin purportedly brought to Shakespeare. Shakespeare, said Baldwin, was not *his* history, at least not in any hegemonic sense, but neither was his history strictly that of Africa. In Baldwin's words, he "had certainly been unfitted for the jungle or the tribe [and] . . . would have to appropriate these white centuries . . . would have to make them" his.[30] Baldwin's *appropriate*, I would argue, is no casual word. It means not only to take without permission but to "take *to* oneself as one's own property or for one's own use" (*OED*, emphasis in dictionary). Appropriation stands against abjection. In such a culturally laden context the act of appropriating, of taking, is saturated with a sense of violence, as is made emphatic by the term *taking* in "taking" the likeness, the representation, of Queen Elizabeth I, in the 1563 edict designed to prohibit the same. In Baldwin *appropriate* connotes violence, a sense of rape—the black man as stealing the white body and corpus.[31] Such is the reality of blackness, especially of the black man, caught in the productions of racism. In this instance, Baldwin rhetorically performs his entrapment between objectification, his being made into a mere "thing of darkness," and his presumed agency in a very long discursive tradition of the black man as black rapist, not that these categories are really mutually exclusive. And because dominant discourse will so often have it that the black man is either one or the other, realpolitik justifies its violent objectification of him by reading it as a preemptive strike against what it sees as his pathological preoccupation with the rape of whiteness. Having said all this, I insist too that nothing here should suggest that African-American scholars and readers read Shakespeare or the early modern period in the same way or from the same intellectual position or with the same critical and theoretical objectives. And even though this book is marked with traces of the personal, it is finally less a testimonial than a book thoroughly committed to the materials and methods of literary and cultural studies. The Shakespeare of this book speaks to the very complexity of cultural positioning and posturing—culture's margins and centers, its rationales and contradictions, and sometimes its radical instabilities. Without over essentializing or aggrandizing my own identity or my place in Shakespeare and early modern studies, my conspicuous selves have given me a sense of critical and intellectual urgency not found in the current dominant strands of American Shakespeare and early modern criticism, which—with new historicism at its vanguard—has pushed for an early modern world more idiosyncratic and arcane than comprehensible.[32]

Ultimately, I think, we as readers learn to discern (or at least approximate) how we read *through* the personal not in a space simply chastised, that is, made free, of it. Beyond the particulars of my own person, Anglo-American criticism could stand, I think, to name and theorize still further the ways the coupling of race and gender lends formative material to the complexities of Shakespeare's literary, theatrical, and cultural vision. Much exciting recent work has been done, most notably the studies of Ania Loomba, Margo Hendricks and Patricia Parker, and Kim F. Hall.[33] Part of what I seek to do here is to continue their work, as well as to take to the other side of the Atlantic the project of Toni Morrison, who has cogently shown and troubled how "the lavish exploration of [American] literature" by some of the academy's foremost critics "manages *not* to see meaning in the thunderous, theatrical presence of black surrogacy—an informing, stabilizing and disturbing element—in the literature they do study."[34] Without disregarding the different historical and cultural specificities, one could say as much for the study of English literature, the study of Shakespeare not excepted. Although this book is most explicitly concerned with only three of Shakespeare's plays, a number of other works from Shakespeare's oeuvre would benefit from more sustained attention to their perhaps more limited but not inconsequential or insignificant use of a racialized aesthetic: *Love's Labor's Lost, The Taming of the Shrew, A Midsummer Night's Dream, The Merchant of Venice, Much Ado About Nothing, The Winter's Tale, The Tempest,* and *The Rape of Lucrece.* Some of these will receive passing attention in this study. In shaping my own agenda, I am invested here in early modern England's real and imaginary uses of race and the ways blackness, the black body in particular, provides a dense and extensive web of material for Shakespeare's aesthetic and cultural critique. As the leading words of my main chapter titles attest—*picturing, witnessing, framing, (re)posing*—I am especially interested in *seeing* the body in its visibility, as well as in all its invisibility.

The stage serves as more than a convenient site for my inquiry. Such historically and culturally minded critics as Jonathan Dollimore (1984), Catherine Belsey (1985), Leonard Tennenhouse (1986), Linda Woodbridge and Edward Berry (1992), and Gail Kern Paster (1993), just to name a few, have argued for the stage as a place to display the body, work out the body's uses—the deployment of its possibilities in the self-fashioning agendas of early modern England. The stage increasingly pressures the body, visualizes it, into full cultural service, pulling it more explicitly into conversation with other cultural texts—chronicles, travel narratives, writings on nationalism and imperialism, medical texts, pictures, and so on. Nonetheless, in poring over the narratively white or not-so-white bodies of Lavinia and Antony and the black or not-so-black bodies of Othello and Cleopatra, I insist on close and extensive readings of these characters' respective plays, not so much to dress this book in formalist clothing but to stress just how discursively complex, nuanced and "sophisticated" (that is, capable of sustaining a place as part of the culture's elliptic- and ironic-speak) is early modern England's constructions and manipulations of race.

From my discussion of the word *jungle* here to its implicit presence throughout this book, I intend the word to signal my consciousness, my own personal performative act—my own "camp" gesture (see Chapter 4)—as a gay African-American scholar reading and writing about Shakespeare. Beyond the self-referential, its titular use intends to keep in serious play the incongruous relationship between "Shakespeare" as iconic placeholder for a non-ethnographic universalism and the very present issue of alterity as located, read, and dramatized in many of Shakespeare's works. To keep in the foreground the supposed disparity, the critical chaste thinking, between a more classically based aesthetic criticism and a more putative sociological application of the literary text. Too, the evocation of the jungle here may seem a bit of an anachronism, a linguistic and ideological stretch, since the word *jungle*—Hindi *jangal*, from the Sanskrit *jangala*—doesn't popularly enter the English language until the eighteenth century, a linguistic consequence of British imperial relations with India, I assume. Beyond its more etymological reference to a desert or a wasteland, the word has come to mean a densely overgrown land. The word's connotations, however, are the raison d'etre here: the jungle as "a dense confused mass," "a bewildering complex or maze," "a place or milieu characterized by ruthless competition or struggle for survival," and, my favorite, "a place where hoboes camp."[35] The term's almost natural propensity toward hybrid forms is no less a part of its attraction, its rhetorical density and messiness, including such terms as *jungle -bear, -bunny, -cock, -fowl* (and a host of other animals), *jungle gym, jungle lodge, jungle market, jungle nail, jungle wood, concrete jungle, blackboard jungle*, and, my favorite, Froot Loops with *Jungleberry* Swirls.

   Among these terms is of course the eponym of this project, jungle fever, which means, according to the *Oxford English Dictionary*, "a form of remittent fever caused by the miasma [that is, poisonous particles floating in and polluting the atmosphere] of a jungle." In popular parlance, the expression refers (with disapprobation of course) to the "disease" of having become sexually curious about (and involved with) someone from a race other than one's own, recalling those old black-and-white B-movies in which some white damsel-in-distress finds herself displaced in a jungle from which she must be rescued before the dark or indigenous people euphemistically sacrifice (that is, rape) her. (King Kong is the noblest and most poetic cultural sublimation of these terrifying personages.) I grew up with these movies. But I first "got it" when I learned this term and its reference to intimate interracial relations from Spike Lee's film *Jungle Fever* (1991), which opens with a Stevie Wonder song in which we learn that some unnamed black he has "gone white girl crazy" and some unnamed white she has "gone black boy hazy." The term refers most deprecatingly and popularly to whites who become sexually and emotionally involved with black bodies. Morrison makes use of this reading in her study of the signifying place of blacks in American literature when she argues that blacks played a role that extended far beyond them as "objects of an occasional bout of jungle fever."[36] I may be accused of simply exploiting a term, since referencing Shakespeare, a black novelist and intellectual, and a contemporary black film in the same paragraph does seem to have an almost-too-self-conscious amount of "raciness" (all definitions and puns intended) for a subject I am at least imagining we would like to think through in terms more formal and recognizably early modern. However so, I evoke the expression "jungle fever" for its many significances, its conjurations of pollution, wild terrain, national and imperial competitiveness, incivility, animalism, and racialized boundary crossing, sacrificing, and rape. All these are the subject of this study.

To say nothing yet about Shakespeare's England, Shakespeare's Others *are* jungle folk. And it is perhaps a recognizable point but one that I wish still to underscore and pause over that especially in Shakespeare's most obvious plays and displays of racial Others—including along with the three main texts of this study *The Merchant of Venice* and *The Tempest*—black and blackened bodies come most frequently into signification through bouts of jungle fever, especially ones accompanied with threats or acts of violence, especially of rape. What all this adds up to is that understanding the workings of Shakespeare's bodies of alterity means being critically careful not to over essentialize those bodies or critique them as having embodiments or bodies separate from the cultural pollution attending their interracial interactions. The jungle and its fever—looming large in the English imagination—will literally and figuratively get mapped out in and across all the wild and potentially wild places of Rome, Venice, Egypt, Africa, and Ireland, these places variously figuring as the jungle of a nationally and imperially anxious England.

I wish to turn my attention here to a series of quotes, two from Shakespeare's day and two from our own, not only to demonstrate the kinds of rhetorical and cultural maneuvers and tensions involved in England's national and imperial self-fashioning but some of the professional and intellectual challenges that come to bear on one's attempt to carry out a critique of Renaissance alterity. Caught up as they all are in our habits and practices of reading, these issues are not unrelated. A more extended inquiry, especially into the former, lies ahead as one of the main preoccupations of this book. The brief discussion that follows here is intended partly to clarify further my evocation of a jungle fever, and I wish it ultimately to point less to an interracial sexual dynamic per se than to the cultural and multicultural anxieties giving rise to these scenes as sites and sights through which England as nation and empire chooses to name and visualize itself.

To begin, the juxtaposing of a quote from Richard Hakluyt's very popular *Principall Navigations, Voyages, and Discoveries of the English Nation* (1589)— "the Prose Epic of the modern English nation"[37]—and a quote from Elizabeth's latest edict to "de-jungle-fy" her England of Africans, to deport them, points to England's desire to invent itself at once in terms both global and insular. Jungle fever would become only one of the most horrifying and intimate scenarios in which England could imagine keeping a proper national and imperial balance between itself and its outsiders. Whereas Elizabeth focuses her national-imperial vision inward, toward definitive cultural boundaries, Hakluyt pushes for a more expansive and encompassing construction of England: "So in this most famous and peerlesse governement of her most excellent Majesty, her subjects through the speciall assistance, and blessing of God, in searching the most opposite corners and quarters of the world, and to speake plainly, in compassing the vaste globe of the earth more then once, have excelled all the nations and people of the earth."[38]

It should surprise us less than it does the historian Kenneth R. Andrews that "when Hakluyt wrote these words . . . Englishmen had indeed made some considerable contributions to European exploration of the world, but they had hardly done enough to justify that boast."[39] But Hakluyt's words are more than a boast, and they are certainly not "true," at least not in any strict historical sense. They are, however, a performatively necessary national and imperial fiction, what I discuss in Chapter 3 as a realpolitik nostalgia.

England "excels" not so much because it has circumnavigated the globe but because at least in its mind—in its newfound rhetoric and picture of itself, that is—it has been predestined to lay claim to the globe. In his call to action Hakluyt pre-scribes, boasts only in the sense that he presumes to prewrite the truth, the foregone conclusion of England as imperial. To talk like an empire is to be an empire. (Perhaps this should be the other way around.) In a single enthusiastic gesture Hakluyt argues not only that England has surpassed all others by traveling more than any other nation or people but that its searching, its ethnographic studying of the globe, has revealed England to be far superior to "all the nations and people of the earth."

If Hakluyt's England has discovered itself as having the "most famous and peerlesse governement" and, by extension, as being the most civilized or the least jungle-like nation and people, then Elizabeth's edict pushes to protect England from what it argues has become the jungle in its midst:

> Whereas the Queen's majesty, tendering the good and welfare of her own natural subjects, greatly distressed in these hard times of dearth, is highly discontented to understand the great number of Negroes and blackamoors which (as she is informed) are carried into this realm since the troubles between her highness and the King of Spain; who are fostered and powered here, to the great annoyance of her own liege people that which co[vet?] [*sic*] the relief which these people consume, as also for that the most of them are infidels having no understanding of Christ or his Gospel: hath given a special commandment that the said kind of people shall be with all speed avoided and discharged out of this her majesty's realms; and to that end and purpose hath appointed Casper van Senden, merchant of Lubeck, for their speedy transportation.[40]

Taken together, Elizabeth's edict and Hakluyt's boast typify the quandary faced by England's national-imperial vision: how to be part of the world and yet separate from it. Elizabeth's edict is no simple protest: the jungle (with hints of a fever) encroaches on her rhetoric, displacing her "natural subjects," those whom she argues elsewhere are "natural to this clime." This emerging jungle has perverted her England from the nurturing "tendering" of her people into its fostering of Africans. As Edmund Spenser argues in *A View of the State of Ireland* (1598 [1633]), a text I discuss in Chapter 3, fostering produces hybrid bodies. ("Tendering" also evokes a sense of Elizabeth's being able to "hold" on to her subjects, versus what are presumably the more unruly Africans.) Moreover, Negroes and Blackamoors have a way of rapidly reproducing themselves as their "great number" works easily into England's "great" distress and annoyance. Even though Elizabeth doesn't argue for the Africans as the explicit cause of England's "dearth," they do clearly contribute to the severity of what she identifies as England's ecological imbalance. And as if turning back on them their "consuming" of England (and the English), Elizabeth in a bit of scatological maneuvering pushes for England to "avoid and discharge" them. In the end Elizabeth's desire to have these persons quickly deported from England works with and against the urgency found in Hakluyt's text for England's imperial consumption of the globe. The jungle problematizes even as it lends shape to England's national and imperial self-fashioning.

But England's chastising desires carry over into our own chastising consumption of England, especially here of "the Renaissance"—the Renaissance as an embodiment, an enclosure, of the classical (not only in a Greek or Roman sense but in a Bakhtinian sense as well). In this formulation an early modern jungle exists as Other to the Renaissance. The Renaissance and Shakespeare, as icons of chastity, get it from both sides, so to speak—from those who wish to claim a more secure intellectual and institutional place for multicultural studies and from those who wish to protect the canonical status of much Renaissance literature.

Using a language not unlike that of Hakluyt and Elizabeth, Bate lays out for us the Renaissance ideal:

> The truth is that, with the fading of the Renaissance ideal through progressive stages of specialism, leading to intellectual emptiness, we are left with a potentially suicidal movement among "leaders of the profession," while, at the same time, the profession sprawls, without its old center, in helpless disarray.
>
> One quickly cited example is the professional organization, the Modern Language Association. . . . A glance at its thick program for its last meeting shows a massive increase and fragmentation into more than 500 categories! I cite a few examples: . . . "The Trickster Figure in Chicano and Black Literature," or (astonishingly) "The Absent Father in Fact, Metaphor, and Metaphysics in the Middle Generation of American Poets." . . . Naturally, the progressive trivialization of topics has made these meetings a laughingstock in the national press.[41]

Bate offers his own imperial truth, his own realpolitik nostalgia as he witnesses the "fragmentation" of a vast professional Renaissance empire, overrun by the "helpless disarray" and the "thick[ness]" of an emerging intellectual and professional jungle. And, like Hakluyt and Elizabeth, he draws on an affective rhetoric of nation—the scopic nation in the case of Hakluyt, the heavily rhetorically laden "natural" one in Elizabeth: Bate's "naturally . . . national press" (however oxymoronic) evokes or longs for a nation that is both natural and scopic. The Modern Language Association (MLA) "sprawls," like Los Angeles, perhaps. And, like L.A., in its mythic identity (as opposed to its real one), multiculturalism and (again) the "thick"—those jungle bodies—overtake it. Specialisms—like special rights—reign in place of a universal nonethnocentric humanism. And, again like L.A., this time the real one, the MLA betrays itself—indeed, the profession—by showing itself to be both progressive and trivial (even though here one term already seems to include the other). And perhaps like an Antony who must pause because he can't hold his gaze on the ripped and torn body of Julius Caesar—Bate can only "quickly . . . glance" at the mangled profession—the minstrelsy, the "laughingstock." The jungle has inverted the Renaissance: instead of excreting black bodies, it "empt[ies]" itself of intellectual matter. And in "the fading of the Renaissance ideal," what I would call "the fading of *a* Renaissance ideal," a kind of brutish and cult-like "suicidal movement" claims the place of a more classical, emblematic, and culturally sanctioned self-sacrificial act.

It may seem to some unfair that I use Bate's quote to illustrate what he effectively sees as the jungle infiltrating the MLA in particular and most alarmingly the professional study of literature more generally. After all, Bate wrote these words nearly twenty years ago. From the stance of Bate's argument, however, the MLA has only gotten worse; and, more important, the Renaissance (one of many disciplinary periods) remains still discrete—a more serious and more substantial—entity. And even our very influential new historicism (one of our main critical events since Bate's note of intellectual and professional Armageddon)—advocating a critical democratization and interdisciplinarity of the early modern—has not been so interested in or capable of interrogating the virginal ascriptions of the Renaissance in early modern times or contemporary ones and has been even less interested in exploring the function of race (and racism) in the fashioning of early modern subject- and nation-hood or in the shaping of our reading of the same.[42] However much the early modern is read and played with, the iconic Renaissance remains an arcane entity still. There really is no central place in Renaissance studies from which to see altars of alterity, that is, sites where early modern processes of racializing, racial othering, and finally racial exorcisings inform the aesthetic suppositions of the Renaissance. By being unable or by refusing to imagine such a place, I argue that we ignore one of the Renaissance's most nuanced and revealing aesthetic devices. (My use of the phrase "early modern" [as opposed to "Renaissance"] through most of this study, is not meant to suggest that this project belongs to the domain of the one and not the other.)

Brian Vickers would most likely agree with Bate. Writing some ten years later and with a broader cultural lens than Bate, Vickers's nemesis is from abroad and his understanding of Shakespeare's (or the Renaissance's) place is less sure and more fraught. For Vickers, the problem springs not exclusively but first and foremost from the "critical upheaval emerging from Paris" in the late 1960s, and his sense that Shakespeare *should* keep some kind of commanding place in the midst of all these contemporary methodologies and issues:

> At one level, of course, it is right and proper that Shakespeare criticism should, albeit belatedly, reflect the general current of ideas. Considering that specialists in Shakespearian [*sic*] and Elizabethan drama have all too regularly constituted their subject as a self-contained enclave, cut off even from broader studies of Renaissance literature and history, any *outside influence* might be thought an improvement. But unfortunately the *fragmentation* and consolidation into individual and rival groups has meant that critics have adopted the theory, method, and terminology of whichever group has won their allegiance. . . . Instead of a critical model opening up a field to fresh enquiry, these approaches effectively close it down, recasting it *in their own images*. . . . Each group has a specific ideology, a self-serving aim. . . . Shakespeare's plays, for so long the primary focus of the critic's and scholar's attention, are now secondary, *subordinated* to the imperialism and self-advancement of the particular group.[43]

For Vickers, the universal-imperial rights of Shakespeare have gone amok in the jungle of would-be critical imperialists, who seem to indulge in a kind of blasphemous reverse discrimination (if they have any discrimination at all). My point here is not to badger Vickers but to question, to make more salient, the *cultural territory and capital* on which such arguments are built and stake their claims.

It would not totally surprise me were the peruser of this introduction to think my readings have taken liberties with Hakluyt, Elizabeth, Bate, and Vickers. I would like the reader to think otherwise. The admittedly by-no-means ludic playing with their language tries to exemplify and get at least some of the ways cultural discourses effectively and affectively cross and absorb or resonate with each other. I suspect it is needless to say that intentionality (theirs or mine) is not an issue. Notwithstanding this, the Renaissance has been made to work as a kind of cultural shorthand, a corrective force to intellectual and political correctness. And the conversation continues. Henry Louis Gates Jr., for example, uses the Bate quote to open his edited study of race and writing: in this instance the quote is used to show how Ethnic Studies is perceived, almost without comment, in opposition to the more rarefied and intellectual critical weightiness of Renaissance Studies. Tzvetan Todorov, in an essay included in Gates's text, will ask in response to the question of whether only blacks can critique black authors, "Should we judge Renaissance texts using nothing but Renaissance concepts, and medieval texts by medieval concepts?"[44] However much we may applaud the multicultural casting of Shakespeare in recent years, Shakespeare remains even more than the Renaissance itself a cultural shorthand. Dinesh D'Souza, in his book *The End of Racism: Principles for a Multicultural Society* (1995), poses the question in the form of a chapter title: "Is Eurocentrism a Racist Concept?" He then follows the earnest pretenses of his interrogative main title with a subtitle whose declarative posture means to deliver an assaulting and satiric "no": "The Search for an African Shakespeare." Although D'Souza's underlying tropic question—Is there an African Shakespeare?—should be taken seriously as trope, the question itself is serious only in the way it *plays, performs.* Such questions, as Eve Kosofsky Sedgwick has argued, are

> revealing only, however, for those of us for whom relations within and among canons are active relations of thought. From the keepers of a dead canon we hear a rhetorical question—that is to say, a question posed with the arrogant intent or maintaining ignorance. . . . Has there been, ask the defenders of a monocultural curriculum, not intending to stay for an answer, has there ever yet been a Socrates of the Orient, an African-American Proust, a female Shakespeare?[45]

And although such questions as D'Souza's intend to delineate and alienate an African difference, they perform first and foremost the link between a constructed white culture and an even more constructed white identity, laying claim in the process, too, to Shakespeare as both universal and white.[46] The fact that there is *literally* no African Shakespeare supports and justifies, for D'Souza, a politics protecting and guaranteeing a European and white superiority. Presumably coming from a different political place, although no less telling, is a recent television commercial for Sprite: A group of African-American men are playing basketball on an outdoor urban neighborhood court. When a director yells, "Cut," the viewer learns that this is no scene of black male authenticity. Not only do the athletes all turn out to be rather peevish when "not acting," but one of them deconstructs the identity politics even further: "I played Shakespeare at Cambridge." Shakespeare functions here as much a marker of whiteness—not a marker the commercial really wishes to explore—as much as basketball a marker of blackness. What these moments (a handful of many) point to is a tropic and disciplinary white Renaissance and white Shakespeare that are themselves in need of interrogation. Without fantasizing that I speak for all Other readers (and I would like to think of the Other reader as a complexly constructed position more so than an essentialized one), the very matrices of dominant cultural realities predispose the Other reader almost "naturally" to hear (to perceive) the ways dominant-culture speak refracts. That is, the sense that he or she willingly or contentedly submits his or her identity (or identities) to this fragmentation, this seemingly civilizing ritual of *sparagmos* (see Chapter 1). The Other offers himself or herself to a dominant culture's illusive and elusive finished and whole—that is, classical—subjecthood.

I am aware that this direction—this potentially over scrutinizing of dominant-culture speak, of its quibbling—could *possibly* lead the reader to ascribe to this project what Sedgwick would, I imagine, discern as the genre of paranoid criticism, a "hermeneutic of suspicion."[47] My own professional, personal, and intellectual grounding has taught me that a little paranoia never hurts. If Renaissance and/or early modern readers find the exaggerations—the paranoia—of this study to direct us toward a more sobering corrective of the chastising and corrective strategies at work on Shakespeare's stage and in Shakespeare's nationally and imperially anxious England, then (from the point of view of its author) this book has more than accomplished its aim or justified its publication.

In the end, of course, the lofty or not-so-lofty goals of a book must be realized through its exploration of particulars. I have set this book up as an analysis namely of the bodies of Lavinia, Othello, Antony, and Cleopatra, respectively. Chapter 1, "Picturing the Hand of White Women," examines the narrative and cultural spaces shared by the rape of and the hand of white women, the hand being iconographically the authorizing agent of the woman's stealing back her whiteness and virginity. This chapter troubles too the narrative causality between rape and sacrifice. Which one produces the other? Comparing the classical aesthetic representation of Lucrece to the horrific stage presence of Lavinia in *Titus Andronicus*, this chapter interprets the figuring of the latter as a rereading of the former. Lavinia explodes the vision of corporeal re-closure that the dominant appropriation of Lucrece fails in the end to secure. In reading Lucrece and Lavinia, this chapter foregrounds the racial narrative in depictions of Lucrece and in Shakespeare's dramatization of Lavinia. By further attending to the racializing informing early modern rape narratives, this chapter takes a significant part of its impetus from the fact that in many plays the most catastrophic incident is the rape of a white woman and the most infamous character is a black man, who always somehow fails to be the actual rapist or finds himself at least a person or two removed from it. How the erstwhile or newly found virginal white woman disappears from the symbolic picture of the nation and empire she transforms is one of the questions driving this chapter.

Chapter 2, "Witnessing Whiteness," looks at the efficacy of drawing a comparison between early modern England and early modern Venice, at least England's perception of Venice as it is depicted in *Othello*. After establishing the Venetian city-state as a multicultural rendering of London and after considering what may be termed England's far more embryonic multiculturalism, a multiculturalism no more "successful" than England's realization of its imperial ambitions, I ask whether we have fallen short in our critical attention to the play by conceptually failing to move it beyond our own surprise of an African presence in early modern England. England, to be sure, was not overrun with thousands or even hundreds of Africans, despite Elizabeth's annoyance with their number. But what do we do with our critical rubrics, especially those we bring to *Othello*, when it becomes clear (as it has) that a black body was not an anomaly in early modern England? What would happen to *Othello* were we to consider it a drama taking place not at a critical juncture of London's inclusion of black bodies but of its exclusion, its deportation of them? (Our particular cultural moment here in the United States could prove a critically enlightening one.) From here the chapter traces how scenes of traumatic sexual encounters—the consequence of a raging jungle fever—inform Othello's blackness; the chapter then goes on to consider Othello's implication in the tradition of the black rapist. Othello as first black rapist of a white woman in early modern drama? Turning more explicitly to the play's metadramatic and metatheatrical possibilities (and to such possibilities in other black characters on the early modern stage), I ask what theoretical space can we or should we assign at least in our critical understanding of the play to the white actor who plays/played Othello, the black rapist, murderer, and sacrificer. I finally read Othello as a black character being made a forced witness to the performative nonperformativity of whiteness.

In Chapter 3, "Framing Antony's Anatomy," the first of two chapters on

Antony and Cleopatra, I use the term *framing* to connote both the imaging of Antony (his relationship to the picturing of Roman masculinity) and his being framed, his being set up, by Caesar to portray Antony as falling short of Rome's idealized image of its corporeal self. This chapter begins by reminding its readers not only of England's fashioning itself through what it sees as its emulation of Rome, its perfecting of Rome's imperial designs, but its adoption of a white Roman anatomy as well. Attending to the importance of Rome as a site of both *virtus* (masculinity) and *civitas* (civility), I argue that England represents the ideal male as possessing a body that is masculine to be sure but characterized by a tempered masculinity, one that does not stretch beyond the bounds of civil decorum, that is, into the realm of the jungle. Giving careful study of the nostalgic imaging of Antony by Caesar's Rome, I show how this imaging locates Antony as fluctuating unpredictably between an excessive masculinity and an embarrassingly pathetic effeminacy. Antony is either too much the brutish man or too much the emasculated man of the boudoir. It almost doesn't seem to matter which. How the gendering of Antony by himself and others frames his sacrifice is one of the concerns of this chapter. More than this, I examine how Rome figures Antony as an impostor, how Rome, Shakespeare's Rome, distinguishes between the physical whiteness of Antony and the more important signifying and ideological whiteness of Caesar.

To make sense of Antony's ideological whiteness, I turn to what I argue is a rich reservoir for reading Antony's whiteness, that is, most pointedly, England's shaping and visualizing itself against what it sees as its own impostors, the Gaelic Irish. Several centuries of anti-Irish writing and sentiment had made it clear that in their comportment and cultural habits the Irish were very much akin to the African. They too were jungle folk. One way England justified its colonial agenda in Ireland was by claiming that it would mercifully save the Irish the way Rome had once conquered and saved, that is, civilized, the English. The English would sacrifice the Irishman, the brute, in order to save the man. By offering an analysis of Spenser's *A View*, the culminating and most sophisticated text of early modern England's racializing of the Irish, I argue that Caesar—especially through his exploitative troping of the cannibalistic and the starving Irishman—in effect stresses a racial difference between himself and Antony. And more specifically than this, Caesar seems adamant in fashioning himself in the voice and guise of the New English, the putatively racially and culturally pure English, as opposed to the Old English (those English persons long established in Ireland and whom the New English argued were racially suspect, a mixed people of

Irish, Spanish, and African constitution). I suggest that Shakespeare's linking of Caesar to the New English, to those advocating the starving of the Irish, ultimately compromises and complicates what Caesar fashions as the classical aesthetic of his new masculine and civilized imperial Rome.

Chapter 4, "(Re)Posing with Cleopatra," draws on a rather dense repository of meanings, moving in and around the term *(re)posing*. The word works rather nicely to lay out what I argue is Cleopatra's polymorphous perversity, her *polyglossia*. Her place in Shakespeare's play moves from her posing to her posturing: from her posing (as in sitting to have one's picture taken) to her reposing, sexually stretched out in her barge; from her posing to her reposing, her repositioning of herself in response to a Western positioning of her; from sexual positioning to her sexual posturing, that is, her indulgence in the "preposterous" discourse of transvestism and sodomy. At once Cleopatra speaks a language, utilizes a grammar, organized around land and organized around sex. Beginning with a study of Cleopatra's racial fluidity and the fact that Shakespeare imagines his Cleopatra as black, this chapter stresses the importance nevertheless of keeping in mind that whether racialized as white or black Cleopatra, from the days of Augustan propaganda through today, sports a body of hybridity. Whether white or black Cleopatra finds herself the object of racial passing. Shakespeare's Cleopatra, one of the playwright's most radical theatrical and metatheatrical creations, uses her sacrificial death to reposition the positioning of her in Roman narrative, particularly the fixing of her in Enobarbus's pornographic and ethnographic fantasies. Her hyperperformative response to Rome's functionally invisible performativity works finally to critique the latter's condemnatory picturing and poeticizing of not only Cleopatra but Egypt and Africa. The staging of her highly theatricalized death reigns as one of Shakespeare's most unpredictable cultural and erotic scenes. Her self-slaughter unravels, or at least makes profoundly messy, the efficacy of sacrifice and the signifying weight of alterity. Perhaps England is already more of a jungle than it recognizes. In addition to thinking about Cleopatra in the context of the racial fluidity of black women in early modern drama—on several occasions they sacrifice themselves and become white—this chapter emphasizes Cleopatra's polymorphous perversity by arguing that she appropriates and challenges a mix of representational selves, offering herself not only as a legendary and dark Cleopatra but as a white boy actor, the Virgin Mary, and Queen Elizabeth. All this argues finally that Shakespeare's Cleopatra offers an alternative reading of her position, her being positioned, invitingly stretched out, in the Western imaginary.

ONE

Picturing the Hand of White Women

According to the closing lines of the second quarto, the tribulations in *Titus Andronicus* begin with Aaron:

> See justice done on Aron that damn'd Moore,
> From whom our heavy haps had their beginning:
> Then afterwards, to Order well the State,
> That like Events may ne're it Ruinate.[1]

These lines do not appear in the main text of our contemporary editions of Shakespeare's play, but I want to read them *back* into the play to examine the signifying and significant place they ascribe to Aaron, especially in Lavinia's rape, the most ruinating and consequential deed in this particular rendition of Shakespeare's Roman state. I want to ponder for a moment whether the absence of these lines in our contemporary editions gives us an Aaron who is less a product of Roman textuality than of our own cultural assumptions: without these lines we are, perhaps, less prepared to read the fictions circulating in Shakespeare's Rome and more prone to accept quietly an unproblematically villainous Aaron. The argument I put forward in this chapter suggests that Shakespeare's Aaron steals the show, the picture, making him the primary actor in Lavinia's rape and in her father's (that is, Rome's) and England's sacrificial stealing back of her chaste or virginal body.[2] In the end this chapter foregrounds the working ideological narrative in this and many other early modern texts, especially dramatic ones, in which staging the black rapist and the raped white sacrificial woman becomes an expedient and conspicuous way for England to prove and picture its national and imperial character.

A good place to get a first look at Aaron is in Henry Peacham's peculiar brown-ink drawing (figure 1), his reading of *Titus Andronicus*, done on one page of a folded folio sheet, containing below it some transcribed text from

1. Drawing by Henry Peacham from *Titus Andronicus*, c. 1595. Marquess of Bath, Longleat House.

the play, including especially Tamora's plea for the life of her son Alarbus (1.1.104–20) and Aaron's braggadocio about his many crimes (5.1.125–44); written vertically just on the other side of the fold is "Henrye Peachams Hande—1595." This presumed signature text makes a particularly enticing addition to a play that has so much to do with hands and signature texts. And, of course, hands are important iconographic objects in Peacham's drawing, where the openness of Titus's hands contrasts sharply with Tamora's pleading ones and the tied ones of her sons. What remains especially curious in this drawing is Aaron, who at once completes and challenges the symmetry: his facing left complements and provides the closure for the Roman figures facing right, yet he stands in a different plane from the three Goths, breaking the balance that sets them in opposition to the three Romans.

In short, even as Aaron stands out in the drawing, he remains marginalized. Aaron's black hand firmly grasps and holds up his sword as he boasts (judging from the transcribed text) about how he orchestrated Lavinia's rape. Peacham's drawing is most explicitly about the iconography of the hand, and Aaron's hands are the most conspicuous ones, not only in their brownness, their blackness, but in their triumph: Titus extends his open right hand, displaying the hand he will himself cut off. Tamora raises her supplicating hands, hands that will ultimately prove ineffective. Only Aaron's hands, gripping the penetrating and mutilating object of rape, will remain effectively in place by the end of the play. If (as I am suggesting and will argue more explicitly later) Aaron emerges as the black rapist here and in Shakespeare's play, then where is Peacham's Lavinia, who has the most constitutive body and hands in Shakespeare's play? What does it mean to see or not see Lavinia, whose body we literally do not see but whose body is everywhere written into these cut-off, ineffectual, and rapacious hands? This chapter explores the representation of Lavinia, not her depiction (or lack thereof) in Peacham's drawing but in Shakespeare's play, and I am especially interested in the relationship between the Lavinia body raped by the Goth and African outsiders and the Lavinia body sacrificed by her father.

By attending to the ongoing interplay between rape and sacrifice I wish to read her with and against the narrative and visual representation of Lucrece, who, I argue, is Shakespeare's most iconographic "source" for Lavinia. In fact, Lavinia functions in this chapter as an elaborate example of the picturings of Lucrece circulating in a number of early modern texts and points the way to how such a figure comes to forge and reify a national and imperial identity by laying claim through her death to both whiteness and virginity.

Before turning to Lucrece and then Lavinia I would like further to spell out the relationship between rape and sacrifice because only by understanding the relationship Rome forges between rape and sacrifice do we have a context for appreciating and deciphering Rome's self-fashioning gesture of castigation, of picturing (and writing) the ideological and cultural difference between them. Although Mieke Bal has argued convincingly, with reference especially to Lucrece, that "rape is *like* self-murder . . . because rape *leads* to self-murder,"[3] it would be misleading to take too literally Bal's structural causality. Not without their classical Roman antecedents perhaps,[4] some early moderns were able to imagine if not actually advocate a normative link between rape and death. William Roper's biography of Thomas More (1626), for example, recalls the classical story of the offending virgin:

> An Emperour that had ordained a lawe that whosoeuer comitted a certaine
> offence (which I nowe remember not) excepte it were a virgine, should
> suffer the paynes of death, such a reuerens had he to virginity. Nowe so it
> happened that the first comitter [of that offence] was indeed a virgine,
> whereof themperour hearinge was in no small perplexity, as he that by
> some example fayne wold haue had that lawe to haue ben put in execution.
> Whereuppon when his councell had sate long, solembly debatinge this case,
> sodenly arose there vpp one of his councell, a good playne man, among
> them, and said: "Why make you so much adoe, my lordes, about so small a
> matter? Let her first be defloured, and then after may she be devoured."[5]

The jingoistic erasure here of any ideological or cultural difference between *defloured* and *devoured* replays itself in early modern dramatic texts in less jingoistic fashion but in no less succinct and definitive terms. In Beaumont and Fletcher's *The Tragedy of Valentinian* (1610–14), for example, a play thoroughly invested in the link between rape and sacrifice, the emperor Valentinian says to Lucina, whom he has just raped, "And your daring husband / Shall know h'as kept an offring from the Empire, / Too holy for his Altars" (3.1).[6] When her husband, Maximus, enters, he finds the raped Lucina alone and reads in her look what has transpired. He reasons that "we are too base and dirty to preserve thee" and without hesitation tells her to go outlive her rape if she dares. She responds as quickly, "I dare not" (3.1). This is, of course, the expected response: as Maximus argues, were she to choose life,

> When they read, she liv'd,
> Must they not ask how often she was ravish'd,
> And make a doubt she lov'd that more than Wedlock?
> Therefore she must not live. (3.1)

And, after her death, he admonishes, "Did she not dye to tell ye / She was a ravish'd woman!" (3.3). Without the woman's self-slaughter there is no rape. Maximus's reasoning may be put a little differently: was she not raped in order to provide the man in her life with ocular and definitive proof of her virtue? And even in more succinct fashion is Cyril Tourneur's *The Revenger's Tragedy* (1607), in which Lord Antonio draws back a curtain, as though showing a picture, to reveal the body of his wife, who has poisoned herself after having been raped: "Violent rape / Has played a glorious act: behold, my lords, / A sight that strikes man out of me" (1.4.3–5).[7] This is the only time the on- or offstage audience sees Antonio's wife; she appears in the play at one and the same time as raped and sacrificed. And although we may assume that actual early modern women did not see such a foregone link between rape and sacrifice, we do know that as late as 1631, in the much publicized trial of the earl of Castlehaven, who was found guilty and executed for assisting in the rape of his own second wife and his son's twelve-year-old wife (mother and daughter) by the earl's servants, the raped woman, the countess of Castlehaven testified, as a protestation of her innocence perhaps, that she "would have killed herself afterwards with a knife, but that hee tooke it from her."[8] The real-life example aside, rape does not necessarily take place or get pictured before death: it appears at one and the same time or, as in the classical examples, the imminence of death becomes the impetus for rape.

Stripping and Scripting for Death; or, The Arts of Lucrece

Lucrece is the most seen and emblematic of sacrificially raped women. She enters signification through the sacrificial visualization of herself. As William Painter writes, she becomes seen through her "wound, which gushed out with aboundance of bloude."[9] Her body gets laid out for Romans to gawk at and becomes one of the most frequently represented figures in early modern art. We may apply to other Lucreces, as well as to other raped women, Coppélia Kahn's claim that more than any other Shakespeare character Lucrece is inscribed in and controlled by a scopic economy.[10] And Catherine R. Stimpson does not exaggerate when she writes with an eye to the pornographic that "like murder, rape also pictures a helpless victim, powerless vulnerability. Because rape's violence is sexual, an audience watching it can live out voyeuristic fantasies."[11] In Chaucer's telling of the Lucrece story in *The Legende of Good Women*, Tarquin enters through Lucrece's opened bedroom window, "giving the alert reader," according to the masculinist criticism of Roy W. Battenhouse, "a hint as to her knack for leaving windows open, through a negligence due perhaps to sub-conscious motive."[12] The semiotics of Lucrece are very much about seeing her, about the viewer peeping through frames and windows to get a good look. As the most frequently represented sacrificially raped woman in early modern European culture, she is put on display not only for the immediate Roman onlookers in the narrative but also for the early modern viewer, who could both vicariously "see" through those narratives and gaze more immediately at pictures of Lucrece. As the emblematic sacrificially raped woman in early modern culture, Lucrece embodies a story not just about being raped but about being seen. I want to argue as one of my main points here, however, that her story about being seen is *officially* about her not being seen, her being inscribed in an invisible pornography; or, in other terms, what is seen *corporaliter* is meant to be seen *spiritualiter*.[13]

Before going further, let us recall the story of Lucrece, which takes place in 509 B.C., during the tyrannical reign of Tarquininus Superbus.[14] One night, while his noblemen and soldiers are encamped outside of Ardea, the noblemen—including Tarquin (the king's son) and Collatinus (Lucrece's husband)—begin to boast competitively about the virtues of their respective wives. To settle this dispute the noblemen ride back to Rome and find all the wives, except Lucrece, frolicking and amusing themselves. Inflamed mostly by Lucrece's chastity, Tarquin later steals from the camp and returns to Collatinus and Lucrece's house, where Lucrece, unsuspecting of any of

Tarquin's designs, gives him a room for the evening. During the night, he enters her bedchamber and tries to seduce her, but she rejects him. He then threatens to kill a slave (in some versions a black slave), put him in bed with her, and publish that he killed the slave after finding him in bed with her. Lucrece protests, after which Tarquin rapes her and then leaves. She sends for her father and her husband, each of whom arrives with one trusted companion (as instructed by her). They find her in a state of mourning. She tells them what has happened to her, speaks of her polluted body, then stabs herself. Brutus (the putative imbecile) takes the dagger from her body and vows to overthrow the tyrannical household of the Tarquins. Lucrece's body is put on display in the marketplace as a sign of Tarquin's tyranny and her virtue. After Brutus (with the aid of many other noblemen) overthrows the Tarquins, Rome becomes a republic.

Although the contest-rape is of course the constitutive event in Lucrece's history, with her rapist Tarquin and her husband Collatinus being the main culprits, we should not overlook the ways in which this moment seems to be always leading to Lucrece's self-sacrifice. There is no real difference between the contest-rape and the self-slaughter. The latter does not simply signify an unforeseen turn in events. The complicity between these two narratives deserves emphatic attention. Like the common proliferation and repetition of false or failed sacrifices before the real and final one, the story of Lucrece is marked with a false closure: the contest continues to loom over the narrative like a Freudian masterplot, marking both the beginning and ending of the story.[15] Only when Lucrece kills herself does the contest of women's virtue come to an end, since the only definitive (that is, conclusive) way to prove integrity is through self-slaughter. Notwithstanding, the contest over the virtue of their wives (if the contest is about the wives at all) is concomitantly a contest over Rome's own masculine political integrity.

Lucrece's wound is the visible proof of the end of her rite of passage. Mieke Bal speaks to this point in her reading of Livy: "The red stain on the white gown, the sign of the suicide that proves her chastity, can be seen as an allusion to a very old tradition of visual positivism: the widespread practice of showing the bloodstained sheets after the wedding night as evidence of the bride's virginity."[16] From the perspective of sacrifice, then, the contest over Rome becomes a postsacrificial celebration, an epilogue performed over Lucrece's dead body. The husbands' contest and Lucrece's rape and death are not locked into any linear causality. There is also a synchronic story, a story in which Lucrece's sacrificial proof (made possible by Tarquin) signifies not merely the consequence but the originary evidence of Collatinus's boast.

In typical sacrificial fashion, Lucrece, and not the men around her, de-mands her sacrificial death. She insists on killing herself because, although her mind is innocent, her body is guilty. She cannot live with this kind of potentially deconstructive reading of not only her patriarchal body but that of a patriarchal body politic. As she says in Livy's account, stabbing herself and splitting herself from her body, "As for my part, though I cleare my selfe of the offence, my body shall feele the punishment: for no unchast or ill woman, shall hereafter impute no dishonest act to Lucrece" (Painter, 24). Or in Shakespeare's *Rape of Lucrece*, "'No, no,' quoth she, 'no dame hereafter living / By my excuse shall claim excuse's giving'" (lines 1714–15). Or in the more extended *declamatio* Lucrece offers in Coluccio Salutati's *Declamatio Lucretiae* (late fourteenth century, Florentine), in which her words echo those of Iphigenia speaking of Helen's abduction: "See to it that he also renders other women's sleep safe from so much burning shame. If you are too neg-ligently lacking in this, unrestrained lust will spread, and the Roman women, not only while their husbands are absent but even in the embraces of their husbands, will be pressed by the violence of shameless youth. For indeed, what woman will be safe if Lucretia has been raped?"[17] And she finishes too by resisting the (anti-)social uses of her body: "Let not Lucretia be given as an example to Roman women, so that, on account of my life, they may con-vince themselves that life is lawful for the unchaste."[18] Lucrece dies for her chastity, and her final words testify to her resolve. It would be useful to con-sider here the concept of "chaste thinking," which Stephanie H. Jed reads as a site of conflictual thought represented on one side by the impulse to touch and on the other by the impulse to be cut off from contact.[19] These dual im-pulses are germane to my reading of Lucrece narratives and pictorial repre-sentations and to my reading of *Titus Andronicus*. Chaste thinking reveals the interdependency of the pornographic—that is, the urge to touch and ex-pose—and the state's demands of chastisement.

Chaste thinking informs Shakespeare's poem as well. After Lucrece has killed herself and the men look on, the narrator writes that "some of her blood still pure and red remain'd, / And some look'd black, and that false Tarquin stain'd" (1742–43).[20] As a sacrificially raped woman, she is marked, too, with the double signification of the bleeding virgin. (Hence, Pseudo-Albertus Magnus writes in his late-thirteenth- or early-fourteenth-century natural philosophy/medical text, *De Secretis Mulierum* [The secrets of women], "You should know that the menses is of a double nature: one part is pure, and one part is impure.")[21] Such distinctions do break down. A single image comes to represent both the sacrificial and the pornographic. This breakdown in distinctions is made especially clear when Lucrece's body is taken to the marketplace. Ovid comments in *Fasti*, for example, "*Volnus inane patet*" (the empty wound stood open [line 849]), that is, in more readable prose, that Lucrece's "gaping wound was exposed for all to see."[22] (The Latin word *inane* [empty] makes emphatic a visible invisibility, not only one looking back to a virginal Lucrece but one whose emptiness, whose openness (*patet*) displays the evidence that she has been penetrated.) In Chaucer's *The Legende of Good Women* Brutus says, "And openly let cary her on a bere / Thurgh al the toun, that men may see and here / The horryble dede of hir oppress-youn" (1866–68).[23] These two impulses also collapse in Livy's narrative: "The body of Lucrece was brought into the market place, where the people wondred at the vilenesse of that facte, euery man complayning vppon the mischiefe of that facinorous rape, committed by Tarquinius. . . . Then the lustiest and most desperate persons within the citie, made themselves prest and readie, to attempte any enterprise" (Painter, 24). In Livy's narrative Lucrece's body, for all its purity, has become the sign of Tarquin's vileness, his pornographic objectifying of Lucrece's body. And the daring and "lustiest and most desperate" onlookers seem simply to have usurped Tarquin's place.

Lucrece's move to "cut off" her life also restages her being touched. Two points Bal makes about the role of touching in Rembrandt's paintings (1664 and 1666) of Lucrece's suicide apply to other Lucrece representations. Bal writes that "the male rivals literally need to *touch* the woman's body—to partake in its rape,"[24] and she argues that in these paintings "the touch of the maker is represented as strongly as is the touch of the rapist."[25] Paintings of Lucrece insistently beg Lynda Nead's question in her study of the female nude: "What happens when the gaze turns into a stare, when the desire to see becomes the need to touch?"[26]

Before going on with my discussion of Lucrece, it is worth noting that Nead's question may be applied here to more than Lucrece, to more than legend. It may be one of the greatest ironies of Elizabeth's reign that the queen (against the kind of advice Henry IV gives to Hal [*1 Henry IV* 3.2.39–91]) pictures herself as a way of rendering herself nearly invisible, a rarity. The iconography of her portraiture insists that the Elizabeth we *see* is the unseen Elizabeth. The Elizabeth in Cornelius Ketel's *Elizabeth I as a Roman Vestal Virgin*, the "Siena Sieve" portrait (c. 1580), for example, holds a sieve in her hand—her hands are often presented grasping the objects of her power, her representational essence. (The Vestal Virgin Tuccia proved her chastity by using the sieve to carry water to the Tiber; despite the vessel's porous nature, it remained sealed.) The painting shows us what we do not

see. The story of the foreign Dido, painted on a pillar behind Elizabeth, signifies not only the affinities between Elizabeth and Dido but their differences. With Elizabeth's arm in effect pushing Dido into the background,
Dido's sacrificial story, told through a series of miniatures filled with activi-
ties, contrasts with the stalwartness and stillness, the ideological nonrepre-
sentability, of the leaking or lacking Elizabeth, to whose left stands a globe
with the motto, "*Tutto vedo e molto mancha*" (I see all and much is lacking).
Elizabeth insists not only that she does the looking but that her corporeal
"lack" is lacking, an object not to be seen. Her body, in effect, boldly pictures its invisibility, its nonpornographic nature.[27]

Nead's question works especially with regard to the 1563 edict "Prohibiting Portraits of the Queen." According to this document, Elizabeth, who has
been reluctant to sit for an authorized portrait but "being herein as it were
overcome at the continual requests of so many of her nobility and subjects
whom she *cannot well deny*,"[28] will permit some "cunning" (that is, knowl-
edgeable) man to make a portrait whose pattern "known men of understanding" may imitate, but only when they are hired by "some perfect patron," the "head officers" of their dwelling places. (The word *cunning*
probably hints at "craftiness.") Others, the proclamation states, "should not,
without, attempt the same."[29] Seeming to give in to a publicly arranged marriage proposal, if not a private rape, Elizabeth is "overcome" by men (I pre-
sume) "whom she cannot well deny."

Throughout, a language of licentiousness dominates. Like a courtroom
testimonial, the document recalls how the "natural desires" of "*all sorts* of
subjects"—"all manner of painters," "all manner of other persons," some
"noble," some "mean"—wish and "do daily attempt" to "procure" the picture not just of the queen but of the "Queen's majesty's *most noble and loving
person* and royal majesty." As the passage moves from one possessive to the
next, it seems more and more to penetrate the very privacy of Elizabeth's
corporeal self; we may note this most particularly in the image of her "most
noble and loving person." Her body (subject in representation to "errors and
deformities committed by sundry persons") must be protected from "*the
showing or publication* of such as are *apparently deformed* until they may be re-
formed which are reformable" (*reform* being a particularly laden word for
Elizabeth, whose portraiture essentially replaced the presumably idolatrous
deformed Catholicism associated with images of the Virgin Mary).[30] Here,
in the closing words of the proclamation, one senses a deliberate collapsing
of bad portraits and bad artists (that is, "committed" persons) prying for
transgressive access to Elizabeth's image, to her body. When Elizabeth decides

that "some special commission painter might be *permitted, by access* to her majesty, *to take* the natural representation of her majesty, whereof *she hath been always of her own disposition very unwilling,*" all begins to sound a lot like her marriage proposals that would become one of the leitmotifs of her reign. Here, however, she does not turn away her suitors. She gives in.

But more important than her giving in (one could easily argue that she doesn't have much of a choice) is the anxiety here about how easily a marriage proposal moves to a rape, particularly if that suitor is foreign and Catholic. And in a pamphlet written against Elizabeth's proposed marriage to the Catholic French Alençon, *The Discovery of a Gaping Gulf* (1579), a title ripe with pornographic implications, John Stubbs evokes a more explicit sense of France as rapist of England. His text works well, too, to draw together issues of pornography, sacrifice, woman, and nation/empire. As the cunning scribe imagines it: "The very foundations of our commonweal [would be] dangerously digged at by the French; and our dear Queen Elizabeth (I shake to speak) [would be] led blindfold as a lamb to the slaughter."[31] He comes closest to envisioning such a marriage as a rape of national and imperial proportions when he argues that the French "have sent us hither, not Satan in body of a serpent, but the old serpent in shape of a man, whose sting is in his mouth, and who doth his endeavor to seduce our Eve, that she and we may lose this English paradise."[32]

As for the painting of Elizabeth, the queen has been (and, of course, remained) "very unwilling" to give a suitor access to her body, and anyone "permitted" access to her would need penetrate her corporeal space very carefully and very knowingly; one would need to be not only a "perfect patron" to a knowing painter but a perfect subject to one's own perfect patron, that is, to Elizabeth herself. More significant still for my purposes is the way the proclamation insists, discursively, on a link between Elizabeth's authorized/natural representation and her virginity or, to put it in other but similar terms, on the unauthorized/unnatural *taking* of her image and the violent sexual act of raping her, of *taking* her body. Jean-Joseph Goux's reading of the Roman cult of Vesta has more than a passing relevance here: "Vesta's virginity and her unrepresentability are both protected at once. A man (*vir*) should neither penetrate, nor see, nor imagine. The inviolable virginity and the strict unrepresentability are identical, as if there were a complicity, on some opposing plane, between 'rape' by manly sensual desire (the Priapic appetite) and the visualization, which would be a phantasm and an impious fraud."[33] As Elizabeth herself seemed to understand, being nonpornographic, being made nonviolable, is not so easy. It's about more than just saying "no."

In 1596, for example, more than three decades after this prohibiting edict, the Privy Council were still going about the business of finding and destroying "unseemly portraits of the Queen."[34]

Such a gaze entraps Lucrece, threatening to rape her yet again. The public gaze upon Lucrece and the desire to touch her body cling together in Botticelli's *The Tragedy of Lucretia* (c. 1499), one of the earliest and most comprehensive paintings of Lucrece (figure 2). In Botticelli's triptych the central image shows the Roman men gathered around Lucrece's body, which is stretched out on its altar with the dagger (re-)inserted into her breast; she appears locked in by pillars, by borders, as though Botticelli's public framing of her intends also to let the viewer peep through Lucrece's private bedroom window while she sleeps, while she—to re-evoke Battenhouse— "awaits" her rapists.[35] The image to the left shows Tarquin attempting to rape her, and the image to the right shows the four witnesses gathered around her as she collapses from her suicide. Tarquin touches her; the witnesses touch her. In the center image, the largest of the three, two figures close to her stretch their hands toward her body as though they will touch it; and behind her and, pictorially, close to her breast and the dagger, two hands, almost disembodied, are drawn in toward each other as though they are in the act of resisting touch.

This cross-purposed voyeurism typifies the numerous paintings and drawings of Lucrece, both the representations of her being raped by Tarquin and those in which she mortally wounds herself. And however much the viewer may be asked not to touch—not to read pornographically the pictures in which both Lucrece and Tarquin appear—Tarquin's aggressive hands are no less a part of the visual narrative than Lucrece's resisting ones. (I will say more about Lucrece's hands in a few moments.) These depictions are often completed with their own staple voyeur, whose presence invites further indulgence in the scene's salaciousness, its pornographic possibilities, as in Felice Ficherelli's *Tarquinio e Lucrezia* (figure 3). However subtle or not so subtle the voyeur presumes to be—in the background in Ficherelli's painting but in the foreground of Artemisia Gentileschi's *Tarquin and Lucretia* (late 1640s) (figure 4)—he complements other signs pushing for the viewer's pornographic attention. These include especially the presence of phallic objects—most obviously Tarquin's dagger but also his rigid and spatially demanding hand and arm and sometimes his knee—and plenty of soft and vibrant folds usually involving the canopy over Lucrece's bed and/or the bedsheets.

2. *The Tragedy of Lucretia*, by Alessandro Filipepi Botticelli, c. 1499. Isabella Stewart Gardner Museum, Boston.

3. *Tarquinio e Lucrezia*, by Felice Ficherelli (mid-seventeenth century). Accademia Nazionale di San Luca di Roma.

In the image of a resisting Lucrece, particularly with her staying-off hand, the viewer supposedly locates "his" resistance to the proffered pornographic narrative. The act of viewing Tarquin's aggression becomes the viewer's aggressive act of just saying "no." One of the most striking depictions of this cross-purposed voyeurism in representations of both Lucrece and Tarquin is Agostino Veneziano's *Tarquin and Lucretia* (figure 5), in which Tarquin wields a dagger in one hand and grips a phallic-like knot (from the canopied bed) in the other. Lucrece pushes him away with one hand, so prominently pressed against him, whereas her other hand, hidden by Tarquin's thigh, acts simultaneously as Lucrece's castrating and self-chastising arm and an extension of Tarquin's phallic self (that "third" leg of which some men like to boast). In the spirit of the open and closed, the seen and unseen contestations over Lucrece's body, casements and latches compete for visual dominance. And the phallic-like knots surrounding Lucrece and Tarquin seem to pull open the canopy as the viewer watches. The vaginal rendering of the canopy is quite explicit and made even more so with the fire burning just above it and with the sodomizing dogs (with visible penetrating penis) to the right and in the foreground. Although Veneziano's drawing may be more explicit, more pornographic, than most other early modern depictions of Lucrece and Tarquin, the difference between it and many less explicit representations remains an issue of degree not of kind.

But by far the most common way of depicting Lucrece is without Tarquin and in the act of committing suicide. And however much this moment presents a more virginal Lucrece, a Lucrece in the act of self-chastising, the pornographic narrative is no less part of these representations. In these images Lucrece, often fully or partly disrobed (often with at least hints of red clothing), stands facing the viewer's gaze, holding a dagger that she prepares to plunge into herself, if, indeed, she has not already done so. The diachronic dimensions, the temporal range, of her story are always under threat of erasure, becoming fixed and framed by this single gesture. With the dagger plunging toward her chaste and unflinching breast, even the rape seems elided or cut off from her self-sacrifice. Sometimes she stares out at her viewer, content and perhaps triumphant. Sometimes she, like so many representations of Christian martyrs, stares heavenward in supplication or downward in humility. Only rarely does her face show pain.

The raison d'etre for the body's being exposed to the viewer's gaze depends on the presumption or the pretense that the viewer sees double, that is, sees not only Lucrece's chastity but simultaneously the *loss* of that chastity. The "vilenesse" one sees because of Lucrece's body is also the "vilenesse"

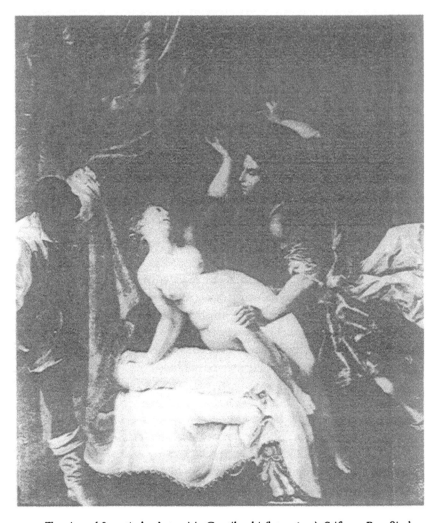

4. *Tarquin and Lucretia*, by Artemisia Gentileschi (late 1640s). Stiftung Preußische Schlösser und Gärten Berlin-Brandenburg/Bildarchiv.

that one actively cuts off from her body. Present here too is what Lynda Nead (reading through Derrida) has called the "double inscription" of the female nude, "a kind of surface within a surface."[36] For my argument it is the female body being pulled between two seemingly opposite narratives. Giovanni Battista Moroni's painting *Chastity* (1555–60) is a rather pointed example. Chastity is allegorized as a woman, seated and holding a sieve filled with water that stays contained within it. The woman's breasts are exposed, but her middle body remains well draped. Her legs, especially her lower legs, are visible, and her right foot rests on a stone or plaque that reads, "*Castitas infamiae nvbe obscvrata emergit*" (Chastity emerges from the dark clouds of infamy). The viewer is asked to read Chastity's body as a double inscription, as a body inscribed in a narrative of chastity as well as in a narrative about the (possible) loss of that chastity.[37] Lucrece's body in and out of pictorial images is also encoded by this double reading. As Mieke Bal has written, "The chaste Lucretia, thus, has become public property by her rape; she has been opened to the public. The visual representation of the woman at the moment of her self-killing partakes of this 'publication.' Lucretia is put on display for the eyes of the indiscreet onlooker."[38] The viewer is supposed to see Lucrece as yet another body double, another *parthenos aparthenos* (in Greek language and culture, "a virgin who is not a virgin").[39] The dagger now plunging or about to plunge into her body and mark her with blood signifies her chastity; it also replicates the penetrative act of the rape itself.

The double inscription is most explicit in paintings in which Lucrece seems iconographically to use her blood to write her chastity upon her breast.

5. *Tarquin and Lucretia*, by Agostino Veneziano (early sixteenth century). Graphische Sammlung Albertina, Wien.

Her dagger (trained on herself) becomes her pen, her tool of inscription—
her subjectivity.[40] With her pen in hand she is seen as writing herself out of
pornographos, out of a "writing *about* whores," a writing about the seenness of
the woman's body. Thomas Middleton's *The Ghost of Lucrece* (1596–98) represents the most extended example of Lucrece's suicidal writing (539 lines of
it), since she (as a ghost) is the poem's sole voice, excepting the epilogue, in
which her death is blazonly described. The poem figures itself as a picture of
her chastising hand, her authorizing fingers, as she attests near the end of the
poem:

> Lucrece (alas, thou picture of thyself
> Drawn poor and pale by that old painter, Time)
> . . .
> Bleed no more lines, my heart! This knife (my pen),
> This blood (my ink), hath writ enough to Lust.
> Tarquin, to thee (thou very devil of men)
> I send these lines; thou art my fiend of trust;
> To thee I dedicate my tomb of dust;
> To thee I consecrate this little-most,
> Writ by the bloody fingers of my Ghost. (498–99, 505–11)

In Middleton's poem and elsewhere Lucrece is pictured as (subjectively)
rewriting the generic woman's story, but, as I have already argued, this chastised figuring goes hand in hand (so to speak) with her viewer's more salacious knowledge about Lucrece's raped body. A good example of the signature painting is the sixteenth-century *Lucrecia Romana* (figure 6), by a follower
of Lucas Cranach, in which a bold script (above and flanking Lucrece's
head) dominates the upper part of the painting: "*Satius est mori qvam indecore
vivere*" (Death is enough when to live is disgraceful [or unsightly]).[41] And
below these words is her name, as though Lucrece has just penned her resolve in an epistle: "Lucrecia Romana." When read from the top down, more
perhaps the way one would enter the hermeneutics of a written text than
those of a painting, Lucrece's body becomes secondary to the patriarchal
script for which she dies. This more literal signature, "Lucrecia Romana,"
becomes even more pointed, however, when it is read with the other words
flanking Lucrece's head: on the left, "Indecore Lucrecia," and on the right,
"Vivere Romana." From this perspective, only Lucrece's self-sacrifice, her
pinning her body up between *Lucrecia* and *Romana,* seems capable of resisting any kind of playful or deconstructive desire to forge a relationship between *Lucrecia* and *vivere.* Such a relationship would also produce an affinity

6. *Lucrecia Romana*, by a follower of Cranach (sixteenth century). Photographed when in the Philipson Collection. Photograph Courtauld Institute of Art.

between *indecore* and *Romana*, precisely the text that Lucrece's suicide attempts to keep out of circulation.

The Lucrece signature painting may be found too in the portrayal of the real Lucrezia Persaro in Lorenzo Lotto's *A Lady as Lucretia* (c. 1534). Her face is characterized by an unflinching resolve, and her right hand seems incidentally to cover, almost to clutch, her genitalia, while also pointing casually to a drawing she holds in her left hand. The drawing depicts a nude Lucrece with disheveled hair, who is about to plunge the dagger into herself, perhaps into her genitalia, which she covers partially with some kind of drapery she holds on to with her left hand. And on the table beneath the drawing is Lucrece's signature text: "*Nec vlla impvdica Lvcretiae exemplo vivet*" (Never shall Lucretia provide a precedent for unchaste women to live). Although Lucrezia Persaro is and remains *decorous* (that is, untouched), unlike Lucrece in *Lucrecia Romana*, both paintings use rape and death to signify or prove the woman's chastity. Most clearly foregrounded in the Persaro portrait, and, I would argue, also foregrounded in the *Lucrecia Romana*, is the sacrificial story. Her wound becomes a kind of *signum*, not just a sign(ature) but a "cutting into."[42] In these paintings Lucrece's cutting into herself or cutting off herself frames her and her hand in the act of self-signing or self-signifying. She writes herself into being as a subject in the very gesture she uses to erase her subjectivity.

Lucrece becomes emblematic of the raped woman in early modern literature and painting who finds herself corrected, contained, and obliterated. I refer here less to the woman who becomes no-body, the mere object in the hands of her rapist, than to the raped woman who is made to chastise, frame/aestheticize, and erase herself by killing herself after she has been so violated. When Lucrece kills herself, she signifies doubly: her body is simultaneously scripted in two narratives, one literally pointing with the dagger back to the violable act of rape and the other, paradoxically, to the impenetrability of her body. Like the hymen in Jacques Derrida's hymeneal fable, her virginity signifies a (subjective) self that is "*always* intact as it is *always* ravished, a screen, a tissue."[43] We may begin to do more than suspect that Lucrece does not die because she is raped but that she is raped because she must be gloriously sacrificed. As true here as in classical tragedy, "Women's glory in tragedy was an ambiguous glory."[44]

A more explicitly pornographic user of Lucrece's suicide is Lucas Cranach, who created (between 1510 and 1538) more than thirty pictorial images of a practically nude Lucrece in the act of committing suicide. His repeated touch of Lucrece's chastity brings into focus more than any other single

artist (of whatever genre) the ornamental use of Lucrece's suicide. Patriarchy's sacrificial narrative becomes inseparable, indeed, indistinguishable,
from what it proffers as the pornographic narrative. (This is also and more
than conveniently evident in Livy's account in which Collatinus, Lucrece's
husband, is eventually forced into exile because he too—Tarquinius Collatinus—is a descendant of the Tarquin family.) Cranach's Lucrece paintings,
some of the most reproduced paintings of Lucrece, fully exploit her double
inscription as raped and as chastised. If explicitly voiced nowhere else, this
double inscription is articulated by Michel Leiris, the early-twentieth-
century French ethnographer, on the cover of his study *Manhood: A Journey
from Childhood into the Fierce Order of Virility* (1939). Glossing the Lucrece
painting, Leiris writes:

> Lucrece, pressing to the center of her white chest, between two marvelously
> hard, round breasts (whose nipples seem as rigid as the stones decorating a
> gorget or cuirass at the same place), the narrow blade a dagger whose tip is
> already beaded, like the most intimate gift appearing at the end of the male
> member, with a few drops of blood, and about to annihilate the effect of
> the rape she has suffered by a similar gesture: one that will thrust into a
> warm sheath of flesh, and for a bloody death, the weapon at its maximum
> degree of stiffness, like the rapist's inexorable virility when it enters by force
> the orifice already gaping between her thighs, the gentle pink wound—
> deeper, wickeder too, but perhaps even more intoxicating—made by the
> dagger will release, from Lucrece's very heart as she faints or fails, a torrent
> of blood.[45]

However unseen Lucrece is supposed to be in her many pictures, it remains
true not only in Cranach or Leiris's use of Cranach, or in the early modern
period or the twentieth century, that Lucrece is seen as a pornographic object, her rape fully evident. Huston Diehl argues convincingly that Cranach's
Lucrece paintings belong to the period of Cranach's conversion to Luther-
anism and that "Cranach employs an iconoclastic rhetoric that, because it
both exemplifies and seeks to contain the erotic power of images, is profoundly disturbing. Lucretia's mournful intentionality as she plunges the
dagger into her heart is, in a sense, the artist's own as he repels the viewer
from the powerful image he so lovingly portrays, 'killing' his own creation,
perhaps so that another Rome can be purified."[46] But Diehl speaks with too
much hesitancy, I believe, in arguing that these paintings "may well anticipate and even help to construct a modern male gaze that takes a pornographic pleasure in the image of a woman who is both pure and violated,

chaste and abused."[47] Images of Lucrece (Cranach's too) partake of this double inscription, this cultural space that not only makes possible but also gives expression to this early modern invisible pornography. If Cranach stages anything, it is this troubled space in which the conversion never really does become a completed experience. As in the many images of Lucrece, his and others, Lucrece is pictured (as in the central image in Botticelli's painting) not as dead but as caught in the very active act of dying.

However ambiguous may be Lucrece's sacrificial glory, less equivocal is the cultural and racial self-defining proof her sacrifice pictures and reifies. Leiris's description of Lucrece's "white chest" is, for example, no immaterial detail. The miscegenational rape or the possibility of it sits right at the basis of national, imperial, familial, and social fears. Elizabeth herself would give her suitor, Alençon, such ominous foreign names as "little Moor" and "little Italian,"[48] and Stubbs would argue that Elizabeth's marriage to Alençon would in effect be an act of miscegenation: he shudders to think of Elizabeth commingling with a French atheism imported "from those eastern parts." Such fears shape a number of Lucrece representations that stress a racial difference between the Roman Lucrece and the Etruscan Tarquin. Although the critical tradition has given scant attention to the interracialism at the foundation of Rome's republican freedom, the racializing of Lucrece's rape is evident in the picturing especially of Tarquin, who is often represented as noticeably darker and/or more exotic than Lucrece. Pictorial representations of Lucrece's rape are more likely to flesh out this racial story than to shy away from it. The cultural gist of Ian Donaldson's remarks about Titian's *Tarquin and Lucretia*, for example, typifies many representations of this rape:

> Despite the high colour of her face, Lucretia is pale beside Tarquin's darker skin—a tonal contrast which possibly hints at the racial, as well as purely sexual, oppositions of the story: Lucretia is a Roman, Tarquin an Etruscan. Yet Tarquin is also dark in other ways: the shadow falls across part of his face, and there are depths of shadow behind him. The light catches his back: the scarlet of his stockings, the plum breeches, the ginger beard, the fiery reds that indicate his temperament.[49]

Although many paintings that depict Lucrece and Tarquin do stress the cultural and/or racial difference between them, more conspicuous and frequent still is the racial difference between Lucrece and the witnessing slave, who usually exists on a different plane from the rape itself. He, more than Tarquin, adds ethnographic color to the rape, providing the scene with a symbolic set of pornographic eyes. His presence testifies to the cultural and racial alteration brought on or proven by the act of rape. This persona appears often, from Botticelli's painting through at least G. B. Tiepolo's *Tarquin and Lucretia* (1745–50), in which an ominously erect black bedpost looms with a black voyeuristic and phallic presence. (The copulating dogs in Veneziano's drawing provide much the same function in a more explicit fashion.)

And more than simply emphasizing the cultural and sexual violation of white female virginity and chastity, the dark voyeur, sometimes the ethnographically black voyeur as in Gentileschi's painting, also makes clear the racial cleansing that must (or does) take place in the excising of the pornographic from Lucrece's body. Lucrece's chastity, her unseenness, is on a par with her whiteness. These representations of the raped Lucrece (who appears of course with Tarquin and, usually, a darker or more exotic voyeur) may be considered alongside those paintings and drawings of the sacrificial Lucrece, who appears alone. In this context Lucrece sacrifices herself not only in the name of chastity but in the name of whiteness. In fact, the two are culturally inseparable. And if this were not the case or less the case in the earlier days of the Lucrece legend, the twinning of Lucrece's chastity and whiteness would become more and more realized during the early modern period.

Redirecting Nancy J. Vickers's reading of the heraldic colors in the face of Shakespeare's Lucrece, I would argue that this racialism figures in the imagery of Shakespeare's *Lucrece* as well. Vickers argues that "Lucrece's body as shield stands between Tarquin and Collatine to deflect blows, to prevent direct hits."[50] But it is not only Collatine's family name, or a family name so exclusively, that Lucrece's body protects. In more than a dozen references to Lucrece's whiteness her sexual redness struggles with her virginal whiteness, and as the poem climaxes, the narrator admonishes Tarquin for battering such an "ivory wall" (464) and continues stressing the color of Lucrece, "Who o'er the white sheet peers her whiter chin" (472) and inquires "under what colour he commits this ill" (476). (He responds, "The colour in thy face, / That even for anger makes the lily pale / And the red rose blush at her own disgrace" [477–79].) Heraldic images are surely at work here, but so too (if not especially) are images of Lucrece's white corporeal self trapped in the rapacious grip of the jungle:

. . . the picture of pure piety,
Like a white hind under the gripe's sharp claws,
Pleads in a wilderness where are no laws. (542–44)

And later,

> The wolf hath seiz'd his prey, the poor lamb cries,
> Till with her own white fleece her voice controll'd
> Entombs her outcry in her lips' sweet fold. (677–79)

More tellingly, she herself racializes Tarquin, pushing her reading of him from a metaphorical to a physiological blackness. Before the rape, she talks about her and Tarquin's social contract, that is, about his "black payment" for her hospitality (576), and then about his desire, his "black lust" (654). Following the rape, she refers to Tarquin (who has now departed) as "night's child" (785), that is, a child of blackness, and then proceeds to draw out Night's (and Tarquin's) anatomy. First, she talks about its "black bosom" (788), and then in one of several apostrophes she sees or reveals, I argue, the penis, the black penis, that has landed her in Shakespeare's sacrificial narrative:

> O night, thou furnace of foul reeking smoke,
> Let not the jealous day behold that face
> Which underneath thy black all-hiding cloak
> Immodestly lies martyr'd with disgrace! (799–802)

(Relevant too is her apostrophe to Opportunity [876–1036].) If not fully realized in Shakespeare's poem, the racial possibilities of Lucrece's apostrophe are teased out by the Queen Mother in Thomas Dekker's *Lust's Dominion; or, The Lascivious Queen* (1600):

> Fair eldest child of love, thou spotless night,
> Empresse of silence, and the Queen of sleep;
> Who with thy black cheeks pure complexion,
> Mak'st lovers eyes enamour'd of thy beauty:
> Thou art like my *Moor*, therefore will I adore thee,
> For lending me this opportunity,
> Oh with the soft skin'd Negro! heavens keep back
> Thy saucy staring day from the worlds eye,
> Until my Eleazar [the Moor] make return. (3.1.1–9)[51]

After Shakespeare's Lucrece kills herself, the orgasmic black penis is seen as having partly contaminated her physiology: "Some of her blood still pure and red remain'd, / And some look'd black, and that Tarquin stain'd" (1742–43). Race enters here as a way of visually marking in terms of the cultural Other a physiological truism from Hippocratic through early modern medicine: sexual intercourse changes one's physiological self. Beckford Sylvester suggests a medical reading of Lucrece's blood: "It is because Lucrece thinks herself physically divided that she sees herself as a living rebuke to her husband."[52] Maria calls on such a physiological reality in Dekker's *Lust's Dominion*, when she threatens to take the life from her "ivorie pallace" (2.6.1366), that is, to kill herself:

> Then this ensuing night shall give an end
> To all my sorrows, for before foul lust
> Shall soil the fair complexion of mine honor,
> This hand shall rob Maria of her life. (2.6.1357–60)

As mentioned earlier, Magnus writes of the menstrual flow's "double nature," one part pure, one impure.[53] And in 1651 we find the famous physician William Harvey in his work *On Generation* summarizing experiments he has done to prove false such suppositions about the mixture of male and female fluids and arguing against the Aristotelian proposal that healthy blood is red whereas blood "vitiated either by nature or disease . . . is blacker."[54] When representations of Lucrece's rape are considered in this context, Lucrece's black blood also tells a racial story. The racial Other is a significant figure in narratives and pictorials of Lucrece's sacrifice and rape. The act of killing herself, of dividing herself, permits Lucrece to cut off and chastise her black self, in fact to achieve virginity and whiteness in one fell stroke; and she attains her prominence most emblematically by displaying her white hand, a hand that contrasts sharply, say, to that black hand flaunted by Peacham's Aaron.

In Botticelli's painting, for example, the whiteness of Lucrece's emerging sleeve and her nearly autonomous hand, the hand that has chastised the touching that has been done to her, are made conspicuous against the darkness of her dress. A similar interpretation of Lucrece's powerful white hand may be reached from its foregrounding in *Lucrecia Romana* (where one hand is lower and turned toward the viewer with palm open and with a confident hold on the colorful and invasive hilt, the other hand effectively closed, although it grips the blade, with its whiteness in prominent and easy view) or from the white hand, the light center of the painting, splayed before the viewer in Ficherelli's *Tarquinio e Lucrezia*. As one among many examples from drama, the sacrificially murdered Mariam in Cary's tragedy finds herself lamented in such emblematic terms: "She's dead, hell take her murderers, she was fair, / Oh, what a hand she had, it was so white, / It did the whiteness of the snow impair," and as Nuntio, the messenger, concurs, "'Tis true, her hand was rare," and as Herod further protests, "Her hand? her hands; She had not singly one of beauty rare, / But such a pair as here where Herod stands, / He dares the world to make to both compare" (5.1.149–56). And in the folio of *The Countess of Montgomerie's Urania* (1621), Lady Mary Wroth describes Celina's hands, with their "unmatched whitenesse": "They were to be adored, not put to use unlesse to cherish hearts, their softnesse knowing no hard worke, could not be cruell, but gentle to wounds, by themselves especially given."[55] The hand becomes a kind of signature of racial and sexual purity. More than as static synecdoche for the woman's sexual and racial purity, the white hand *works* as the primary penning and pinning agent—authorizing and flaunting, securing and insisting on the white woman's claim to sexual and racial purity.

Picturing Lavinia; or, The Story of the Pit

Lavinia's rape is no more an accident to republican Rome than is Lucrece's. The official Roman world wishes to tell the story otherwise, and it is precisely this fiction—of how Lavinia's sacrifice counterbalances, corrects, or chastises her rape—that Rome (not necessarily Shakespeare's play) promotes to the status of a cultural truism. Rome demands Lavinia's rape as much as it demands her sacrifice; these are concomitant acts. Her rape completes the picture, simply becoming the mechanism through which the Roman world defines and celebrates its racial and masculine wholeness and clarity. Already in the opening scene, before the Goths and the African Aaron become part of the Roman drama, Lavinia finds herself the potential object in a sacrificial story when Titus demands that his son Lucius give Lavinia back to Saturninus. Like Virgininus (Titus will also evoke him at the end of the play), who kills his daughter instead of letting the king have his sexual way with her, Lucius says he will return her dead but not as Saturninus's wife (1.1.294–98). And just before the rape Lavinia makes it clear as she begs Tamora to protect her that she prefers death to rape: "And with thine own hands kill me in this place. . . . O, keep me from their worse-than-killing lust" (2.3.169, 175). But it is not only the rape and death of Lavinia that need attention here.

To understand better the participation of Rome in Lavinia's sacrificial rape we need to understand Rome's sacrificial crisis, that is, its need for a sacrifice, for a symbolic act that would establish the difference between, say, pure blood and impure blood. As René Girard defines it, a sacrificial crisis is "a crisis of distinctions—that is, a crisis affecting the cultural order. This cultural order is nothing more than a regulated system of distinctions in which the differences among individuals are used to establish their 'identity' and their mutual relationships."[56] Rome's crisis becomes evident in its confusion of categories: the Roman and the barbarous (as Tamora becomes "incorporate in Rome"), piety and impiety, war and peace, civil war and national war, enemy and ally (Saturninus marries Tamora, Titus kills his son Mutius, the brothers Bassianus and Saturninus struggle with each other for Rome's imperial seat), Tamora's allegiance to both a racial whiteness and a racial blackness, and murder and sacrifice. Lavinia quickly emerges as Rome's symbolic sacrificial object, a body in crisis, caught in its own confused signification between being virginal and being raped. Almost immediately after her entrance she finds herself inscribed in a story of *raptus*, of bride theft, of becoming, ideologically and representationally, a raped body. Saturninus accuses Bassianus of rape, of stealing Lavinia, whom Titus has just promised to Saturninus, reneging on his earlier promise of giving Lavinia in marriage to Bassianus, "'Rape' call you it, my lord, to seize my own" (1.1.405). Lavinia's body becomes one of indistinction because in stealing Lavinia Bassianus steals her back, in effect rechastising her instead of raping her. Still, Lavinia's body is caught between these two readings, and Rome finds itself without any real strategy for distinguishing between *raptus* and the more proper patriarchal bestowal of marriage rites.[57]

Furthermore, not only Lavinia but Rome itself will come to remind us of Lucrece. When the play opens, the brothers Saturninus and Bassianus, each with his army, are debating rather intensely about which of them should become Rome's emperor, Saturninus proposing a strict patrilineage system (which would favor him) and Bassianus a government by election (which would presumably favor him):

Saturninus (to his followers):
Noble patricians, patrons of my right,
Defend the justice of my cause with arms;
And, countrymen, my loving followers,
Plead my successive title with your swords.
I am his first-born son that was the last
That ware the imperial diadem of Rome;
Then let my father's honours live in me,
Nor wrong mine age with this indignity.

Bassianus (to his followers):
Romans, friends, followers, favourers of my right,
If ever Bassianus, Caesar's son,
Were gracious in the eyes of royal Rome,

> Keep then this passage to the Capitol,
> And suffer not dishonour to approach
> The imperial seat, to virtue consecrate,
> To justice, continence, and nobility;
> But let desert in pure election shine,
> And, Romans, fight for freedom in your choice. (1.1.1–17)

But the rhetoric that actually makes their debate cohesive has less to do with the kind of government they represent per se than with their contention about which form of government best replicates Rome's *honor*, a word that comes at least retrospectively in *Titus Andronicus* to call attention to the honor, the virginity or chastity, of the female body. When Bassianus's call to his followers is read also as a response to Saturninus, Saturninus's toying with virginity becomes more obvious. Bassianus's word choice—*dishonour, consecrate, continence*, and *pure*—conjures an image of a chaste body, particularly a virginal body that, having been surprised while on its "imperial seat" (its bed), resists the predacious hands of the rapist. In other words, and we will return to this discussion at the end of the chapter with reference to Lucius, this struggle over whose body will signify Rome echoes Tarquin, Collatinus, and the other Roman soldiers' debate over the purity of their respective wives. The brothers are themselves vying over which of their bodies can best represent Lucrece's honor. To the extent that these contests are the same, the question is not simply whose body will represent Rome but whose body will actually become Rome, incorporate Roman virtue into itself. The republicanism scripted into Bassianus's last line, "And, Romans, fight for freedom in your choice," works especially to recall not merely Lucrece's sacrificial purity but the bed on which she consecrates herself to a Roman freedom.

The focusing of the sacrificial story on Lavinia's body becomes all the more acute after she is raped. The sacrificial principle is not lost on Demetrius and Chiron, who tell her to go hang herself if she can find the hands to help her knit the cord (2.4.1–10). And following the rape, Titus offers the play's most explicit comparison between the sacrificial Lavinia and the sacrificial Lucrece:

> Thou map of woe, that thus dost talk in signs,
> When thy poor heart beats with outrageous beating,
> Thou canst not strike it thus to make it still.
> Wound it with sighing, girl, kill it with groans;
> Or get some little knife between thy teeth,

And just against thy heart make thou a hole,
That all the tears that thy poor eyes let fall
May run into that sink, and soaking in,
Drown the lamenting fool in sea-salt tears. (3.2.12–20)

Titus and Tamora's two sons highlight Lavinia's problem as far as the sacrificial narrative is concerned. At least at this point in the play she lacks a signature text. She cannot speak her innocence nor write her chastity upon her breast. Furthermore, Lavinia serves as a compendium of sacrificial deaths. Between Titus and Tamora's sons Lavinia is envisioned as stabbing, hanging, and drowning herself. Not lost in this play's sacrificial vocabulary after Lavinia's rape are the several mentionings of the word *martyr*, a word occurring only four times in the play but appearing more than once in only one other Shakespeare play. (It appears twice in the second part of *Henry IV*.) And it takes on an even more emphatic significance when it is considered in the context of the other sacrificial words and images saturating the play. As A. Robin Bowers argues, although editors of Shakespeare's play commonly gloss this word to mean "mutilate," the primary meaning of *martyr* is very much evident in the play, as well as in pictorial representations and in other narratives indebted to Lucrece's sacrifice: "Lavinia, like Lucrece, is easily associated with martyrdom as well as mutilation."[58] Furthermore, for the Andronici the word *martyr* acts as more than a euphemism: it serves also to erase the narrative space between her rape and her death. It serves in effect to "cut off" any other narrative possibilities for the raped virgin/woman. To be raped (not just mutilated) is to be martyred.

When Lavinia is taken offstage to be raped, the pit substitutes for her body.[59] It is no longer her wedding night, but the pit completes her sexual passage from virginity to marriage. (As a sign of Lavinia's unwavering virginity, when Saturninus says the morning after Lavinia's nuptials that Titus has blown the horns "lustily" and "somewhat too early for new-married ladies," Lavinia protests and says she has been "broad awake two hours and more" [2.2.14–17]. Figuratively, the sexual bed has yet to consume or perhaps claim her.) The scene in which Martius and Quintius happen on the pit is almost mythic in its recognition of this rite of passage. The "fall" into the pit is no less consequential than the Edenic fall to the extent that the fall into the pit forces Rome to expose its postlapsarian self. As A. C. Hamilton and Albert H. Tricomi have argued, the pit also recalls the classical underworld.[60] In this regard the shift from the nether regions of the underworld to the nether regions of the female body replays such a move in Thomas

Kyd's *The Spanish Tragedy* and anticipates one in Thomas Middleton and William Rowley's *The Changeling*, where (in the latter play) the prying into the secrets of Beatrice-Joanna's body replaces the prying into the secrets of the castle. Frequently in early modern tragedy the play world "falls" into or finds itself confronting the devouring female body. This is one way that the early modern period evinces its misogynistic nightmare: on the stage the female body is seen as incorporating, devouring, or wounding the state.

Titus Andronicus refers three times to this "fell" pit as a mouth. Although it could prove useful to explore more classical associations between mouth and vagina (as Giulia Sissa has done in her study of Greek virginity),[61] the link between mouth and vagina in *Titus Andronicus* is quite visible. The mouth becomes a sign of an invisible pornography. As Gail Kern Paster argues, "The blood flowing from Lavinia's mutilated mouth stands for the vaginal wound that cannot be staged or represented, which has charged these images of warmth, movement, and breath with a peculiar eroticism and horror."[62] Also, Paster reminds us, "vaginal or menstrual blood was thought to issue sometimes from other parts of the body—from breast or mouth" (98). The pit becomes like Tamora, who, according to Lavinia, is beastly and has "no grace, no womanhood" (2.3.182). But the pit is the "bad" vagina magnified, deformed into a gaping and cannibalistic monster—an "unhallowed and bloodstained hole" (210). It is a "fearful sight of blood and death" (216), a "detested, dark, blood-drinking" (224) thing, a "devouring receptacle" (235), a "swallowing womb" (239), a "grave" (240). The female genitalia receive here one of their most horrific depictions in Shakespeare (with *King Lear* providing the most graphic and damning example [4.6.124–29]). The pit also becomes a sacrificial site, a kind of sacrificial cauldron for Bassianus, the "slaughtered lamb" (223), a container for "ragged entrails" (230). In the Oxford edition of *Titus Andronicus* Eugene M. Waith glosses "ragged entrails" as "rough interior," but the phrase refers to entrails that are, perhaps more suggestively, similar to Alarbus's (1.1.144); and also, but perhaps more imaginatively, the phrase evokes for the offstage audience (who are at that moment engaged in the act of *knowing* Lavinia's rape) an enlarged picture of Lavinia's torn and violated vaginal interior.

Despite the horrific portrayal of this pit, this scene has about it a kind of pastoral mythos. When Martius falls into the pit, Quintius says to him,

What, art thou fallen? What subtle hole is this,
Whose mouth is covered with rude growing briers,
Upon whose leaves are drops of new-shed blood
As fresh as morning dew distilled on flowers? (198–201)

And a few lines later the light reflecting from the dead Bassianus's ring will make Martius fancy that "so pale did shine the moon on Pyramus / When he by night lay bathed in maiden blood" (230–31). In these images of virginity and defloration, the body undergoing the rites in this scene is not Tamora's of course but Lavinia's.[63] This rude awakening into the rites of sexual penetration is Lavinia's story. In the image of the pit, the virgin/woman's rape and the virgin/woman's more mythic passage from *parthenos* to *gyne*, from virginity to womanhood, come very close to collapsing the one into the other and recalling in the process the uneasy relationship established earlier in the play between marriage and rape. Moreover, if Tamora is beastly and has no grace or womanhood, Lavinia must expurgate or prove she does not have this aspect of herself. She must in effect "cut off" herself from the kind of Tamora. Lavinia, like Lucrece (or her father), must enact or have chaste thinking enacted upon her own body. More than anything else perhaps, Lavinia's mutilated body signifies a move toward the sacrificial act of chaste thinking. Notwithstanding the blatant nature of the female genitalia imagery in the pit scene, it is not Lavinia's but Bassianus's body that plays through her sacrificial story—his blood stains the leaves and reminds Martius of Pyramus and Thisbe. Bassianus's murder, a kind of Girardian "sacrificial substitution," absorbs the language and impact of Lavinia's rape. In Girard's analysis the "sacrificial substitution" contributes to the "certain degree of *misunderstanding* demanded by the sacrificial process."[64]

The substitution here works to keep Lavinia's body seemingly dissociated from any kind of prurient knowledge. When she reenters mutilated, the signs of rape are on her. In what has become one of the most notorious speeches in the play, Marcus talks to and about the raped and mutilated Lavinia (2.4.11–57). As Bowers has argued, critics tend to neglect the emblematic aspects of Marcus's speech and instead offer up objections to his *dilatio*, his seemingly unending mythopoesis of a traumatized body in need of some kind of urgent response.[65] His speech, situated as it is between the classical cohesion of the first half of the play and the disjunctive immediacy of the second half, commands the emblematic center of the play. Marcus's mythopoesis, his "notoriously Senecan amble" as Helms calls it,[66] does threaten to slow "the usually hectic action to an almost Senecan torpor."[67] But critics are often misdirected in passing judgment on Marcus's speech and in arguing that the speech is *otiose* (to use Helms's word). Marcus's speech is perhaps ineffective in the sense that it does not return Lavinia to her former condition; nonetheless, his speech is far from being a textual distraction.

Marcus's speech is strained to arrest her—to fix her as a Lucrece *pictura*—

but she flies away, turns away, draws back (2.4.11, 28, 56), always resisting the structuration of his speech. He tries to retreat into mythopoesis by evoking Daphne and Philomela, but in each instance the figure simultaneously or quickly deconstructs before his own eyes. Daphne, with her victorious transformation into a tree to protect her from her rapist, finds herself in *Titus Andronicus* "bare" and with her dissevered "two branches" (16–18). And Philomela, says Marcus, "but lost her tongue, / And in a tedious sampler sewed her mind; / But, lovely niece, that mean is cut from thee" (38–40). His lyricism evokes and competes with the spellbinding music of the lavishness of Orpheus, the lyricism of that "Thracian poet" (48–51), but his poeticizing can neither restrain her the way Orpheus's music could wild animals nor restore her to her former self the way Orpheus's music could his wife, Eurydice. By gazing on and lyricizing about Lavinia's mutilated body, Marcus tries to piece her body together even as he blazons it, recalling images of her "rosed lips," "honey breath," "pretty fingers," "lily hands," and "sweet tongue" (24–49).[68] Marcus's *dilatio* is his desperate attempt to establish a picture of Lavinia's chaste body, that is, of Lavinia as a modest virgin/woman who still blushes (31–32).

Calderwood has argued that "in *Titus* [and particularly in Marcus's speech] Shakespeare fails to mold his verbal style to the contours of shifting dramatic occasions; and as a result word and deed become dislocated and often grotesque in their mutual isolation or come together with a disfiguring clash."[69] He is right to the extent that word and deed become dislocated and often grotesque, but this is not a failure on the playwright's part. Marcus's own convoluted, classically inscribed verse suggests, especially to Marcus himself, that there are no poetic words, no myths, to articulate the image of the raped and mutilated Lavinia. There are no paintings or drawings either; this is Titus's point when he gazes on her and says,

> Had I but seen thy picture in this plight,
> It would have madded me; what shall I do
> Now I behold thy lively body so? (3.1.103–5)

This is also Lavinia's point when she comes close to hysteria just before turning to the story of Philomela and Tereus in Ovid's *Metamorphoses* (4.1.1–59).[70] Lavinia's body works against the easy reading of her body within any kind of poetic or artistic mythos or stasis. What the play repeatedly argues and Marcus's speech emphatically marks is a kind of disjunctive mythopoesis, the *failure* of Lavinia's body to fit even those classical tableaux of horrific rape.[71]

Stealing Back Lavinia

Lavinia comes close to these classical representations, particularly to the martyred virgin/woman, when in her signature moment she puts the staff in her mouth and writes "Stuprum" (that is, "rape") and the names of her two rapists (4.1.77), finally opening up and bespeaking the act of vaginal penetration. Here she taps into the classical lexicon of rape, presumably breaking through the silence of her victimization and claiming it as a basis for *her* sacrificial desires. What she signs, in effect, is the warrant for her own death, the willful abandonment of her *self*.[72] It is also, as Marjorie Garber has argued about Caesar's signifying "Et tu, Brute" in *Julius Caesar*, "a survival, a remnant of authentic Romanness, a sign of origin . . . a quotation of a quotation."[73] Following through on my earlier discussion about the relationship between the mouth and the vagina, the staff in Lavinia's mouth places her within an iconic framework similar to that found in representations of Lucrece, whose story frequently gets played out, symbolically and synchronically, through the dagger that writes *and* threatens, rapes, kills, and apotheosizes her.[74] Marcus makes clear the association between the signifying Lavinia and Lucrece:

> There is enough written upon this earth
> To stir a mutiny in the mildest thoughts,
> . . .
> And swear with me, as, with the woeful fere
> And father of that chaste dishonoured dame,
> Lord Junius Brutus sware for Lucrece's rape,
> That we will prosecute by good advice
> Mortal revenge upon these traitorous Goths,
> And see their blood, or die with this reproach. (4.1.83–84, 88–93)

Marcus passes over the fact of Lucrece's suicide, her signature moment. As I have argued throughout, within Rome's logic Lavinia's sacrificial death is a foregone conclusion. When Lavinia writes "Stuprum," she is, as Marcus understands, providing the signature of her own chastity, the call for her own death. It is a coup de theatre, a moment in which Lavinia's pure white hand—however disembodied, however physically missing—still *manages* (etymological pun intended) to inscribe itself in Rome's sacrificial iconography.[75]

Shakespeare's Rome presumes to impress on its audience the horrific nature of rape and the chastising and repatriative spirit of sacrifice. When Titus kills Lavinia in the spirit of sacrifice, he presumably does so *because* of the horrific nature of rape. To accept Titus's reasoning is also, of course, to accept Rome's masculinist fiction, which argues that rape leads to sacrifice. Rome and Titus stress that no matter how "unnatural and unkind" this sacrificial act is, this nonetheless chastising "outrage" (5.3.47, 51), it is merely a mimetic reflection, an undoing, of Lavinia's horrific rape. Girard's point about the "essentially mimetic character of sacrifice with regard to the original, generative act of violence" deserves consideration here.[76] The penetrating penis and the penetrating dagger are both one. Like the child playing through and repeating the primal scene in order to free "himself" from it or to chastise it, the penetrating of Lavinia with the dagger, like Lucrece's self-penetration, plays through that earlier scene of violence. (In the cases of Lavinia and Lucrece this private and unseen scene gets replayed before the pornographic gaze of an on- and offstage public.) In the end Rome insists that a proper understanding of Lavinia's chastising sacrifice, or of Titus's self-sacrifice, depends on an understanding of the truly horrific nature of the crime committed against Lavinia's body.

According to the sacrificial principle, Lavinia becomes free of this private crime by having the crime publicly reenacted on her body. The evocation of the sacrificial traditions of Lucrece and Virginia presumably enables Rome to ensure the strict stage management of Lavinia's death. It allows Rome to affect a correct sacrifice, that is, "to conceal the murder lurking beneath the sacrifice."[77] Within the strictures of sacrifice's mimetic framework, the outrageous and "the unthinkable [become] a recital of events."[78] Rather than create the sacrifice, the horrific act *allows* the sacrifice to happen. The initial violence and the sacrifice are part of the same narrative strategy; both share the same origin.

Although mimesis is undeniably at work in Lavinia's death, the way Lavinia's death also supposes to cut her off from the precipitating event must not be missed. Titus's "Die, die, Lavinia, and thy shame with thee" (5.3.45) cloaks a sexual dying in a mortal one. This being cut off from contact, of being chastised even as she is violated, is one of Jed's primary arguments and one given too little attention by Girard.[79] (It is also an argument not understood by Augustine.)[80] Shakespeare's Rome insists on establishing some kind of logical continuity from rape to sacrifice; it insists also on cutting off contact between them and affirming their ideational or ideological differences. The sacrificial story must be protected from contamination by the rape story. Even as Lavinia sexually and chastisingly dies as her sacrificial self reaches climax, Rome continues to see itself as acting within the bounds of civilized imperium; in fact, the proof of its civilized imperium is the strictly stage-managed killing of Lavinia. Not surprisingly, it is the outsiders, Tamora and now Saturninus, who are shocked by Titus's killing of Lavinia. To be Roman is to be able to sacrifice and be sacrificed. The message is clear: only a chaste Rome truly understands sacrifice. Rape belongs to Rome's cultural Others. Barbarians rape; Rome chastises. This is Rome's other story of chaste thinking, or at least its chaste thinking about Others.

Rome finally kills Lucrece not because her body is polluted but because her mind is pure—"[H]er bodye was polluted, and not her minde"—and Brutus swears to seek vengeance in the name of her "chast bloud" (Painter, 24). And she dies willingly because in her purity even her life opposes any kind of corporeal contamination. In this respect Lucrece is like those sixteenth-century criminals who on the scaffold publicly confess their crimes to ask for forgiveness before welcoming the execution.[81] The execution does not punish them for their crimes, then, as much as it becomes evidence of their willing intervention between the state and its pollutants. This is precisely the place of Lavinia, who from the beginning of the play to its end has inscribed herself and has allowed herself to be inscribed in Rome's story of intervention. From Rome's perspective Lavinia dies as a Roman, not as a barbarian. When Titus kills her, he replays the sexual violence by masturbating her with his sacrificial knife and reenacts both the rape and the *raptus*. He incestuously steals back her chastity by stealing the place of Tamora's sons and Aaron, making himself the agent of Lavinia's rape, transforming it into his own orgasmic experience—"And with thy shame thy father's sorrow die" (5.3.46). Like Ravenscroft's play, with its "greater Alterations or Additions," Shakespeare's play, at least Shakespeare's Titus, insists that this second rape of Lavinia displaces the obscene crime with an invisible pornographic scene. As Ravenscroft writes in his preface to the reader, in order to show the Popish Plot and such, he has forced himself to stage this play: "Which were the reasons why I did forward it at so unlucky a conjuncture, being content rather to lose the Profit, then not to expose to the World the Picture of such knaves and Rascals as then Reign'd in the opinion of the Foolish and Malicious part of the Nation."[82] He exposes in order to chastise, or so he says. Shakespeare's Titus effectively strips Lavinia again, chastises her, cuts her off not only from the rape but from a foreign and "barbarous" contamination. In Shakespeare's Rome, incest is better than miscegenation. Lavinia dies not as the (raped) body stolen by the Goths and the Moor but as Rome's sacrificial property.

Black Rapists and White Redemption

The dominant culture emphatically marks the difference, the official difference, between rape and sacrifice, even as it forges the relationship between them. Catherine R. Stimpson has made a point I wish to generalize; she has argued that "Shakespearean rape signifies vast conflicts: between unnatural disorder and natural order; raw, polluting lust and its purification through chastity or celibacy; the dishonorable and the honorable exercise of power."[83] The question becomes, how does this conflict end? What finally makes, decides, and visualizes the difference between an unnatural and polluting rape and an honorable suicidal or homicidal chastisement? I will argue as I end this chapter that a racial blackness enters textual play, especially in early modern tragedy, as a way of culturally marking and proving the difference between sacrifice and rape. Nonetheless, cultural or racial difference as signifying the difference between rape and sacrifice is not new to the early modern period. In Euripides' Greek tragedy *Iphigenia in Aulis*, for example, Agamemnon and Iphigenia concur that more horrific than rape per se is the fact of being raped by a barbarian, a cultural or racial outsider:

> O child, a mighty passion seizes
> The Greek soldiers and maddens them to sail
> With utmost speed to the barbarian place
> That they may halt the plunder of marriage beds
> And the rape and seizure of Greek women. (1263–67)

And, after some serious thought, she agrees:

> Because of me, never more will
> Barbarians wrong and ravish Greek women,
> Drag them from happiness and their homes
> In Hellas. (1379–82)

Through the guises of enthusiastic consent and good stage management, Iphigenia's sacrifice presumes silently and in tricky fashion to return rape to the community. Being raped by one's own isn't really rape. (Hence, the difficulty of prosecuting husbands and other family members for one's rape in present-day society.) After all, real white men don't rape. Barbarians do. (Hence, my book's first epigraph.) In classical and early modern culture rape happens primarily to the woman perceived as man's property, not to the woman perceived as an individual subject with her own claims to the boundaries of her body.[84] In this respect rape by a member of one's own community fits all too well into men's ongoing negotiations about their various inventories. To be raped, to be stolen, by one's proprietor becomes an ideological conundrum. Following the same logic, to be raped by an outsider, to be claimed by one who has or is given no local claims, signifies nothing less than an act of aggression against the body politic itself. Within the misogynistic frame of the nation-empire, rape really comes to mean something when its perpetrator comes from the outside; and rape comes into its most visual, catastrophic sign when it is committed by a *black* outsider. Lavinia's chastity is implicated in her racial whiteness, her pure Romanness or Englishness. Like England, or like Elizabeth I herself, Lavinia must rise from the emerging cultural and racial complexities as a symbol, an ornament of national and imperial purity. Her role is similar to that of Elizabeth, whose Protestant portraiture presumes to protect her body from the potential miscegenational contamination of Catholics and especially of the French and the Spanish. (I will say more about the explicitly *white* Elizabeth in Chapter 4.) Lavinia's imperial virginity is also presented as something that must get cut off from the kind of miscegenation imported "from those eastern parts," for the telling of which John Stubbs sacrifices his own hand. Lavinia, like Elizabeth, becomes the advocate too for a white England, one populated only by its "natural subjects."[85] Tamora's miscegenated body and miscegenated affair become potential titillating stepping-stones to Lavinia's body. Tamora's national-imperial claim once she becomes empress—"I am incorporate in Rome" (1.1.462)—her sexual relationship with Aaron, and her urging her sons to rape Lavinia toy together with the easy move from one kind of racial contamination to the next. The danger of the racial Other leads all too easily from one racial pollutant to one that is presumably even more racially contaminating.[86] All too easily interracial bodies and interracial sex get visualized as a scene of miscegenational rape.

The black man has an almost omnipresent place in early modern rape drama but, not surprisingly, is never actually allowed to rape the white woman. For some examples in addition to *Titus Andronicus* we may consider Dekker's *Lust's Dominion*, in which Eleazar threatens to rape the virtuous Isabella; the second part of Thomas Heywood's *The Fair Maid of the West* (1631), in which Mullisheg desires to rape Bess; or William Rowley's *All's Lost by Lust* (1619), in which Mulymumen first tries to marry Jacinta after revenging her rape by the Spanish king Roderigo. After her refusal, however, Mulymumen comes close to raping her, pursuing her across the stage as she answers his protestations of love, "Love thee? as I would love my ravisher" (5.5.1–10).[87]

Throughout early modern plays, the black man maintains a peculiar relationship to the rape narrative: although often enjoying the role of most nefarious and flagrant villain in a play in which a rape is the most catastrophic and constitutive act, his black body and the woman's white one become the twain that never do meet. His blackness serves to mark rape with racial pollution without insisting on a literalization of this contamination. Does the sexism of patriarchal culture require racial difference in order to make rape truly (that is, emblematically) violent? Without race the catastrophic nature of rape remains too ambiguous, too enfolded in cultural narratives of a natural masculine domination. Furthermore, the presence of the black body becomes a way of visualizing, of fantasizing, the pornographic narrative across the border of racial difference. Blackness makes rape happen. The black body simultaneously enables and distances (makes foreign) the pornographic story. By the end of *All's Lost by Lust*, for example, horror at the very possibility of even consensual sexual contact between Mulymumen and Jacinta overshadows and overwhelms the play's constitutive act, her rape by the white king. Mulymumen's presence both defines the play's pornographic threat and conspicuously marks Spain's difference from pornography.[88] The black bodies in these rape plays help accentuate this racializing.

Rape often pollutes or visualizes its pollution by racially marking the body. *Valentinian*, *All's Lost by Lust*, and William Heminge's *The Fatal Contract* (1640) exemplify a range of racializing possibilities. In Beaumont and Fletcher's *Valentinian*, which has no black body, Lucina insists on locating her rape in a black corporeality that signals the black race (and not just allegorical coloring) by effectively contrasting the emperor/rapist to a (white) blushing face and through a catalogue of invectives often used to describe the lecherous African infidel:

> Wilt thou not kill me, Monster, Ravisher,
> Thou bitter bane o'th' Empire, look upon me,
> And if thy guilty eyes dare see these ruines,
> Thy wild lust hath laid level with dishonour,
> The sacrilegious razing of this Temple,
> The mother of thy black sins would have blush'd at,
> Behold and curse thy self. . . .
> . . .
> Women, and fearfull Maids, make vows against thee;
> Thy own Slaves, if they hear of this, shall hate thee. (3.1)

A disguised Jacinta kneels before her father, Julianus, in *All's Lost by Lust*, hypothesizing and visualizing her rape in unmistakable anatomical terms:

Say that some rapine hand had pluckt the bloome,
Jacinta like that flower, and ravisht her,
Defiling her white lawne of chastity
With ugly blacks of lust; what would you do? (4.1.72–75)

Lest we forget, the black Mulymumen is the play's *diabolo incarnato* (devil incarnate), but the white king, Roderigo, is Jacinta's rapist. And, finally, taking one step further Ben Jonson's concealment from his audience of the boy bride's gender in *Epicene, or The Silent Woman* (1609–10)), the end of *The Fatal Contract* reveals to the audience on- and offstage that the black eunuch and villain, Castrato, is really the raped white Crotilda, whom the audience has only heard about in passing. Her black male disguise not only presumably frees her to revenge her rape and commit villainous acts but to perform more far-reaching cultural work. It forges a schizophrenic or hysterical link between the raped Crotilda and the rapist Castrato,[89] effectively turning the white Crotilda, who has been raped by the white king, into her own, nevertheless black, rapist. Were he himself no eunuch, Castrato muses,

I'd search the Deserts, Mountaines, Vallies, Plaines,
Till I had met *Chrotilda*, whom by force
I'd make to mingle with these sootie limbs,
Till I had got on her one like to me. (1.2.59–62)

(Throughout, Castrato echoes Shakespeare's Aaron, except Heminge allows Castrato to voice a more explicit desire to rape the best virgin or, at least, the best virgin-that-was.) Rape racially pollutes.

Sacrifice, however, racially purifies. All three plays I have discussed here, for example, stress the raped woman's sacrificial death as "returning" her to the purity of a racial whiteness. In *Valentinian* Lucina's very name originates in whiteness (in "light" [Latin]), and her husband quickly sends her off with his sacrificial approbation and shrouds her in a discourse of whiteness, calling her a "Lilly," a "sweetly drooping flower," and a "silver Swan" (3.1). When Mulymumen of *All's Lost* "tricks" the blinded Julianus into stabbing Jacinta,[90] Julianus's own daughter, Julianus offers what is presumably the play's official aphoristic and chastising/whitening response: "Forgive me, my Jacinta, 'twas in me / An innocent act of blood, but tyranny / In that black monster" (5.5.184–86). And in *The Fatal Contract*, with the uncovering of the fact that Castrato is really "no sun-burnt vagabond of *Aethiope*" (5.2.463), Crotilda wills her sacrificial/sexual return to whiteness at the hands of the man who raped her:

Thou injurd'st me, and yet I spar'd thy life;
Thou injurd'st me, yet I would dye by thee;
And like to my soft sex, I fall and perish. (5.2.484–86)

Crotilda's whiteness is underscored in her femininity. The sacrifice of these raped women knowingly reinscribes them in a discourse of whiteness. The violence of their deaths works most decisively to cut them off from a racial pollution.

More obviously, rape informs Lavinia's rape-sacrificial story. She too must be cut off from Rome's racial Others, these outsiders who do not invade Rome but are forced into it by Titus. Early in the play Titus especially emphasizes a chastising and chastised Rome; thus, his bringing the Goths and the Moor into Rome seems somewhat counterintuitive or at least somewhat extravagant. But the role of the racial Other has a use value and is far from being a mere ornament or curiosity. The racial Others are part of Rome's ethnographic allegory—its humanistic chaste thinking, its sacrificial redemption. Their entrance is no less significant than Titus's: they all participate in Rome's chastising and chastised agenda. On an ethnographic allegorical level, by admitting the Goths and the Moor into Rome, Rome does nothing less than guarantee the presence of rape and mayhem in the imperial city. For Rome (and for England) this is what racial Others are for: they are the bearers of national, imperial, familial, and social violence. This is the perennial story of "them" and "us." Like Shakespeare's other Other rapists, Aaron cannot be totally closed in by the allegorical or ethnographic tradition for which he not only presumably stands but for which he *presumes* to stand. Although not enough time is spent in critical studies, including this one, on the myriad implications of Aaron's seeking "to identify himself as a character outside a preordained allegory,"[91] I would like to think here about how Aaron nonetheless participates in Rome's and Shakespeare's ethnographic allegory. Notwithstanding his new son's being a sign of Aaron's adulterous relationship with Tamora, the child also allows Aaron to be seen in his own youth, his own innocence. Aaron can be "pictured" through reproduction, whereas Lavinia, whose chastised picturing is such a concern to Rome, can only be pictured through sacrifice and death.

In *Titus Andronicus* Tamora's two sons and Aaron with his "slavish weeds and servile thoughts" (2.1.18) have roles that are respectively analogous to those of the Etruscans and the slave voyeur in the myth of Lucrece. Tamora's sons rape Lavinia, and Aaron watches from the margins. The Goths are only half-barbarous, half-foreign. After all, they will ally themselves with Lucius in his attack on Saturninus and Tamora. Tamora, a Shakespearean prototype for Cleopatra, is herself doubly racialized: although Romans see her as effectively black, her sons see her (and themselves) as white. Saturninus is taken with her "different hue," but her sons are flabbergasted when she produces a black child with Aaron. Also, as doubly racialized, Tamora both makes possible the rape of the white Lavinia and stands between Aaron and Lavinia, providing a sexual barrier between them. Aaron is, presumably, the total barbarian, the fully signifying black Other. Even though Tamora's sons rape and mutilate Lavinia, Aaron is the most vilified character in the play and in its criticism. Marion Wynne-Davies, for example, has recently referred to him as "the Moor, who repudiates all moral standards and stands in the play as an incarnation of evil."[92] But how does he stand? Where? Perhaps erect over Lavinia?

As the sexually potent mastermind behind Lavinia's rape, Aaron is the play's real rapist, a sentiment as emotionally emphatic in the closing lines of the second quarto as it is visually affective in Peacham's drawing. He belongs to what becomes Shakespeare's ongoing commentary on or participation in the Western ethnographic tradition in which the racial male Other is *seen* as someone who is a rapist, a rapist especially of white virgins: Caliban is so depicted by Prospero, Othello by Brabantio; and then there is the "valiant" (that is, conquering) prince of Morocco, who seems parodically to indict himself when he suggests to Portia that he has had sex with the "best-regarded virgins" of his clime (*Merchant of Venice* 2.1.10). (Suggestively, Morocco threatens perhaps to darken or blacken Portia the way Shakespeare's Lucrece is supposed to be contaminated by someone of a different hue.) Dismissing Aaron simply as a *diabolo incarnato* is to displace him too quickly from the miscegenational rape narrative to which he belongs. It also marks a neglect of the complexities of the ethnographic aspects of Shakespeare's allegorical devil.

Such superficial readings fail to account for Aaron's role in Lavinia's sacrificial rape, making Aaron too Other to be truly integrated into the sacrificial and rape semiotics of Shakespeare's play. As Helms writes, Aaron "turns the traditional blackness of the stage devil into racial difference."[93] And as Wynne-Davies herself argues, when Aaron refuses the sacrificial killing of his own child—"My mistress is my mistress, this myself, / The vigour and the picture of my youth" (4.2.107–8)—the sympathy he arouses "can hardly be reconciled with [his] demonic role."[94] Similar to his speaking of himself as a lamb or his refusal to sacrifice his own child (Aaron may be no biblical Abraham but neither is Tamora's Rome part of any biblical covenant), Aaron seems poised throughout the play to mock Rome's sacrificial seriousness and hypocrisy, as, for example, in his exchange with Lucius in the last act of the play:

> Aaron: They cut and ravished her,
>   And cut her hands and trimmed her as thou sawest.
> Lucius: O detestable villain! Call'st thou that trimming?
> Aaron: Why, she was washed and cut and trimmed. (5.1.92–95)

Lucius's horrified response to Lavinia's trimming, her getting barbered—cut and groomed, "O barbarous, beastly villains like thyself!" (5.1.96)[95]—tells at best only a partial story and conveys only an officially sanctioned sentiment. All along, Rome (not Aaron) has been adamantly trimming Lavinia, sacrificially preparing her. Such sacrificial trimmings would become an almost voyeuristic stamp in a few of Shakespeare's plays: before the discovery of Juliet, for example, who has presumably already trimmed herself in her sacrificial scene: "Go awaken Juliet, go and trim her up" (*Romeo and Juliet* 4.4.25); as a capstone to Cleopatra's own sacrificial drama: "I found her [Cleopatra's gentlewoman] trimming up the diadem / On her dead mistress" (*Antony and Cleopatra* 5.2.341–42); and most vividly in Shakespeare's Hotspur, who speaks first of a "certain lord, neat and trimly dressed, / Fresh as a bridegroom" (1.3.33–34) and later urges,

> . . . Let them come.
> They come like sacrifices in their trim,
> And to the fire-eyed maid of smoky war
> All hot and bleeding will we offer them.
> The mailed Mars shall on his altars sit
> Up to the ears in blood. (*1 Henry IV*, 4.1.112–17)

Such sacrificial preparations allude, too, to Revelations 21:2: "And I Iohn sawe the holie citie newe Ierusalem come downe from God out of heauen, prepared as a bryde trimmed for her housband."[96] Lavinia, whose wedding to Bassianus has been cut off, finds her own marriage rites prolonged, as her trimming readies her for sacrifice. As King has argued about Greek wedding rituals, they share many elements found in the preparation of a beast for sacrifice, including "cutting hair, washing, giving a sign of consent and wearing a garland."[97] Lavinia's trimming recalls these other trimmings. Aaron exposes and mocks the lie that is Rome's fantasy of trimming, of chaste thinking—of cutting off ideological and narrative contact between rape and sacrifice, between Romans and outsiders. Aaron argues that however marginal he may officially be to Rome's community, it is he (*as* community member) who has prepared and stage-managed Lavinia's sacrificial Roman death.

Besides Lavinia, Aaron is the most visible character in Rome. It is perhaps for some Shakespeare audiences a relief (and a little surprising) that Aaron the Blackamoor, the icon of libido and rapaciousness, does not rape Lavinia. In any event, Aaron in his visibility stands in a role similar to that of the black servant in several representations of Lucrece. He is also the play's most voyeuristic character, watching and plotting without a word, for example, through the entire first act. Also in *The History of Titus Andronicus* (c. 1594), the chapbook prose story, the author points out that during the rape Aaron is set "to watch on the outborders."[98] On the "outborders" is also, one may recall, where Aaron is located in Peacham's drawing. Aaron stands in the margins with his black hands in full evidence, and his sword points to the kneeling and bound Chiron and Demetrius as he reveals not only his managing role in the rape and mutilation of Lavinia but also his iconographical place in pictorial representations of Tarquin and Lucrece.

Although the Romans find it expedient to racialize and differentiate Chiron and Demetrius from themselves, they also find it necessary to keep Aaron's blackness at a distance from Lavinia. This miscegenational rape would be no less horrifying to Chiron and Demetrius: they may rape and mutilate Lavinia, but they are disgusted and shocked into disbelief when they see the proof of Aaron's consensual sexual affair with their mother. (White-on-white rape is also more acceptable than consensual interracial sex.) Even though Aaron does not rape Lavinia, he stands in the play as *the* visible sign of the cultural otherness that Rome attempts to chastise with Lavinia's death. He becomes the horror that Rome claims it cannot imagine even as it does. Notwithstanding the importance of the Roman imagination, there can be in the play no literal racial contamination of the pure white Lavinia, just as there can be no such contamination of Lucrece. As foreign as Rome's and Shakespeare's ideological constraints will allow, Lavinia can only really be contaminated by a white Other. In a semiotics more nuanced perhaps than that of a racial conversion from white to black or from black to white (fairly available tropes in early modern England), Lavinia *is* a white woman who is made functionally and temporarily to pass as a black woman. Stretching, perhaps, the limits of my analogy, I suggest that Lavinia's body becomes for the moment like the octoroon in Joseph Roach's analysis, whose "nearly invisible but fatal blackness makes it available; [whose] whiteness somehow makes it clean."[99] In short, Roman contamination, like Roman sacrifice, is a story about symbolic relations (as opposed to real or literal ones), with Rome bringing in Aaron both to mask and to help expedite its symbolic story of sacrifice. But to leave the argument here seems to cheat somewhat the affectivity of the racial and pornographic story of Lavinia's (or Lucrece's) rape. There is something literal about Aaron's raping Lavinia, just as there is something literal in those many other early modern depictions of black men raping white women. In the rape-sacrificial story, in which the community is always at pains to separate its desires for the sacrifice from its desires for the rape, his black body is the textual trick, the incorporation of the sacrificial hoax, the *misunderstanding*, that differentiates rape from sacrifice. However much Aaron may be on the textual or representational border, Shakespeare's Rome consistently conceptualizes and imagines his body at its textual center. Given this play's obsession with the sociopolitics of identifying oneself as a brother, an early modern audience would most immediately recognize Aaron's name as belonging to the brother of Moses. This biblical Aaron helped Moses liberate the Israelites from Egypt (Joshua 24:5, 1 Samuel 12:6, 8; Psalms 77:20; 105:26), assisted him and the elders at significant sacrificial events (Exodus 18:12, 24:9–11), and served as the first high priest of the children of Israel (Exodus 31:10; 35:19; 38:21; Leviticus 13:2; Numbers 18:28). Admittedly, Shakespeare's Aaron is no high priest, and Shakespeare's Rome may have its reasons for finally reading Aaron's body as the real body threatening the palisading of white virginity—hence the closing lines of the second quarto. But in the end what makes Aaron no mere allegorical object is the fact that the metatheatrical Aaron knows and manipulates his place as sacrificial hoax and host.

At the end of Shakespeare's play Rome fantasizes that Lucius recovers not only Rome's virginity but its whiteness. As Calderwood has argued, Lucius, who is not in any of Shakespeare's conjectured sources and whose name means "light," functions as Rome's "political redeemer" and stands in contrast to Aaron, the nonlight, the Blackamoor.[100] To become Rome's redeemer Lucius leaves the city and stages a reentry. In the most classical tradition of the sacrificial victim, he is the outsider who is also an insider.[101] As the redeemer, Lucius emerges as the cultural product of Rome's ethnographic allegory. By being put in contradistinction to Aaron, he assumes a crucial role in what Clifford calls a "redemptive Western allegory." He is more than Rome's political redeemer in any abstract sense. By stepping in at the end to save the scattered (that is, "mutilated") body of Rome from doing "shameful execution on herself" (5.3.66–75), Lucius is also Rome's final substitute victim. Whereas Marcus himself pulls back from Rome's sacrifice of

itself, its proof of its purity, Lucius offers up himself and symbolically inscribes the Lucrece story on his own body:

> I am the turned-forth, be it known to you,
> That have preserved her welfare in my blood,
> And from her bosom took the enemy's point,
> Sheathing the steel in my advent'rous body.
> Alas, you know I am no vaunter, I;
> My scars can witness, dumb although they are,
> That my report is just and full of truth. (5.3.108–14)

In two gestures, figuratively taking the sword from the raped woman's body
and putting it in his own, Lucius becomes Brutus and Lucrece. After all,
Brutus's full name is Lucius Junius Brutus. Shakespeare's Lucius emerges as
the latest incorporation, the latest picture, of Lucrece's chaste body. But he
does not simply imitate his namesake. Instead of simply taking the dagger
from Lucrece's bosom and going on to sacrifice his own sons (Brutus would
kill his sons who did not support Rome's move to republicanism), Lucius
symbolically sacrifices himself. He brings the sword to its final resting place,
to a final resolve, by symbolically "sheathing" it in his own body, turning
this Roman drama into a political morality play.[102] Through him Rome becomes male and female—more accurately, the male body incorporates the
female body into itself. Lucius's determined move here to a symbolic understanding of Rome's chastity transforms sacrifice from a physical act into a
discursive practice. In a more cynical view of Rome's achievements at the
end of Shakespeare's play, one may perceive sacrifice not just as a discursive
practice but as a discursive trick, a theatrical trick, that allows Lucius to picture himself as both Brutus and Lucrece, Titus and Lavinia. He is both the
wounded soldier returning from battle and the wounding, self-sacrificing,
and preserving Lucrece. And as in Peacham's drawing, Lavinia loses her corporeal place in the story. In his coolness Lucius has chastised Lucrece, remembering the actions of her white hand, her sacrifice, her invisibility, even
as he forgets her rape.

TWO   Witnessing Whiteness

The white realm of Venice was not *the* white realm (of England), but with its own imperial ambitions and as the last Western European bastion of civilization before what was understood to be the darkness of Africa, Venice could be seen by the English if not always as an exemplary state then most certainly as a warning. The two republics were similar enough. Both promoted themselves as virgin territories, Venice driven by its cult of the Madonna, England by its cult of the virginal Elizabeth, a cult that acted in many ways of course as a palimpsestic picture of the Virgin Mary. Notwithstanding their official theological differences—via a religious Catholicism and a secularized Protestantism—they arrived at a similar or at least a sympathetic place, since what distinguished Venice's devotion to the Virgin Mary (its self-fashioning as the *Venezia Vergine*) from other Italian cities was, as Rona Goffen has argued, "a particularly complex and thoroughly Venetian blend of civic and sacred conceptions."[1] Not surprisingly, this has also meant that Venice, like England and classical Rome, could more vividly imagine the threat to its borders as a threat of rape.[2] In terms of a realpolitik, the English did perceive the Venetian Republic as sharing some of England's governing principles: Venice had its Council and England its Parliament.[3] But from the perspective of a Protestant England, Venice was at best a liminal and conflicted space: although standing as the last stronghold against the Ottoman Empire, it was still nominally Catholic and home to many Jews and other non-Christians. And although Venice *was* Catholic, it was also politically anti-papal.[4] In a final analysis, however, the Venetians were, for the English, decisively not English. Even though both cities promoted themselves as virginal cities, for example, Venice, with its seeming propensity for more relaxed moral attitudes, was more famous for its courtesans (and homosexuals) than for any real or symbolic virgins.[5] More important, Venice, with its extensive cultural and racial plurality—its own brand of multiculturalism—

would be seen by the English as (in this respect especially) a less chastised state. England fantasized bringing to fuller fruition the imperial and cultural vision of a classical Rome. Present-day Rome may have been England's danger "above all,"[6] but its decisive differences from Protestant England made it less a mirror through which early modern England could glimpse itself. Or, to put this in other terms, Venice was a more productive example for England's national-imperial purposes. In short, Venice figures as an imperfect picture of England, the inheritor of classical Rome's imperial self-fashioning but not its cultural and racial purity, its true virginity—its cultural and racial whiteness.[7] In the English reading of Venice, the openness of Venice's mercantile and sexual markets represents its most enviable strength and its most profound horror:[8] although this city-empire inserts itself in and becomes a nexus for a global marketplace, it also risks losing even the pretense of an identity separate from these same encroaching environs. As Murray J. Levith has summarily argued, "Venice was the hub of Italy for Shakespeare and his contemporaries. One could love it as the locus of excitement and progressive culture . . . or hate it as the seat of excess and decadence, a Catholic Sodom and Gomorrah. Most English undoubtedly saw it as a bit of each."[9] Venice was a city-empire that England at once envied, imitated, and had to chastise, to cut off from itself.

Stratagems: Courting Deportation

Both of Shakespeare's Venetian plays stage Venice's imperial identity as being at a point of crisis—in Girardian terms, at a juncture demanding at least a sacrificial gesture to give Venice *back* a discrete and enclosed sense of itself. As Jack D'Amico has argued, "These plays address a basic conflict between cultural pluralism and [a] strong tendency in the ruling class of any society to return, under pressure, to a more limited, perhaps clearer, definition of its social, racial, and political identity."[10] This city-empire tries to reconcile its pull in two directions: on the one hand, it draws cultural outsiders into the ambit of its powerful gaze, exploring and consuming their materials and their laboring bodies; on the other hand, it deports, expelling or erasing, cultural outsiders from the inner sanctums of Venetian culture. In *The Merchant of Venice* (1596–97), Portia, disguised as the lawyer Balthazar, asks, "Which is the merchant here? And which the Jew?" (4.1.174). The Venetian pursuit of fair contracts and equitable exchange leads to a cultural melding, a loss of a hegemonic Venetian imperial distinction. And in *Othello*, where a Moor (assuming the role of general) acts as the new fortified paterfamilias for the state, going even so far as to marry its prized daughter, the Venetian Empire finds itself compromised, sexually and culturally opened up, made "pliant" (1.3.152), by the very martial and marital exigencies that are supposed to protect it. The vital presence of Othello in Venice's making of war, or of Shylock in its conducting of commerce, underscores the city-empire's crisis of identification.

The Merchant of Venice proves a rather mythic example, with Venice playing out the colonial/imperial nightmare of hybridization, showing itself to be a society contractually trapped by its own global aspirations. If the presence of Shylock, the outsider, signifies the danger looming on the Venetian horizon, then Antonio's claim to a place at the center of Venice's economy, its main hold, hints how such cultural mixing has come about. Antonio turns of course to Shylock for help, and perhaps Shylock speaks not so unwittingly about the unjust irony of his place and placelessness in Venetian society, when he notes that "[Antonio] hath an argosy bound to Tripolis, another to the Indies . . . a third at Mexico, a fourth for England—and other ventures he hath, squand'red abroad. But ships are but boards, sailors but men; there be land rats and water rats, water thieves and land thieves—I mean pirates—and then there is the peril of waters, winds, and rocks. The man is, notwithstanding, sufficient" (1.3.17–25). Shylock describes a potentially very unstable Venetian market, one that may reach into many areas of the known world but that is practically at the whim (if not the mercy) of other men—not to mention the weather. He presents a Venetian world that is not only extremely vulnerable but that seems profoundly reckless. Moreover, for Shylock the fact that Venetians eat pork only begins to describe their barbarity, their cultural perversity (1.3.31–33). By contracting to take a pound of Antonio's flesh, Shylock satirizes the ritual foundation of Venice's Catholicism, its Eucharistic basis—its consumption of Christ's sacrificial body. And Antonio, whose own cultural place is always a highly ambivalent one, insists too earnestly on submitting himself to (what I would argue is for him) a homoerotically driven sacrifice. In other words, Shakespeare depicts the cultural and racial plurality and sexual liberality of Venice as pushing it to the critical point where Shylock and Antonio—which one *is* the merchant, which one the Jew?—collude to undermine the sacrificial principles on which the cultural and sexual identity of the empire depends. In the end, however, Portia doubly trumps Shylock and Antonio's potentially devastating cultural, sexual, and theatrical coup. First she thwarts Antonio's own Christ-like drama, allowing him to give his flesh but not his blood (4.1.304–11). And immediately thereafter she evokes a deus ex machina in the form of a law that effectively turns Shylock's contractually granted payment or sacrifice into a debt or an act of murder, a killing against, not for, the state: "If it be proved against an alien / That by direct or indirect attempts / He seek the life of any citizen," he or she should lose half his or her goods and find his or her life at the mercy of the duke (4.1.347–55). (Portia effectively renders Venice Protestant and heterosexual.) Portia, herself a kind of deus ex machina, reminds Venice that however vulnerable and penetrable it may seem, however playful and fluid it may advertise itself, it finally must not compromise its imperial Venetian essence. No proper Venetian law or ritual would demand such a thing.

It should not surprise us that the Elizabethesque Portia, the central authority to whom mighty Other nations must curtsy, instructs Venice in the error of its ways. She presides over Belmont, a city-empire that serves as Venice's fantastic counterpart. In essence, Belmont solves Venice's global quandary, its desire to have the world but not belong to it. Although Belmont may figure as an older and more feudal England,[11] Belmont is finally shaped not so much by any romanticized English wistfulness as by an imperial English fantasy, partaking in what I elaborate on in the next chapter as a realpolitik nostalgia. Portia's name calls up more than a Roman imperial lineage (1.1.166), even though it does that too. Her name also connotes, of course, "port," in her case, the divinely vested white center of intercultural commerce: "From the four corners of the earth they come / To kiss this shrine, this mortal breathing saint" (2.7.39–40).[12] And her suitors submit themselves to the casket test with the proviso that if they choose wrongly they will never marry (2.1.38–42). Not surprisingly, outside of Bassanio, her casket drama focuses mainly on the Catholic prince of Aragon and especially the infidel prince of Morocco, whose dark complexion repels Portia (2.7.79) and whose aggressive claim to the virgins of his clime borders on rape (2.1.8–11).[13] The Moroccan prince's choosing incorrectly renders him impotent, effectively castrated, yet an observer of Portia's sexual proprietorship. In other words, the prince essentially marries Portia, contracts himself to her, but is unable to have sexual relations with her. He belongs to Portia; in Portia's chastised vision of the empire, which is at once open and closed, he owes his allegiance, his body, to Belmont but can make no demands on it. He is obligated to submit to it but is not allowed to adulterate it, to blend in culturally. When Portia expels him, bids him a gentle riddance (2.7.78), she finds herself a step closer to achieving an imperial (im)balance between deporting and exploring the bodies of cultural Others. Through chance— which turns out to be a kind of universal determinism—Belmont remains culturally and racially pure even with its doors seemingly liberally thrown open for commerce and socialization.

Othello becomes Shakespeare's dramatic culminating point in this narrative of racial chastisement, with Othello effectively getting deported from Venice and shipped off to Cyprus, right to the edge of Africa, perhaps, back to Africa. (Contributing to and helping to shape and make more ominous the darkness of Cyprus, this outpost, would have been the fact that the Turks conquered Cyprus, taking it from Venice in 1571.) The Florentine Cassio is his counterpart, a near fantastical figure of whiteness. Cassio, like Othello, is a foreigner in the Venetian community, but whereas Othello represents the sinister outsider, the Florentine Cassio signifies a kind of white knight from abroad. He is the courtier par excellence, more "gentleman" than any Venetian. Iago has it out for both Othello and Cassio, one representing blackness and the other a kind of mercantilist untainted whiteness. Iago pushes for a Venetian whiteness that is not as courtier oriented, not as ungrounded and fanciful, as the whiteness of Florence.

Venice is trapped by its reliance on Othello. Unlike Venice, England was not in the habit of using outsiders to lead its military. Even so, Othello's public presence and his participation in Venetian private life would most likely raise the question for Shakespeare's early modern audience about the interdependency and intermixing of England's public interests and its expectations with respect to its private everyday interactions. The Venetian senators seem not to understand the tragic depths of the cultural infiltration signified by Othello and Desdemona's marriage. As further evidence of their failure to read the full impact of this marital-sexual violation, they also miss the way Othello's winning narrative of seduction draws Othello's onstage audience into a kind of rhetorical homosocial if not homoerotic love fest. (Hence, the duke's displaced response about how Othello's narrative would win his daughter too [1.3.170].) As in *The Merchant of Venice*, racial and sexual deviancies become intertwined signs of a community in crisis.

When we consider the black Othello in Shakespeare's play as a historicized racial subject, we most often think about him with respect to a black or African presence in early modern English culture, studying the size of the black population and its social or economic status before and/or after blacks arrived in England.[14] However necessary and legitimate such inquiries are, perhaps we need to ask a different question when studying Shakespeare's *Othello*. When the play opens, Othello is already settled in Venetian society, as evident by his frequent visits to Brabantio's house, his ample opportunities to court Desdemona, the senators' comfort and familiarity with him, and the fact that Othello himself can confidently rely on the state's knowledge of the services he has rendered. Notwithstanding the paucity, the near nonexistence of sympathetic black characters on the early modern stage, Shakespeare's play seems less daunted by the presence of the black Othello in Venetian society than by the events and stratagems through which Othello comes to be excluded, effectively deported from Venice. All this, even as the Venetians reach into Cyprus and beyond. I would like to suggest, as a way into *Othello*, that the play concerns itself less with the fact of Othello's mere black presence (an aspect of the play by which we often seem to get critically paralyzed) than with the drive to exclude him.

However few blacks there may have been in Shakespeare's England, Shakespeare finally seems less driven by the existence of blacks in England than by the move to deport them, to mark them as indefensibly different and dangerous. As Ruth Cowhig has argued, "The sight of black people must have been very familiar to Londoners. London was a very busy port, but still a relatively small and overcrowded city, so Shakespeare could hardly have avoided seeing them [that is, blacks]."[15] Or, in the words of Eldred D. Jones, "Not only is it certain that Shakespeare, living as he did in London and being so much a part of his times, would have had the opportunity to see Negroes, it seems impossible that he could have escaped seeing them."[16] In other terms, to say nothing about the quality of their experiences, from about the mid-sixteenth century onward blacks from North Africa and West Africa were a part of early modern English culture. There were clearly enough of them to motivate the Privy Council to order the deporting of eighty-nine of them. The council issued its warrant on July 18, 1596:

> Considering the reasonableness of his requestes to transport so many black-amoores from hence, doth thincke yt a very good exchange and that those kinde of people may well be spared in this realme, being so populous and numbers of hable persons the subjectes of the land and Christian people that perishe for want of service, whereby through their labor they might be mayntained. They are therefore in their Lordship's name required to aide and assist him to take up suche blackamoores as he shall finde within this realme with the consent of their masters, who we doubt not, considering her Majesty's good pleasure to have those kinde of people sent out of the lande.[17]

The eighty-nine black persons needed to fulfill this warrant were not the only blacks residing in England, as is evidenced by the fact that the council's primary objective here is to give Casper van Senden only as many Africans as Englishmen he has procured from Spanish and Portuguese prisons and brought back to England. The council makes it clear that, whatever their numbers, "those kinde of people may well be spared in this realme."

The ruling racial sentiments were unambiguous, and the antiblack or anti-African language only intensified a few years later, when Elizabeth issued her second edict on the subject around January 1601 (her first in 1599), this time without any capitulation to "reasonableness." I won't quote from that document here, since I used an extended piece of it in my introductory chapter. In the edict, however, the focus moves from compensating van Senden to vilifying and deporting all blacks out of the good and natural province of England. Passing the Africans on to van Senden serves here more as a convenience than as an impetus. However unsuccessful Elizabeth and the English were in deporting blacks from England, such proclamations do suggest that in the early years of the seventeenth century more saliently pressing than the presence of blacks in England was their expulsion from the naturally white "realme."[18] For evidence, real or imaginary, blacks became a sign of England's own growing unease with an increasingly more complex and diverse marketplace and especially with its particular place in it. With this agument as my constitutive point, I examine not only how the Venice of Shakespeare's play places Othello's blackness but how it dislocates it and transforms Othello into the ideological and theatrical instrument of its white sacrificial narrative. In the end I wish to argue that Othello's courting of Desdemona ushers in an elaborate theater of transported and deported bodies.

Uncovering the Black Scene

Shortly after Iago convinces Othello that evidence of Desdemona's guilt needs only ocular proof, Iago tells Othello that a woman's honor is "an essence that's not seen" (4.1.16).[19] From this point on Othello attempts to see this unseen essence, zealously searching for the origins of Desdemona's honor, that is, the original symbolic intactness of her hymeneal or undivided body. His examination of this unseen body simulates the play's interrogations of Othello's own metaphorical black body, unseen and missing despite his physical black presence. The duke offers the official reading of Othello's body when he proclaims to Desdemona's father, "If virtue no delighted beauty lack, / Your son-in-law is far more fair than black" (1.3.284–85).[20] In other words, Othello's physical blackness should not be read as ocular proof of his cultural blackness. And the full effect of the duke's "lack," that is, Othello's lack of whiteness, depends on an audience's understanding of Othello's entrapment in a discourse of lack. Either he is "far more fair than black," and therefore does not have a metaphorical black identity, or he really is black and is therefore entrapped by those pre-textual histories of blackness as an essential absence. Whether attention is focused on a theological or aesthetic racism, the presence of Othello's self depends (in the play and in criticism) on the success of culture to render invisible itself and its "racialist ideology."[21] It depends, finally, on the ability to accuse Othello the man rather than the culture that damns him from the start, thereby making personal the definition of Othello as savage and libidinous Other. To define Othello's blackness as personal is to argue that it does not metaphorically represent blackness but is literally the thing itself. But, as Othello's country-men will finally have it, no amount of rhyming or coupling (or punning) will leave unseen the black Other whom the audience suspects is hidden within Othello. Like Othello's search for Desdemona's honor, the play probes his blackness, always scrutinizing and presumably moving toward the origin and essence of his black presence.[22] To the extent that blackness in *Othello* is allegorical, it functions as Shakespeare's pre-text, what the audience knows before it comes to experience the play.[23] Shakespeare's play is the text that will at once unsettle and fill in, substantiate and resolve what the audience suspects it already knows about the essence of blackness as the savage and libidinous Other. But blackness is also Shakespeare's *pretext* in the more common sense of this word. Blackness is Shakespeare's pretense, the metaphor to which onlookers, both the audience and characters onstage, can pretend to react only as the image is produced before them.[24]

The three crucial structural elements of Shakespeare's play are Othello's blackness, his marriage to the white Desdemona, and his killing of her. These elements are, of course, related. The meaning of Othello's murdering Desdemona depends on their marriage, and their marriage's meaning is thoroughly invested in Othello's blackness. Each element is in effect a repetition of the other two. However so, the sexual coupling of Othello and Desdemona serves as the definitive picture of Othello's blackness. The scene of sexual intercourse between them functions, for the on- and offstage audiences alike, as the sexual site and sight of the play's racial anxieties.[25] And especially Iago, Venice's self-appointed cultural savior, re-presents these anxieties by mocking the sexual coupling of Othello and Desdemona and by associating it with scenes of horrifying sexuality, such as bestiality, and with culturally questionable sexual practices, such as homosexuality.

Iago draws on but does not invent a language of racism for his critique of Othello's blackness. Some kind of horrific history is already in place, deeply embedded or suspected to exist in the very physicality of black bodies. Iago's promise to "bring this monstrous birth to the world's light" (1.3.395) draws on a rich and complex semiotics of blackness (and whiteness).[26] Origin myths and theories linked blackness to Africa's proximity to the sun, to the light.[27] Especially during the early part of this period, England popularized the classical myth of Phaeton as a story about the origins of blackness. As Ben Jonson tells the story in his *Masque of Blackness* (1605), before Phaeton's "heedless flames were hurled / About the globe, the Ethiops were as fair / As other[s]." Now, "black with black despair," Ethiopian dames roam the world in search of their missing beauty, their lost identities.[28] Although other stories and theories superseded the popularity of the Phaeton myth, the myth remained in circulation at least until the late seventeenth century. In John Crowne's masque *Calisto* (1675), for example, one African nymph laments to another,

> Did not a frantic youth of late
> O'erset the chariot of the sun? . . .
> It is he that hath undone us. . . .
> And now we range the world around . . .
> To see if our lost beauty can be found.[29]

More than signifying a different identity, blackness throughout the seventeenth century came to represent a lost identity.

The mythic reading of blackness was only one of several explanations of origin. As "scientific" evidence became increasingly the official, or real, proof of the day—and as England's black population flourished—there developed a need for more such scientific histories.[30] Of particular interest was George Best's *Discourse* (published in 1578 and reprinted in Richard Hakluyt's *Principall Navigations* in 1600), which meticulously maps out God's condemnation of Ham, who, against the commandment of God and Ham's father, Noah, copulated with his wife while in the ark. God presumably punished Ham by making his son, Chus, and all Chus's offspring "so blacke and lothsome, that it [that is, their blackness] might remaine a spectacle of disobedience to all the worlde." Best also tells of another spectacle: "I my selfe have seene an Ethiopian as blacke as a cole brought into England, who taking a faire English woman to wife, begat a sonne in all respects as blacke as the father was." He concludes by arguing that the blackness of the child was owing to some "natural infection" in the father.[31] Sir Thomas Browne confronted the same issue in *Pseudodoxia Epidemica* (1646), raising objections to many of these earlier explanations and suggesting that "in the generation and sperm of Negroes, that being first and in its naturals white, but upon separation of parts, accidents before invisible become apparent; there arising a shadow or dark efflorescence in the outside."[32]

These typical examples assume that whiteness functions as the originating construct of a racial self and that blackness signifies some later horror, a kind of accident or aberration, a kind of jungle infestation. Further, a traumatic sexual encounter informs many of these scenes, hinting at something sexually bungled or impolitic. The disobedient white Ham secretly copulates with his white wife, who then gives birth to a black child. Best has a voyeuristic encounter with miscegenation, saying in effect that he has *seen* a white English woman give birth to a black child; his not ending the sentence until he has explained the source of the infection (the black father) also licenses him to see this scene, this moment of the infectious Other. And Browne's biological explanation brings before the onlooker's eyes the initially unseen bad seed (the bad copulation), thereby repeating in his writing the move from invisibility to visibility. As Ambroise Paré writes in a chapter entitled, "An Example of Monsters That are Created Through the Imagination," in his *Des Monstres et prodiges* (1573), "Hippocrates saved a princess accused of adultery, because she had given birth to a child as black as a Moor, her husband and she both having white skin; which woman was absolved by Hippocrates' persuasion that it was [caused by] the portrait of a Moor, similar to the child, which was customarily attached to her bed."[33] As Newman has pointed out, in both Shakespeare's play and European travel accounts of Africa, blackness becomes nearly synonymous with a perverse sexuality,[34] the site and sight of a monstrous birth. All too naturally and frequently black identity finds its origins in a scene of horrific copulation.

Many of these attempts to define blackness, to discover its origins, revolve around the effort to decide the naturalness or unnaturalness of blackness. Even so, as Bartels has argued, the gesture really seems intended to show the instability (and therefore untrustworthiness) of blackness, as it slips, often surreptitiously, from one category to the other.[35] The site and sight of blackness finally *is* the interminable interplay between the natural and the unnatural. Uncovering or discovering the original accident of blackness would achieve a nonpareil collage-like summation from John Bulwer in his *Anthropometamorphosis: Man Transform'd; or, the Artificiall Changeling* . . . (1653), in which the animalism and the sexual and heliocentric readings of the origins of black Africans would spring from a single explanation:

That it may be the seed of *Adam* might first receive this tincture, and became black by an advenient and artificial way of denigration, which at first was a meere affectation arising from some conceit they might have of the beauty of blacknesse, and an Apish desire which might move them to change the complexion of their bodies into a new and more fashionable hue, which will appear somewhat more probable by divers affectations of painting in other Nations, . . . And so from this Artifice the *Moores* might possibly become *Negroes*. . . . For thus perhaps this which at the beginning of this Complexion was an artificiall device, and thence induced by imagination, having once impregnated the seed, found afterwards concurring productions, which were continued by Climes, whose constitution advantaged the artificiall into a natural impression.[36]

Bulwer's theory not only argues for the natural unnaturalness of blackness but, and I will return to this point at the end of this chapter, the virtual theatricality of blackness. From this perspective especially, Othello's pre-texts include a host of dramatic Others, most famously "Belial the blake" in *The Castle of Perseverance* (early fifteenth century), Prince Muly Mahamet in George Peele's *The Battle of Alcazar* (1589), and Shakespeare's own Aaron in *Titus Andronicus*. However well black African bodies may perform blackness, blackness remains an artificial and performative thing, at once imitable and inimitable. Theatrically, blackness becomes a kind of racial testing ground for whiteness, most immediately for the white actor. Not in spite of the racist sentiments driving the nineteenth-century Mary Preston's protestations with respect to Shakespeare's play—"I have always *imagined* its hero *a white* man. It is true the dramatist paints him black, but this shade does not suit the man. It is a stage decoration . . . We may regard, then, the daub of black upon Othello's portrait as an *ebullition* of fancy, a *freak* of imagination . . . the single blemish on a faultless work. Othello was a *white* man!"[37]—it becomes more than necessary to hypothesize, to at least try to trouble (to un-chastise) that space between Othello's ethnic and theatrical blackness, that is, that difference between Othello as black character and Othello as white actor—or, perhaps, between Othello as unnatural black man and Othello as natural white actor.

Black on Display

Blackness figures as an unending exchange between Othello's literal black presence and his metaphorical black absence; throughout, his blackness continues to elude. It is not an isolated issue in the construction of this single character;[38] it informs and is informed by every other object and event in the drama. And what brings objectness (presence and visibility) to his blackness is nothing less than his own confrontation with objects—namely, the bed and the handkerchief. These objects are thoroughly inscribed in both the presence and the absence of his blackness, an identity at which the play will often only hint. Unlike his blackness, the bed and the handkerchief are so explicitly and frequently imaged throughout the play that they do not seem so critically elusive.[39] In the end, however, the meaning of the bed and the handkerchief, like that of Othello and Desdemona's marriage, hinges on what the audience already knows to be the meaning (or emotional content) of Othello's blackness.

As both Michael Neill and Lynda E. Boose have argued, the bed (along with its sexual couple) finally emerges as an object that the play has all along been bumping into or trying to maneuver its way around.[40] It stands before the audience as visible and climactic. I am inclined to agree with Stanley Cavell, whose "hypothesis about the structure of the play is that the thing *denied our sight* throughout the opening scene—the thing, the scene, that Iago takes Othello back to again and again, retouching it for Othello's enchafed imagination—is what we are shown in the final scene, the scene of murder."[41] But, as Neill demonstrates, it is first and foremost the bed—and not the murder—that the play persists in dangling before our eyes and repeatedly snatching away. Although Lodovico's response to the tragic loading of this bed—"The object poisons sight; / Let it be hid" (5.2.360–61)—may attempt to return the bed to its hiddenness, it also figures this bed as an object always represented as a textual negotiation between presence and absence.[42]

The handkerchief, even more than the bed, appears and disappears repeatedly. It acts as a kind of prefatorial object, providing a visible token of one of Shakespeare's pre-texts, Leo Africanus's *A Geographical Historie of Africa* (1600).[43] In his *Historie*, Africanus relates the custom in which "a certaine woman standeth before the bride-chamber doore, expecting till the bridegroome hauing defloured his bride reacheth her a napkin stained with blood, which napkin she carrieth incontinent [that is, immediately] and sheweth to the guestes, proclaiming with a lowd voice, that the bride was euer till that time an vnspotted and pure virgine."[44] Steeped in consummation ritual from a culture of the Other, the napkin has at least a dual function: it speaks to Othello about the displacement of his marriage and to the audience about the exoticism and out-of-placeness of Othello's blackness in Western European culture. Rather than having a meaning that "may well lie hidden in rituals and customs which were accessible to Elizabethans but have since been lost,"[45] the handkerchief most likely already functioned when the play was written as Shakespeare's token of lost or hidden rituals.

Like the napkin in Africanus's text, which exhibits the woman's loss of virginity, the napkin in Shakespeare's play is thoroughly invested with issues of loss and displacement.[46] First of all, only after Othello and Desdemona lose the handkerchief does it become a significant object. This happens, of course, almost immediately. Lost a few lines after its first appearance, the handkerchief enters the play as a displaced object (3.3.285–88) and is, in essence, about its own absence. Further, its origins are textualized in a loss of life:

> There's magic in the web of it.
> A sibyl that had numbered in the world
> The sun to course two hundred compasses,
> In her prophetic fury sewed the work;
> The worms were hallowed that did breed the silk,
> And it was dyed in mummy which the skillful
> Conserved of maidens' hearts. (3.4.69–75)

Othello himself comes into possession of it as he loses his mother: "She, dying, gave it me" (3.4.63).

And the nature of its enchantment depends on whether it is lost or, instead, properly bestowed. Othello tells Desdemona that if his mother "lost it / Or made a gift of it, [his] father's eye / Should hold her loathed" (3.4.60–62). Bianca also reads the handkerchief as a sign of loss. When Cassio gives it to her and asks her to copy the pattern, she blames his absence on the handkerchief and its owner: "This is some token from a newer friend. / To the felt absence now I feel a cause" (3.4.180–81). The pattern continues. There is a certain lack of objectness to this cloth. Rather than representing some real corporeal thing—a body part, for example[47]—the napkin turns Othello's enchafed mind back to the presence or absence of a first sexual scene between Desdemona and himself, what I have argued elsewhere is the play's primal scene.[48]

In its origins, as well as in its ritualistic propriety, the handkerchief conjures up an originary sexual moment. It encourages the audience's return to Africanus or to some such pre-text and to narratives of foreign rites of devirgination found in those pre-texts. More incisively than any other critic, Boose has argued for a relationship between the cloth and some scene of sexual intercourse. She quite rightly links the handkerchief to the "ritual origins of marital blood pledge [that] stretch back into man's ancient consciousness." As she points out, the allusion to the phallic worms that made the cloth and the "mummy . . . Conserved of maidens' hearts," which made the spotted-strawberry (or bloody) pattern on it, "*repeats* the picture of the handkerchief." And as "an antique token / [His] father gave [his] mother" (5.2.213–14), this napkin represents "that which every husband 'gives' his bride."[49] In his psychoanalytic reading of the play Peter L. Rudnytsky argues more explicitly for the handkerchief as a substitution for the primal scene.[50] As Boose and Rudnytsky insist, the absent/present napkin, like the matrimonial bed itself, works to summon the audience again and again to the missing scene of the sexual coupling.

The handkerchief does not simply substitute for the sexual scene of Othello and Desdemona. Rudnytsky reads the cloth as a symbol of "all the 'displacements of affect'" throughout the play, that is, as the thing that replaces what the audience is not allowed to see; but the significance of the napkin is less in its being a symbol and more in its being a distorted representation than Rudnytsky's argument allows.[51] Both Othello's forced attempt to translate this untranslatable object and what Othello sees as the transferring of this nontransferable object threaten to transform the handkerchief's sacrificial cultural potency or assignation into something exotic and cultish. Too, the handkerchief trivializes the much larger wedding-bed sheets, even as it publicizes and makes small their culturally traumatizing significance. The mere presence of the handkerchief pushes the matrimonial bed and couple from a private into a public arena, where their marriage is itself subjected to and doomed by public scrutiny and cultural prejudice. The rites of marriage, instead of belonging to Othello and Desdemona alone, seem always to be displaced and possessed by whoever possesses the napkin. The displaced cloth comes to represent the displaced bed, which represents the displaced couple; and these objects and the couple of Othello and Desdemona are significant *because* they are displaced.

Displacement, like Browne's reading of the accident of blackness, is signified by its visibility. The primal scene is the site and sight of such displacements, such emergences from invisibility. The couple that effects such a displacement is, of course, Othello and Desdemona. Nonetheless, their difference depends on the sameness of Desdemona and Cassio, who throughout serve as a kind of originary couple. Of the women and men found in this play, Desdemona and Cassio function as this Venetian play world's most natural pair. As Stephen Greenblatt has argued, "It is eminently probable that a young, beautiful Venetian gentlewoman would tire of her old, outlandish husband and turn instead to the handsome, young lieutenant."[52] Cassio and

Desdemona have about them a social legitimacy that grants them cultural invisibility: without Desdemona's marriage to Othello, she and Cassio would be the play's most probable and conventional couple.

Iago iterates as much shortly after Desdemona arrives in Cyprus and engages in banter with Cassio; Iago watches and comments on their ingenuous parody of courtly affectation. And when at the end of his chorus the sound of Othello's horns is heard and Iago proclaims, "The Moor! I know his trumpet" (2.1.175–76), Iago takes the trumpet as the cue for his own Jerichoan destruction of Othello and his world. He takes it also as a signal to begin his own revelatory trumpeting of Othello's strumpet. Iago's call for destruction announces first and foremost the metamorphosis of Desdemona from a virgin to an adulterous whore. The perfection of Desdemona and Cassio that could have been is forever lost: they are the originary couple that cannot be recovered. The courtly and proper couple is effectively displaced into the sexual and improper couple of Othello and Desdemona. Genteel courtship has been displaced by the bedroom, the most telling and exhibitionistic topos of the primal scene. As already noted, the improper relationship between Othello and Desdemona is in its essence a displacement of the proper relationship between Desdemona and Cassio. The "divided" (1.3.179) relationship of Othello and Desdemona is haunted by the originary oneness of Desdemona and Cassio, who can now offer only a monstrous and grotesque parody of Othello's union with Desdemona. Given Desdemona's *obscene* marriage, the proper coupling of Desdemona and Cassio is now recoverable only as a scene of sexual transgression. Iago attempts to make Othello see his (Othello's) complicity in Desdemona's violation, if not of Venice's real mores, then most certainly its self-fashioning ones. Iago's first words in the play speak of the coupling of Othello and Desdemona: "'Sblood, but you'll not hear me! If ever I did dream / Of such a matter, abhor me" (1.1.4–5). He uses words that draw on a primal discourse of blood, dreams, and whoredom (pun on "abhor"). Before identifying Othello and Desdemona by their names, he conjures them up in the familiarly ominous images of the primal scene. Long before Iago tells Cassio's dream in act 3, the dream of Othello and Desdemona has been put into discursive circulation. But Iago's horror at the possibility of sex between Othello and Desdemona is not his alone. When Brabantio hears that Desdemona has eloped with Othello, he confesses, "This accident is not unlike my dream" (1.1.139). Brabantio's dream is one that presumably murders him before the "sight" (that is, of the couple on the bed) would, according to Gratiano, have forced him to "do a desperate turn" (5.2.204–6). Each of these dreams is a "foregone conclusion"

(3.3.425), a fait accompli, before the play ever opens. These are the Venetians, perhaps the proper ones (the ones of a more fortified Venetian past), whose nightmares have already anticipated Venice's new plurality, its inability to keep its doors shut against outsiders (1.1.82, 102–3), against the jungle.

It is Iago, however, who most adroitly pushes Othello toward understanding the signifying density of blackness, its cultural, racial, and sexual range. He understands blackness as well as would Bulwer (from whose *Anthropometamorphosis* I quoted earlier) or as well as would Samuel Purchas, who refers in *Hakluytus Posthumus* (1625) to the "filthy sodomites, sleepers, ignorant, beasts, disciples of Cham, Balaam, and Core . . . to whom the blacke darknesse is reserved for ever."[53] In act 3, scene 3, especially, Iago presents and re-presents to Othello the horrific phantasm of Othello's own perverse and violent sexual coupling with Desdemona. The scene opens with Iago's distortion of Cassio's conversation with Desdemona and closes with the homosocial and homosexual marriage between Othello and Iago. Voyeuristic imagery dominates the scene: from Othello's failure to see Cassio stealing away guilty like (3.3.38–39) to the pain of his "watching" (line 284) to his demand for "ocular proof" (line 357) and satisfaction (line 387) to Iago's pornographic teasing of Othello and pornographic indictment of Desdemona—"How satisfied, my lord? / Would you, the supervisor, grossly gape on? / Behold her topped?" (lines 391–93)—through Iago's evocation of bestiality:

> Where's satisfaction?
> It is impossible you should see this,
> Were they as prime as goats, as hot as monkeys,
> As salt as wolves in pride, and fools as gross
> As ignorance made drunk. (3.3.398–402)

His bestial references here give further weight not only to his earlier disapprobations of "a Barbary horse" (1.1.108–9), "the beast with two backs" (1.1.114), and the "tupping" old black ram (1.1.85–86) but also to early modern Europe's belief in the bestial sexual practices of Africans and the suspicion that Africans are at least partly beast. The sixteenth-century French political theorist Jean Bodin, for example, writes in his *Method for the Easy Comprehension of History* (first published in Latin in 1566): "Because self-control was difficult, particularly when plunging into lust, [Africans] gave themselves over to horrible excesses. Promiscuous coition of men and animals took place, wherefore the regions of Africa produce for us so many monsters."[54] In 1534 England made bestiality a capital crime, in part because "in popular estimation at least, man was not so distinct a species that he could not breed with beasts . . . [and] the separateness of the human race was thought so precarious."[55] Africans would thus have been thought not only a particularly suspect class of people but a group from whom the English would want racially to chastise themselves—to mark and articulate the Africans' distinctive and unequivocal difference. In short, Iago argues that the coupling of Othello and Desdemona conjures up this bestial drama and uncovers their sexual liaison as worthy of a pornographic freak show.[56] Iago structures the scene so that the voyeuristic story intensifies as the scene continues, moving from Othello's witnessing the missing Desdemona-Cassio scene to Othello's demand for ocular proof—a proof that is represented to him as a scene of bestial sexuality and then as a scene of homosexuality, with this final gesture completing Iago's coup de theatre.

One of the play's most memorable displacements and the most memorable gesture in this scene of Othello and Iago's theatrics is Cassio's alleged dream, which Othello demands to have represented and which Iago feigns a reluctance to repeat:

> I lay with Cassio lately,
> And being troubled with a raging tooth,
> I could not sleep.
> There are a kind of men so loose of soul
> That in their sleeps will mutter their affairs.
> One of this kind is Cassio.
> In sleep I heard him say, "Sweet Desdemona,
> Let us be wary, let us hide our loves!"
> And then, sir, would he gripe and wring my hand,
> Cry "O sweet creature!" Then kiss me hard,
> As if he plucked up kisses by the roots
> That grew upon my lips; laid his leg o'er my thigh,
> And sigh, and kiss, and then cry, "Cursed fate
> That gave thee to the Moor." (3.3.410–23)

"O monstrous! monstrous," responds Othello. "Nay," says Iago, "this was but his dream" (line 424). Iago's account works through a series of repetitions. He foregrounds his own telling of the story by emphasizing how much he begrudges telling it, and then, after setting the scene, speaks about men such as Cassio, who in their sleep will "mutter their affairs," presumably things they would normally not publicize or confess. Only after repeatedly drawing attention to more forthright acts of speaking—"mutter," "say," "cry"—

does Iago quote Cassio, whose words reveal the hidden sex scene between Desdemona and Cassio. A very aggressive oral anxiety permeates various levels of Iago's narrative—his "raging tooth," which somatically replicates and evinces the story he tells; his supposedly begrudged telling of the story to Othello; Cassio's painful and accidental confession in his dream; and the kiss on which this oral anxiety comes to focus: "Then kiss me *hard,* / As if he *plucked* up kisses by the *roots* / That grew upon my *lips.*" The repetition of this oral anxiety brings a sense of coherence to the pastiche that constitutes Iago's narrative.

The image hidden from, but being made visible for, Othello is supposedly of Desdemona and Cassio, but Iago actually presents a homoerotic scene involving sex between Cassio and himself.[57] This moment does not mark Iago's betrayal of any repressed homoerotic feelings toward Othello but rather his perverting of the coupling of Desdemona and Othello into sexual copulation between Cassio and himself, where Iago finds himself seduced and violated by Cassio. As in *The Merchant of Venice,* the fluidity of Venice fuses cultural/racial and sexual identities into a single horrific scene. For Iago, who wishes to push Venice toward a more heterosexual and racially homogenous coupling, this latter sex scene conjures up the homosexuality that is supposed also to be part of Venice's loose sexual mores. Although homosexuality could effectively serve as the ultimate horrific act of sexual coupling for English culture,[58] it works especially well here to mark Venice, this reputed home of the homosexual, as decisively different from England.[59] In this sex act Iago is at once Venetian and English. Still, Iago's allowing himself even to be narratively implicated in this scene only underscores the extent to which he will sacrifice himself in order to bring to light what he sees as the monstrous coupling of Othello and Desdemona. Finally, in the marriage between Iago and Othello (with its caustic vows), Iago finishes the scene by re-presenting the nuptials performed just before the play opens (3.3.450–76); profoundly intertwined is Venice's tolerance of racial mixing and sexual permissiveness. The English-Venetian Iago argues that England should take note.

However sympathetic Shakespeare's Othello may appear for most of the play and however much Shakespeare shows him working against his indelibly marked black body—"Keep up your bright swords, for the dew will rust them" (1.2.58)—and however much Othello may have enough distance from his own blackness in order to allegorize it—"My name that was as fresh / As Dian's visage, is now begrimed and black / As mine own face" (3.3.383–85)—his killing of Desdemona changes all. It brings a cognitive assonance to

the physical blackness the on- and offstage audience has witnessed as disso-
nance:Venice *had* declared him far more fair than black. It also gives the distinct impression that Othello—shocked into a more fully blown recognition by Emilia's calling, perhaps knocking[60]—discovers himself entrapped in
blackness. His murderous deed brings a literalness, a fixity,[61] to those cultural
constructs that have become so familiar during the play's repetition and displacement of his blackness.

Othello is made to create the ocular proof that legitimizes an audience's
guarded response to his blackness. Like the fictions about bestiality or homosexuality evoked or generated by the play, blackness is never literal in
Othello. If anything, blackness figures as the ocular sign of a cultural need to
create and destroy monsters: create them so that they may not create themselves; destroy them so that they may not procreate or multiply. In the nas-
cent imperialism of early-seventeenth-century England, this process is not
merely birth control but ideology control. The black presence in Shakespeare's play makes visible and then amalgamates and critiques those impolitic fictions that become engendered and intermixed in the name of cultural order. Bestiality, homosexuality, and black sexuality (or blackness) are
essentially one and the same horrific trope. The act of making fair fair and
black black becomes itself a dramatic metaphor, hinting at the ways realpolitik uses metaphor in the spirit of literalness.

Abuse and the Great White Act of Raptus

And of course Othello's killing Desdemona pictures more than an act of
murder. It is here, too, where the bed is pushed to center stage and the audience is finally allowed to witness Othello and Desdemona's sexual union,
this act that before had been rendered only through a series of missed sexual
scenes, especially of bestiality and homosexuality. Whatever one's critical
position on Othello and Desdemona's sexual consummation[62]—do they or
don't they—this murder makes tangible and visible the sexual coupling, the
primal moment, that moves titillatingly through the play like some kind of
specter. The scene betrays, too, the play's romantic aesthetic, which has pre-
tended to keep repressed, keep hidden, the violent and more physically raw
reading of Othello and Desdemona's relationship. In returning Othello to
his dramatic inheritance, Shakespeare's play (or Iago) also makes literal, bringing into clearer focus, the threat racial mixing poses to the state's national
and imperial identity. Not only is Othello, unlike his dramatic predecessors,
much more integrated into the dominant community, but, more important,

Desdemona, the truly white Desdemona who "blushed at herself" (1.3.96), differs from her predecessors, those other white—more accurately, non-black—women who become sexually involved with black men. Her involvement with Othello threatens the national and imperial hegemony in a way that the already sexually—and therefore culturally and racially—suspect Queen Mother in *Lust's Dominion* or Tamora in *Titus Andronicus* cannot. In other words, Desdemona is the first major *white* woman character in English drama to have a sexual relationship, however explicit or implicit, with a black man.[63] In the self-preserving instinct of Shakespeare's Venice or Shakespeare's England, a white woman's marrying a black man, or, as in *Antony and Cleopatra*, a white man's falling in love with a black woman,[64] amounts to nothing less than a violation of national proportions. Othello's murdering Desdemona in their wedding-bed sheets, producing an orgasmic "death" that is "unnatural" because it "kills" (5.2.42), brings closure to this drama of *raptus*, of bride theft—of rape.

As discussed in the preceding chapter, black male characters are often made to voice such fantasies of jungle fever, however unsuccessful they are finally in acting them out. And although white women may be feared as the target de jour of the black man's sexual violence, these same Western fears construct the black man as having as natural a propensity toward rape as he had toward bestiality. As evinced by my earlier quote from Bodin's *Method*, the black man's lack of self-control leads to his sexual overpowering of animals. And as late as the early eighteenth century one John Atkins would write, "At some Places the *Negroes* have been suspected of Bestiality with them [apes and monkeys], and by the Boldness and Affection they are known under some Circumstances to express to our Females; the Ignorance and Stupidity on the other side, to guide or control Lust . . . would tempt one to suspect the Fact."[65] Or in Paré's story (quoted earlier) of the woman Hippocrates saves from charges of adultery, a black man leaps from a portrait into the woman's bed and then invades her womb. Othello may not be a rapist in the same genre as Aaron, Eleazar, or these bestial or more phantastic Africans, but I disagree with Ania Loomba's reading (as cogent as it is) that the "myth of the black rapist . . . hovers on the margins of Brabantio's accusations, but is undercut by Desdemona's own powerfully articulated desire for Othello."[66] Can Desdemona and Othello really commit their own act of chaste thinking, isolate Othello from his dramatic forebears? First and foremost, like Neill's understanding of the adulterous nature of Othello and Desdemona's relationship, the language and imaging of Desdemona and Othello in terms of rape inform a social landscape more so than they determine the innocence or guilt of any individual character. Also, and relatedly, the social anxiety that the black man will or at least desires to overpower the white woman does not allow for any real ideological dissociation in black-white coupling between consensual sexual intercourse and rape. Notwithstanding such theoretical positions, Othello's violation of Desdemona, demonstrated first as an act of theft and finally in the confirmation of the murderous rape, has more than a casual hold on Shakespeare's Venetian drama.

Especially through the first act, the Venetians (not only Brabantio and Iago) move uneasily but determinately around a discourse of rape. Brabantio's aphoristic closing of the second scene, for example, echoes Lucrece's plaint to Tarquin, when she tries to convince him not to rape her: " 'So shall these slaves be king, and thou their slave; / Thou nobly base, they basely dignified' " (Shakespeare, *The Poems, Lucrece*, 659–60). Says Brabantio, "For if such actions may have passage free, / Bondslaves and pagans shall our statesmen be" (1.2.97–98). But the characterization of Othello and Desdemona's relationship as having a "violent commencement" (1.3.340), as being an act of theft and abuse, most particularly underscores this Venetian suspicion of rape. Not surprisingly, the words *thief* and *abuse* and their cognates name the crime of Shakespeare's Tarquin: "Ev'n in this thought through the dark night he stealeth ... He like a thievish dog creeps sadly thence" (*Lucrece*, 729, 736). Just a few of many examples from *Lucrece* include the following: "O, let it not be hild [*sic*] / Poor women's faults that they are so fulfill'd / With men's abuses" (1257–59); and " 'Though my gross blood be stain'd with this abuse / Immaculate and spotless is my mind' " (1655–56).

Iago first wakes Brabantio with his cry of "Thieves! Thieves!" (1.1.76, 78), which he follows up with, "Zounds, sir y'are robb'd!" (1.1.83). Brabantio responds, "What tell'st thou me of robbing? This is Venice; / My house is not a grange" (1.1.102–3). In the second scene Brabantio greets Othello with "O thou foul thief, where hast thou stowed my daughter?" (1.2.61). The language of thievery and rape continues in the next scene with the duke's asking Othello what "indirect and forced courses" (1.3.111–12) he used to win Desdemona and concludes with the duke's wallowing in his own sententiousness, perhaps his own loss of any real words (Cf. 1.3.284–85), "The robbed that smiles, steals something from the thief; / He robs himself that spends a bootless grief" (1.3.205–6). The imaging of thievery is made most visibly evident in the handkerchief, this sexually and ritually signifying object that changes from a gift into a stolen object, and it makes sense that it ends up in the hands of Bianca, whose name means "white" but who lives in the community as a courtesan. Othello is finally driven not only by his thievery but by his misogyny as he gives into those suspicions that a woman once raped, once stolen, will be eager to be again so violated. (Lucrece kills herself to argue otherwise.) Of course this patriarchal fear informs Brabantio's warning to Othello: "Look to her, Moor, if thou hast eyes to see: / She has deceived her father, and may thee" (1.3.287–88). And Othello understands how his thievery has returned to haunt, perhaps to punish him, when an enraged Othello asks Iago, "What sense had I of her stol'n hours of lust?" (3.3.335). Othello has stolen Desdemona from her father. She can no longer live in her father's house (1.3.236–39). And however much she may wish to follow Othello to Cyprus, she along with Othello is passively banished from Venice: once she strays from her father's house, which is now closed to her, the newly "consecrate[d]" African-smitten Desdemona properly belongs nowhere if not with Othello in the darker world of Cyprus (1.3.243–54, 270–72).

Shakespeare's text of sexual displacements betrays Venice's vulnerability to *raptus*, its "abuse" through the ear. Othello wins the duke and the senators with his tale, which begins with the preamble, "So justly to your grave ears I'll present / How I did thrive in this fair lady's love, / And she in mine" (1.3.124–26). Following right on the narrative heels of the Anthropophagi, the man-eaters, Othello tells of Desdemona's cannibalistic "greedy ear," an ear that betrays her body as being too culturally and sexually open (1.3.142–49). The word *abuse* and its cognates (used more times in this than in any other Shakespeare play) become a kind of choral refrain for Brabantio through the first act: "Is there not charms / By which the property of youth and maidenhood / May be abused?" (1.1.168–70). In the second scene, "Thou hast practiced on her with foul charms, / Abused her delicate youth with drugs or minerals / That weaken motion" (1.2.72–74), the word *motion* signifying doubly, as "thought" and as "physical mobility." And in the third scene:

> She is abused, stol'n from me, and corrupted
> By spells and medicines bought of mountebanks;
> For nature so prepost'rously to err,
> Being not deficient, blind, or lame of sense,
> Sans witchcraft could not. (1.3.60–64)

Brabantio's sensory speech begs for the conflation of *err* and *ear*, with the latter being quite the site in this play of much cultural, racial, and sexual erring. In the next scene Iago further stresses Desdemona's vulnerability when he echoes Brabantio's argument that Desdemona's "delicate youth" has been abused by predicting that before long her "delicate tenderness will find itself abused" (2.1.230–31). Although the word *abuse* works conspicuously to indict Othello for penetrating Desdemona, motivating Brabantio's labeling him "the abuser of the world"(1.2.77), the term comes most tellingly in the latter part of the play to refer especially to Othello, whose penetrable body in the form of his "open nature" (1.3.390) contrasts with Iago's more guarded disposition. Iago confesses that "it is [his] nature's plague / To spy into abuses" (3.3.146–47), and in such a capacity he sets out "to abuse Othello's ears" (1.3.386), vengefully penetrating the body that has penetrated Venice. Iago aims to make known, to make visible, Othello's rape of Desdemona. In Iago's drama of the improper and violable scenes of blackness—Othello's break into Brabantio's house, his bestial display of human bodies, a man's plucking at another man, and Othello's topping Desdemona—all are one and the same image of rape, one and the same horrific image of cultural, racial, and sexual violence.

The sexual violence running through the final scene is evident in more than the interplay between words of "dying" and "killing." Images of sexual violence sustain the speech with which Othello opens the final scene:

> It is the cause, it is the cause, my soul.
> Let me not name it to you, you chaste stars.
> It is the cause. Yet I'll not shed her blood,
> Nor scar that whiter skin of hers than snow,
> And smooth as monumental alabaster.
> Yet she must die, else she'll betray more men.
> Put out the light, and then put out the light.
> If I quench thee, thou flaming minister,
> I can again thy former light restore,
> Should I repent me . . .
> When I have plucked the rose,
> I cannot give it vital growth again;
> It needs must wither. . . .
> O balmy breath, that dost almost persuade
> Justice to break her sword. . . .
> So sweet was ne'er so fatal. I must weep,
> But they are cruel tears. This sorrow's heavenly;
> It strikes where it doth love. (5.2.1–22)

Othello presumes at once to kill and redeem her, deflower and chastise her. His speech here and his actions throughout this scene move between the phallic "cause," that is, "thing,"[67] and an attempt to save Desdemona's body from losing its whiteness and hymeneal enclosure (however real or symbolic): "Yet I'll not shed her blood." His ramblings about putting out the light, alluding perhaps to the lights of Hymen, show him wondering whether his violation of her will allow him ever to give her back her chastity, perhaps her virginity.[68] Or, as Coppélia Kahn has argued, this "imagery of shrine and holy fire is indebted to the cult of Vesta, which replicated ancient Roman family rituals on a national scale and centered on the maintenance of the sacred altar fire by the vestal virgins."[69]

In any case, as Othello stands over the sleeping Desdemona trying to decide whether to violate her, the scene emblematically figures Tarquin and Lucrece and makes visible the horror of the black man raping the white woman.[70] From the earliest depictions of Shakespeare's play through the twentieth century, paintings, engravings, and photographs, and frontispieces, book covers, and advertisement posters have gravitated toward this scene, titillated not only by its verve as a culminating dramatic moment but by the interracial sex and violence serving at once as cultural fascination, fear, and warning. Like the depiction of Tarquin raping Lucrece (Chapter 1), these images call for a double reading, a full grasp of the pornographic import of this scene, to enable the viewer to comprehend the adverse, the scene's racial and sexual chastising demands.

The scene of Othello killing Desdemona not only conjures up images of Tarquin and Lucrece but partakes of the latter's iconography—in fact, becomes yet another retelling, or at least another indulgence of Tarquin and Lucrece's violent, sexual, and racial entanglements. A 1740 frontispiece provides a rather vivid example (figure 7), replete with the killing black hand and the resisting white one, drapery and folds, sinewy and erect black phalluses in the form of a burning candelabra, suggestions of bestial claws (in the legs of furniture) and snakes, the black penile hilt of the sword, and the protruding knee (albeit and interestingly a white-hosed one).[71] The comparison between these two pairs is undoubtedly there. But the observation doesn't stop there. Othello and Desdemona have more than an easy allusive relationship to the scene of Tarquin and Lucrece. Shakespeare takes the suggestiveness of the latter pair a step further, pushing its cultural, racial, and sexual horror to the fore. Shakespeare has in effect abandoned the darker-than-Tarquin voyeur who hangs out on the borders and in a different plane and whose presence signifies the violent and raw sexual energies and images that are never really allowed fully to take over Lucrece's body. (Veneziano's rather explicit *Tarquin and Lucretia* [figure 5], where the viewer gets more than a gander of a beast with two backs but in the image of copulating dogs, makes

H.Gravelot in & del.   O.Vander Gucht Scul.
V. 8 .P. 229

7. Frontispiece for *Othello*, from *The Works of Shakespeare* (1740). Reproduced by permission of the Huntington Library, San Marino, Calif.

a rather good example of contrast.) *Titus Andronicus*, like so many depictions
of Tarquin and Lucrece, shows the black man as the signifying outsider;
Othello shows the black man in the white woman's bed.

To say the least, Othello is caught in an emblematic identity crisis: his
identity signifies doubly, naming him at one and the same time as Tarquin
the rapist and Brutus the avenger. Throughout this last scene, Othello shows
himself trapped in a Girardian crisis of social discourse. Othello closes his
first speech in this scene in this indeterminacy because he cannot grasp—
because it is not there—the fullness of his own agency: "It strikes where it
doth love." Again, when Desdemona protests her innocence, he exclaims,

O perjured woman! thou dost stone my heart,
And mak'st me call what I intend to do
A murder, which I thought a sacrifice. (5.2.63–65)

And when Lodovico asks what shall be said of the "once so good" Othello
(5.2.287), Othello replies, "Why, anything: / An honorable murderer, if you
will; / For naught I did in hate, but all in honor" (5.2.289–91). Othello finds
himself situated in a language of both murder and sacrifice, working against
Venice even as he works for it, assuring Venice's move out of its present ambivalent cultural, racial, and sexual space.

As a way of addressing Othello's *onstage* sexual violation of Desdemona,
I would like to take up one of the most posed questions by those studying
the signifying racial practices permeating Shakespeare's play: why do critics
and readers spend so much energy worrying through the racial identity of
Othello and not that of Aaron? *Othello* seems daring in its social critique, if
not nearly inconceivable.[72] Aaron belongs to that class of black rapists, who,
as I argued in the last chapter, do not actually carry out the physical deed
however much they participate in the rape's construction, the woman's cultural, racial, and sexual violation. However much Desdemona may be "half
the wooer" (1.3.174), Othello becomes in effect the first black rapist, who,
dramatically, is allowed to violate white womanhood. Despite his smother-
ing Desdemona instead of penetrating her with his dagger, when compared
to those of the orchestrating Aaron in that earlier picture of Shakespeare's
Rome, Othello's murderous-sexual actions show a Venice in the throes of a
more dense and complex social crisis. Whereas the Gothic Tamora may become incorporate in Rome, Aaron is still at least a pace safely removed;
Othello has entered the inner sanctum of Venetian society. And although
Aaron is more clearly morally bankrupt, Othello never really does give up

his ambivalent position in this Venetian story that vacillates between murder and sacrifice. From this perspective, a significant part of the critical tradition has fixed Othello's identity as murderer (and rapist) and has not heeded his tortured articulation of his own ambivalent position.

Such a critical stance moves in what seem two opposing directions that effectively (and not coincidentally) reach the same conclusion. One response to Othello's ambivalence has been to whiten him, to get him as close to whiteness as possible. As Michael D. Bristol has astutely noted, "The history of the reception of *Othello* is the history of attempts to articulate ideologically correct, that is, palatable interpretations."[73] By the time the white Edmund Kean played Othello in 1814, he decided not to risk the ridicule that was being heaped on blackened Othellos: because black body and face paint was then more the material of minstrelsy, he adopted a light brown tint.[74] To lend support to Kean and to the period in which they both lived, Samuel Coleridge, the founding advocate for whitewashed Othellos, argued that Shakespeare could not be "so utterly ignorant as to make a barbarous negro [*sic*] plead royal birth . . . [and that] it would be monstrous to conceive this beautiful Venetian girl falling in love with a veritable Negro."[75] (Blackness of course never gets too far away from being "monstrous.") In this reading, without any real racial difference, the racial drama doesn't really happen.

The other critical direction has been to blacken Othello, at times setting up a competition onstage at least to see how black one could make Othello without pushing him and the play into the sublime or the ridiculous. This reading worked to fix Othello in his monstrosity, make him "radically" real, that is, really, really different. Such a direction especially underscores the performativity of blackness, its lack of familiarity, of complexity and nuance—its effective difference from "our" reality. Hence, its lack of being a *real* menace.[76] Laurence Olivier, that consummate Shakespearean British actor, who would play Othello on stage at the National Theatre (Old Vic) in 1964 and in Stuart Burge's film in 1965, proves an expressive example rather than an exception to this reading. In Olivier's own words:

> As Othello, I would have to start quietly, to come onto the stage first as the most real person the audience had ever seen; then, bit by bit, when I'd won their confidence, I would be able to start riding them. Only then would they accept my roaring. . . . I began to think about the play again, [to] look at it from Othello's point of view. I began to sniff around the man, like an old dog inspecting yesterday's bone. I began to read the play and reread it, worming my way into the text. Scratching at the veneer. . . . To create a

character, I first visualize a painting. . . . I was beginning to know how I should look: very strong. He should stand as a strong man stands, with a sort of ease, straight-backed, straight-necked, relaxed as a lion. . . . Black. . . . I had to *be* black. I had to feel black down to my soul. I had to look out from a black man's world. Not one of repression, for Othello would have felt superior to the white man. . . . Throwing away the white man was difficult, but fascinating. Of course, you can never truly do this, but there were times when I convinced myself that I had. . . . I should walk like a soft black leopard. Sensuous. . . . [Othello is] the greatest exponent of self-deception there's ever been. Othello's self-conscious dramatization of himself as the noble warrior leads him to ignore reality. . . . Hands, eyes, body, a kind of self-flagellation. . . . Black all over my body, Max Factor 2880, then a lighter brown, then Negro No.2, a stronger brown. . . . Then the great trick: that glorious half-yard of chiffon with which I polished myself all over until I shone. . . . The lips blueberry, the tight curled wig, the white of the eyes, whiter than ever, and the black, black sheen that covered my flesh and bones, glistening in the dressing-room lights.[77]

It is no surprise that "Olivier stepped onstage to a collective gasp from the audience."[78] He could take the prize for *being* black in a way that the nineteenth-century black American Ira Aldridge or twentieth-century black American Paul Robeson could not.[79] A black actor changes everything. The black actor points to the fact too that there's no easy symmetry here between the white and black actor. It may be true to some extent that on the nineteenth- and twentieth-century English and American stage Othello came to be "identified as a role difficult for cold 'Anglo-Saxon' temperaments and more suitable for those southern climes," but this observation should not lead too readily to the conclusion that this made it "easier to conceive of a black actor in the role."[80] Perhaps not as true today as it would have been in days past (but still fundamentally resonant), when the black actor plays Othello, his most conspicuous performance centers on his ability to play *Shakespeare*; when the white actor plays Othello, he most conspicuously performs blackness. The black actor finds himself all too frequently trapped in some version—to adopt a 1940s phrase from James Agate—of a "nigger Shakespeare" (a phrase presumably made effective by its supposed oxymoronic nature).[81] I use the phrase here to point to a black actor who is said to play Othello too carefully, with too much elocution, as well as to a black actor whose racialized blackness is said to be responsible (positively or negatively) for the primitivism he brings to the role. The Othello caricature

96

Our Captious Critic

on "OTHELLO" (The Savoy Theatre).

I ADVISE all people who think Shakespeare no longer interesting on the stage to go to the Savoy Theatre to see "Othello." There you will see an ineffective Iago, a caricature of Cassio and a Desdemona who is, though pleasant, lacking the needed poise for this lofty stage. Yet go to this theatre none the less, because there you will see such an Othello as may·never be found again, an Othello whose passion rises and falls with the ease of the wave, whose voice is rich music allied to language the wonder of the modern world; an Othello who, as no white man in this country has ever done in living memory, convinces you of the reality of his illusion concerning his wife, of his belief in the absolute necessity of killing her, of the shattering of his being through the dreadful thought. Your pity for Othello is as profound as his own grief (" The pity of it, Iago ! ") and overpowers your fears for Desdemona. You leave the theatre lamenting that you could not help the Moor to know the truth, not in order that he might refrain from the murder of innocence, but that he might retain the happy peace of his soul. You find yourself wondering if the actors of the past really could create those immense effects which loom gigantic on the historic sky and which you have always derided as fiction, when suddenly you encounter a man named Paul Robeson who justifies that tradition and himself looms majestic, " larger than human," before you on this modern stage.

Technically, this negro's Othello has defects, yet not since Irving has so tremendous a general effect been created by any acting. At the risk of seeming childish I will explain my meaning. On leaving the Lyceum after seeing Irving in " Faust," I had to compel myself to walk on sole and heel, so intensely had that tip-toeing Mephistopheles obtained possession of me. On leaving the Savoy Theatre the other day the " pity of it " hung like a cloud over all the city.

You may say that Robeson might fail with western and northern characters, that his triumph is merely because the simple nature of Othello is that of his own race, the race which boasts " the shadow'd livery of the burnished sun," that his " farewell " and " handkerchief " speeches are not delivered with full understanding and that, in general, where anything but emotion is wanted he falls below the best. Granted. But what is the theatre but a temple of emotion and who troubles himself about accuracy of impersonation, of obtuseness or intelligence of rendering, so long as the joy or fear or pity of the scene being acted enters the watcher's soul ? This is the crown of Paul Robeson's effort, that you rejoice and grieve with his Othello.

Let us, lest great praise be thought blind praise, admit that there are times when this Othello seems to be repeating words he does not understand, like a schoolboy reading from a book, that he puts absurd emphasis on the word " Venetian " in his last speech of all, that he often stands awkwardly for so well built a man and often makes you too conscious of his hands. Yet the very heel and front of his offending hath this extent, no more, and we succumb, as Desdemona did, to the simple nobility of his nature.

The play is acted, for some unexplained reason, on a series of steps and mostly on their upper and more distant parts. Beyond giving certain Venetian gentlemen a chance to strike attitudes with one foot on one step and one on another, these stairs seem a nuisance. The stage is built out over the orchestra space, but is little used there by the actors for establishing a greater intimacy with the audience.

Mr. Maurice Browne's Iago is a man of no importance, who has more gift for talking than persuading. He is just about as devilish as a chartered accountant and seems to be planning his murders because that happened to be his job and a man must live, anyway. His voice is equally colourless whether he wishes to influence his victim by reason, affected passion or by maddening allusions to Desdemona's lechery. How great must be this Othello then, when his emotion can surge up so naturally, although its inspirer is himself so uninspired. " Honest Iago " almost suits this ancient of the Moor's, and " harmless " too, so poor seems his guile. It is a careful performance, lacking strength.

In this production poor Cassio becomes rather a brainless dandy than a smart and honest lieutenant, but from the point of view chosen Mr. Max Montsole acts efficiently and Mr. Ralph Richardson's Roderigo is also capable.

Miss Peggy Ashcroft, though she cannot contrive to be both dignified and natural, achieves the better half of the complete Desdemona by being the latter. She cannot raise her sense with Othello to their full height, because that slightly mannish note which is to be found in Shakespeare's heroines and which, though not admirable in itself, harmonises with his plays, is not within her compass. She is like light chamber music to the full orchestra of the Moor, but she wins our affections to the full, for, in Cassio's words, " indeed, she's a most fresh and delicate creature."

As Emilia, Miss Sybil Thorndike's quality is needed, and is forthcoming, for her outburst in the last scene, where the coarse-minded materialist discovers a death-defying devotion to the pale ghost who was once her mistress, and dies for that virtue in her.

It is to be presumed that if Shakespeare had known that his works would so long outlive their author he would have been careful about his plots as he was about his characters and their poetry. Here we have a cool old soldier-like Iago and who, for motives which even he explains half-heartedly, plots a revenge which can only be kept secret by killing off most of the characters in the play. It was long odds, too, on Othello's strangling him on his first daring to hint at Desdemona's frailty—a consummation devoutly to be wished, as another illogical Shakespearean character remarked.

The "honest" Ancient, who "hates the slime that sticks on filthy deeds": Maurice Browne as Iago.

Two studies of the Ethiopian Moor at the Savoy: Paul Robeson as Othello beside himself with the green-eyed monster.

Desdemona drops a hint: Peggy Ashcroft as the great captain's captain.

" Trifles, light as air, are to the jealous confirmation strong, as proof of Holy Writ." Paul Robeson and Maurice Browne.

Iago puts Othello on the rack.

8. "Our Captious Critic," with caricatures of Paul Robeson as Othello. Reproduced from *Illustrated Sporting and Dramatic News*, June 7, 1930.

9. Early-nineteenth-century caricature of Othello and a black Desdemona.
Reproduced by permission of the Folger Shakespeare Library.

accompanying a favorable 1930 review of Robeson in London's Savoy production speaks very much to the point (figure 8). The effect of blackness, its
disturbing silliness, is made all the more explicit in another caricature, this
time featuring not only a truly black Othello but a truly black Desdemona
as well (figure 9): Othello's "real" blackness has turned the play, and a recognizable aesthetic, into a farce. Of course the part of Othello was written
most immediately to be played by a white actor, a fact that has remained undertheorized even in our more liberal and progressive critical discussions of
Othello's *blackness*. What Olivier shows, I imagine unwittingly, is that in the
metatheatrical world of Shakespearean drama the aim of the actor playing
Othello is to *play* black, and the play challenges the white actor to embody
himself as completely as possible in the body of blackness.[82] Shakespeare
stages this imperial fiction. The white actor's inability or ability to play black
presumes to become, in a final analysis, a very real testament to the stability
or adaptability of whiteness.

In the metatheatrical and socially complex world of Shakespeare's play, a
black man has not really raped Desdemona. Rather, the angelic (5.2.129) and
sacrificially identifying Desdemona—"Nobody—I myself" (5.2.123)—who

"saw Othello's visage in his mind's eye" (1.3.247), has never really let go of the fact of Othello's whiteness. (Perhaps the artist of the 1740 frontispiece was of a similar mind, robing Othello in white and making the phallic object that actually ends up in bed with Desdemona Othello's knee hosed in white. Othello's black phallic arm finds itself beneath her throat. He is of course strangling her.) Othello, who becomes a mere type by the end of the play, a murderous devil—not a nuanced villain but a simple vice figure—becomes himself merely a symbolic portrait, perhaps not unlike the pictured Moor who would find his way into the woman's womb in Paré's story. Whether on Shakespeare's stage or Olivier's, we may adopt an argument made about the blackening of characters in medieval theater: "Such performances also had to make femaleness and blackness 'disappear,' to direct attention away from the real subjects whose signifiers men were borrowing."[83] What the audience witnesses in Othello's and others' references to his blackness—his "thick-lips" (1.1.63), "sooty bosom" (1.2.69), and all—is the actor's calling attention to his makeup, to his confession that he knows that his audience is witnessing the work, the staginess, of whiteness.

The figuring of whiteness in such terms is not particular to Shakespeare's play. From the medieval blackening of the Vice to the early modern blackening of stage villains and, of course, of black Africans, white actors were often in dialogue with their blackness. Black characters were often only a step away from the theatricality of their blackness, the theatricality of blackness, as Claire Sponsler has astutely, even groundbreakingly, argued in her study of blackening in the Middle Ages. Despite my rather lengthy extraction from Sponsler, she puts the issue rather cogently and succinctly:

> The use of blackface and female costume by male performers has usually
> been understood either as a matter of theatrical tradition . . . or as simple
> "disguise" meant to conceal the performer's identity (in the case of carni-
> vals, mummings, morris dances, and other seasonal festivities)—interpreta-
> tions that render these practices unproblematic and unremarkable. But such
> a perspective works to preclude full consideration of the issues of race, gen-
> der, status, and performative subjectivity raised by these theatrical practices.
> It also fails to do justice to their deviance and transgressiveness. When seen
> just as conventions of costuming and make-up, rather than as drag and
> blackface, these theatrical practices are defused and denatured, removed
> from the realm of social and cultural struggle into the safe space of stage
> history where they can be viewed as theatrical devices, hence customary
> and inconsequential.[84]

All this is even more true for the Renaissance. What we have failed to do in reading the presence of "real" (or ethnographic) black figures on the early modern stage is to comprehend the theatricality, the very real theatricality, of that blackness: it is not an either-or proposition, dramatically or ideologically. Bulwer's summarily reading the black body as "artificiall" is a case in point. In *Lust's Dominion*, for example, Eleazar, the prince of Fesse and Barbary exclaims,

> Ha, ha, I thank thee provident creation,
> That seeing in moulding me thou did'st intend
> I should prove villain, thanks to thee and nature
> That skilful workman; thanks for my face,
> Thanks that I have not wit to blush. (2.2.925–31)

And later in the play Prince Philip complains, "Thou left'st me to the mercy of a Moor, / That hath damnation dy'd upon his flesh" (5.4.3340–41). And after the Spanish king's two sons have brought about the death of the Moors Zarack and Baltazar and before they have effected the death of Eleazar, Isabella says: "Phillippo and Hortenzo stand you still, what; doat you both? Cannot you see your play? Well fare a woman then, to lead the way. Once rob the dead, put the Moors habits on, and paint your faces with the oil of hell, so waiting on the Tyrant" (5.5.3581–86). And the Jew Quicksands cleverly argues against his gentile wife's protestations in Richard Brome's *The English Moore* (c. 1630). He puts her in blackface—presumably to protect her from the lustful eye of other men (a plot element that also points to the threat of miscegenation, here from Jewishness to blackness)—and alludes to Jonson's *Masque of Blackness*:

> Why thinckst thou, fearefull Beauty,
> Has Heauen noe part in Egipt? Pray thee tell me
> Is not an Ethiops face his workmanship
> As well as the fairst Ladyes? Nay more too
> Then hers, that dawbes & makes adulterate beauty.
> Some can be pleas'd to lie in oyles & paste
> At Sinnes appointment, which is thrice more wicked.
> This (which is sacred) is for Sinnes prevention.
> Illustrious Persons, nay euen Queenes themselfes
> Haue, for the glory of a Nights presentment
> To grace the worke, sufferd as much as this. (3.1.72–82)

He reassures her: "Be feareles Loue; this alters not thy beauty / Though for a time, obscures it from o'eyes. / Thou mayst be white at pleasure" (3.1.85–87). And calling attention not only to Millicent's theatrical and unnatural blackness, a blackness darker than that of a real offstage black person, but also to blacks' presumed sexual proclivities, Nathaniell says, pursuing the blackened Millicent:

> The handsomst rogue
> I haue euer seene yet, of a deed of darknes.
> Tawny & russet faces I haue dealt with:
> But neuer came soe deepe in blacknes yet. (4.3.85–88)

William Berkeley's *The Lost Lady* (1638) and William Heminge's *The Fatal Contract* provide other explicitly drawn examples. In the latter, Castrato's real blackness and Crotilda's theatrical blackness are one and the same. To argue that "for spectators at the Globe, the stage Moor (a 'white' actor in blackface) was essentially an emblematic figure, not a 'naturalistic' portrayal of a particular ethnic type,"[85] is to fail to appreciate the ideological confluences between real African bodies and the very theatricality of blackness in early modern English culture. It is to miss the theatrical and metatheatrical cultural playfulness and seriousness when he offers Brabantio his rather desperate response—"If virtue no *delighted* beauty lack, / your son-in-law is far *more fair* than *black*" (1.3.284–85). In a fashion at once substantial and whimsical the duke unpacks, even as he explicitly and implicitly conflates, a dense repertoire of images—*light, fair, white, black, Moor*. The duke reminds his onstage and offstage audience that Othello is really white on the "inside." There is no black body on the stage, literally. More important, still, it is to not recognize the paradox that such highly articulate moments of rendering black racial bodies theatrical work too if not foremost to ritualize their deportation from both the stage and the culture. It is, in other words, to miss the ways such moments invent and celebrate whiteness.

In the end Othello discovers himself as witness, as imperial traveler, as the fly on the wall so to speak.[86] Othello discovers *Othello* to be his play, his witnessing of whiteness, of the powers of Venice. We are not surprised that Cassio will assume Othello's place, turn Cyprus away from Africa and toward Venice (and Florence). Othello, who will smote the "malignant and . . . turbaned Turk," "the circumcised dog" who "beat a Venetian and traduced the state" (5.2.349–52), witnesses his own death, his own sacrificial drama, pointing as peculiarly to his Venetian self as to the white actor playing him. However much the bed claims center stage, the final and indicting irony here is that the center stage has been itself deported, pushed off to Cyprus. In the end Shakespeare's Venice has worked its own piece of theatrical and geographical magic. Having sacrificed and murdered Desdemona, Othello, who has protested his dramatic inheritance, his societal exclusion, finds himself not only a black rapist but, like his predecessors in paintings, drama, and other representations, an outsider, looking in from the outborders, literally in Othello's case, from an outpost.

THREE

Framing Antony's Anatomy

Rome serves not only as a model for early modern England's imperial ambitions but as the primary prototype for its cultural and racial character and
masculinity. Coppélia Kahn reminds us in her study examining the uses of
Rome in Shakespeare and his contemporary England that Romanness and
an ideology of masculinity are virtually identical and that the Roman pursuit of *virtus*, that is, virtue (etymologically derived from the Latin *vir* [man]),
"isn't a moral abstraction but rather a marker of sexual difference crucial to
the construction of the male subject—the Roman hero."[1] England's imperial
goals are no more extricable from its masculinist ones. It makes sense, then,
that William Harrison opens his essay "Of the Generall Constitution of the
Bodies of the Britons" (1577) by emphasizing not only the whiteness but the
masculinity of the British anatomy: "Such as are bred in this Iland are men
for the most part of a good complexion, tall of stature, strong in bodie, white
of colour, and thereto of great boldnesse and courage in the warres." It
makes sense, too, that Harrison could substantiate his self-fashioning claims
by immediately evoking Rome, and not just any Rome but a Rome that
had defeated Britain: "As for their generall comelinesse of person, the testimonie of Gregorie the great, at such time as he saw English capteins sold at
Rome, shall easilie confirme what it is."[2] Harrison presumably refers to Gregory I's seeing Christian Anglo-Saxons sold in the Roman slave market and
to his comment that the Britons were "not *Angli* but *Angeli.*"[3] Harrison does
more here than amuse himself with language: the prelapsarian, cultural, and
imperialistic mythology underlying such a quip is that "God . . . had originally created man not only 'Angelike' but 'white.'"[4] Even in enslavement,
Harrison contends, there exists a culturally recognizable *virtus* and an almost
sanctified racial respect between the Britons and the Romans.

The Romans were also of course England's model for civility, for *civitas*.
William Camden's sentiments in his *Britannia* (1586) were shared by many:

civility came from Roman domination. Put simply, "Wheresoever the Romans were victors, they brought them whom they conquered to civility."[5] And as James Harrington would argue more vividly in *The Commonwealth of Oceana* (1656), "If we [English] have given over running up and down naked and with dappled hides, learned to write and read, to be instructed with good arts, for all these we are beholding to the Romans . . . by whose means we are as it were of beasts become men."[6] Civility was in itself, however, no admirable trait but had always to be carefully negotiated with a compelling and convincing masculinity. As Debora Shuger notes in classical discourses of Roman barbarism, "If barbarian society rests on rapine and warfare, civility sinks under its own weight into soft, effeminizing decadence, enervating the free warrior with the comforts of baths, bread, and circuses as well as shackling him to anxious drudgery of the plow."[7] In short, the Romans were *the* model of an imperial and civilizing masculinity, and their empire served as a nostalgic model for an early modern England that strongly desired to perform (and thereby prove) its own imperial and masculine identity. But England's masculinity was always to be of a civilizing sort. Harrison speaks of national character as being shaped by the four humors and of the English constitution as being particularly influenced by phlegm:

> He whose nature inclineth generallie to phlegme, cannot but be courteous: which ioined with strength of bodie, and sinceritie of behauiour (qualities vniuersallie granted to remaine so well in our nation, as other inhabitants of the north) I cannot see what may be an hinderance whie I should not rather conclude, that the Britons doo excell such as dwell in the hoter countries, than for want of craft and subtilties to come anie whit behind them.[8]

Turning to Shakespeare's *Antony and Cleopatra*, I argue that at one and the same time Antony has too much *virtus* or *civitas* or too little.[9] His Roman anatomy draws for its affectivity on an English anatomy, particularly one born out of a nostalgia for a racial, sexual, and gender stability and purity. As this chapter shows, at least before Antony encounters Egypt, his body is presumably well complected, tall, strong, white, and courageous—in essence, he *had* a body primed for imperial things. And in his going or having gone primitive, an argument on which I will elaborate in this chapter, Antony's putative deviation from Romanness does not of course leave him with an abject cultural identity, that is, with a subjectivity that only positivizes him as "*non*-Roman." Antony's abject subjectivity is true in Shakespeare's play only to the extent that cultural Others are figured and fantasized as abject by dominant cultural ideologies. In going primitive Antony goes Egyptian, in effect African.[10] But Antony's English and ostensibly white body, a body that is presumably still physically white at the end of the play, betrays him to be a kind of white African. In the latter sections of this chapter I insist on a reading that puts the sacrificial Antony in dialogue with the sacrificial Irish, the hybrid English in particular.

Contagious Pieces

Not surprisingly, the Rome of *Antony and Cleopatra* seems not merely imbued with manly principles but to have about it an innate, natural, and nondeconstructible masculinity. This masculinity not only contrasts with but depends on Egypt's supposedly more performative, unnatural, and unstable femininity, since gender in no way functions here or elsewhere as a discrete category: it has become more than a critical truism that a culture attempting to dominate another culture will endow itself with masculine qualities and the culture it seeks to dominate with feminine ones.[11] Furthermore, gender, race, and sexuality are of course ultimately inseparable categories and are thoroughly implicated in each other's making. Antony's gender is—as are his race and sexuality—marked as different, not quite culturally proper. Even so, on- and offstage readings of Antony's ethos, his cultural character, are more often than not shaped by his gender, especially his effeminacy. Philo's opening cross-cultural and cross-dressed portrait of Antony argues that Antony has gone feminine. As much is corroborated by Caesar, who, in his first speech in the play, laments (presumably and reluctantly) that Antony "is not more manlike / Than Cleopatra; nor the queen of Ptolemy / More womanly than he" (1.4.5–7).[12] And Antony lends Caesar's observation theatrical proof when late in the play Cleopatra and Eros dress him for battle (4.4.11–15). Antony's feminine and primitive presence supposedly signifies his lost Romanness, and act 3, scene 10 is a virtual litany of his lost and feminized self, his "wounded chance" (3.10.36).[13] There are the epistemological laments of Scarus and Canidius: "The greater cantle of the world is lost / With very ignorance" (6–7) and "Had our general / Been what he knew himself, it had gone well" (3.10.26–27), respectively. And Scarus's words are even more emblematic of Rome's voyeuristic and conspiratorial framing of Antony's Romanness, "I never saw an action of such shame; / Experience, manhood, honour, ne'er before / Did violate so itself " (22–24). Already Rome anticipates the staging of Antony's shameful self-sacrifice, the vilifying inscription of his suicide in the ritualistic erotics of the dying virginal woman. Antony himself continues and intensifies this litany in the next scene—"I / Have lost my way for ever," "I have fled myself," "I have lost command," and more visually, "See, / How I convey my shame out of thine eyes, / By looking back what I have left behind / Stroy'd in dishonour" (3.11.3–4, 7, 23, 51–54).

As the play continues Antony retreats deeper and deeper into and insists more and more on this nostalgic self, which increasingly loses its Roman usefulness as Rome becomes increasingly assured of its success in replacing the lost Antony with the found Caesar. This is Rome's objective from the beginning, and this objective necessitates its nostalgic harping on—indeed, its nostalgic creation of—a lost Antony. Manliness, at least a civilized Roman version of it, always belongs to Caesar and never to Antony. Antony seems always to have too much of it (as evinced in Caesar's Modena speech) or too little (as in Philo's opening gambit).[14] (I will discuss both speeches later in this chapter.) Even as he admits that his authority melts from him (3.13.90), he insists, "I am Antony yet," and he disdains Caesar for disdaining him, "harping on what I am / Not what he knew I was" (3.13.93, 142–43). As the drama unfolds, Antony more and more loses—is (in the sacrificial vein of the play) cut off from—his anatomically phallic self.

Despite Antony's self-fashioning protestations of himself to be "like a man of steel" (4.4.33), it is his anatomical steel that seems to work most arduously against his manly picture of himself. Of the triad of gender, race, and sexuality his gender, the putative loss of his masculinity, seems to be the almost obsessive focus of his critics onstage and off. It begins almost humorously with Cleopatra recalling how she dressed Antony in her "tires and mantles" and took possession of his sword (2.5.22–23). Midway through the play he tells Cleopatra that his sword has been "made weak by [his] affection" (3.11.67), and when late in the play an un-Romaned Antony exclaims, "O, thy vile lady! / She has robb'd me of my sword" (4.14.22–23), he seems to echo closely the victim of *raptus*, of bride theft, who has lost the sword she wishes to turn against herself. By the time Antony tries to use his sword to kill himself, it amounts to little more than a stage prop. And these protestations end with Cleopatra's providing at his death a nostalgic and elegiac (if not bemused) lament of Antony's lost sexual and Roman potency, "O, withered is the garland of the war, / The soldier's pole is fall'n" (4.15.64–65). To lose virulence is to become like a woman, to move from being a political agent to a political object, a piece. Even (and perhaps especially) Cleopatra is talked about as a "wonderful piece of work" (1.2.151–52), and Caesar speaks of his sister Octavia as a "piece of virtue" that will "cement" Antony and Caesar's bond (3.2.28–29). Antony, understandably then, refers to his own defeated soldiers as "bruised pieces" (4.14.42), and Cleopatra finally constructs a dream of Antony as "nature's piece 'gainst fancy" (5.2.99). In the hystericized and hybrid portrayal of Antony throughout the play, Antony has not only become a piece but has gone to pieces.

Antony's piecemeal anatomy conflicts with Rome's masculine picture of itself, and more dangerous than Antony's corruption of himself is his corruption of the Roman state, most immediately of his soldiers, who undergo a gender panic as they imagine their masculine selves transformed into feminine ones. Enobarbus tells Cleopatra that in Rome Antony is "Traduc'd for levity" and is said to have an eunuch and Cleopatra's maids managing his war (3.7.12–15). A few lines later Canidius, Antony's lieutenant general, says to a soldier, "So our leader's led, / And we are women's men" (3.7.69–70); and later in the play Enobarbus, "onion-ey'd," begs Antony, "For shame, / Transform us not to women" (4.2.35–36). Antony's masculinity has become a dangerous and endangered thing. Rome has begun to fear that were its masculinity left in the hands of Antony its rectitude would quickly grow flaccid or that, perhaps in a Circe-like fashion, Roman men would not only become feminine but would be remade into women, transmogrifying Rome into a jungle of sorts.

Antony's Blushing and Leaking Body

Indeed, Shakespeare's play doesn't simply feminize Antony; it begins to reconstruct his gender: his body is said to blush and leak. Antony posits himself as a feminized and racialized object:

> . . . O,
> I follow'd that I blush to look upon:
> My very hairs do mutiny; for the white
> Reprove the brown for rashness, and they them
> For fear, and doting. (3.11.11–15)

In the fearful visual power he ascribes here to Cleopatra, she doesn't turn him (Medusa-like) into stone, but she does make him blush—that is, she makes him feminine—and his mutinous and hybrid coiffure underscores the depth of his cultural and racial betrayal. (He evokes the language Brabantio uses as he imagines the white Desdemona mesmerized by the black Othello.) Through the guise of a nostalgia reified and sanctioned by an imperialistic Roman culture, the now blushing and colorized Antony was *once* masculine, white, and heterosexual.[15] He was, in a word, virtuous.

Antony seems almost to mock the rigidity and seriousness of Roman masculinity: for him, it is, or at least it becomes, transmutable and theatrical. Throughout, he has a feminine affectivity, which we see too in the gender-inflected imaging of him in terms of blemishes, blushing, and shame. Considered as discrete signifiers, these images may not seem for some as deterministically gendered as I suggest here, but collectively and with other feminizing characterizations of Antony they inform and help shape our understanding of Antony's effeminacy. On a couple of different occasions we hear about Antony's blemishes, especially in reference to his Egyptian sexual indulgences. Early in the play Caesar quips quite sarcastically that Antony must have a rare composition indeed if such acts as tumbling on the bed with Cleopatra cannot "blemish" it (1.4.22–23). Later Antony says to Octavia, his new wife, "Read not my blemishes in the world's report" (2.3.5). The other substantive use in the play of the word *blemish* refers to Cleopatra. Caesar's Rome talks about her "constrained blemishes" (3.13.59), fashioning her as a damsel or virgin in distress of sorts in the hope that she will accept the presumed flattery and betray Antony. Antony's blemishes, although not necessarily relating exclusively to his sexual body, do readily define and visualize this body that has been stained by Cleopatra's sexual darkness.

His body gets read within a gender-inflected discourse and takes part in a more generalized blemish affect, a discursive interplay between blemish, blushing, and shame. This blemish affect is present most acutely in Shakespeare's *Rape of Lucrece*, where Tarquin tries to convince Lucrece that it is better she submit to him in private than that he denounce her as an adulteress in public:

> The shame that from them [her kindred] no device can take,
> The blemish that will never be forgot,
> Worse than a slavish wipe or birth-hour's blot. (535–37)

And later in the poem Lucrece thinks her male servant "blush'd to see her shame" and "blushing with him wistly on him gazed. . . . The more she saw the blood his cheeks replenish, / The more she thought he spied in her some blemish" (1344–58). To the extent that Antony's blemish takes part in this blemish affect, his body is presented here as being at least partly feminine.

This blemish affect is perhaps all the clearer in the opening moments of the play, when Cleopatra mocks Antony, who has just received a missive from Rome:

As I am Egypt's queen,
Thou blushest, Antony, and that blood of thine
Is Caesar's homager: else so thy cheek pays shame
When shrill-tongued Fulvia scolds. (1.1.29–32)

(Her words also seem to anticipate Antony's pseudovirginal sacrifice on
Caesar's altar.) The kind of blushing Cleopatra toys with here is that which
the *Oxford English Dictionary* defines as a "reddening of the face caused by
shame, modesty, or other emotion." Antony's blushing is most particularly
caused by his shame and modesty. When Caesar pleas for Antony's "shame"
to drive him quickly back to Rome (1.4.72–73)—ultimately so that Antony
can become a sacrificial figure—Caesar in effect pleas with Antony's modesty, his feminine self. The blemish affect gets evoked again in act 3, scene
11, when a defeated Antony says, "I follow'd that I blush to look upon"
(3.11.12), recalling his modesty here too. Later in this same scene Iras further
substantiates this narrative, observing that Antony is "unqualitied [that is,
"unmanned"] with very shame" (3.11.44).

Antony, like Caesar in *Julius Caesar*, is marked with a "shameful stigmata
of ambiguous gender, especially the sign of womanly blood." Antony's
blushing (as well as his blood that often seems on the verge of overheating
[for example, 1.3.80]) can certainly be read in terms of Antony's womanly
blood.[16] Right now I am interested in Antony's gender, but I would like to
interject here that Antony's blemish affect is finally inseparable from the
"shameful stigmata" of his broader textual body, which, discursively, also gets
marked as homosexual and black. The blemish affect most certainly does
represent Antony's body as feminine. But as the play continues and as Antony confesses in oxymoronic fashion that his "authority melts from him"
(3.13.90)—oxymoronic if we read "authority" as masculine and "melts" as
feminine—it is not enough to think of Antony as feminine. It is not enough
to think of Antony in terms of a "lost" masculinity, as characterized solely by
a gender abjectness.

Antony's body does more than blush. Especially in the latter part of
his life in the play (3.13 onward), Antony changes iconographically into a
woman; that is, he becomes something more representationally graphic than
can be accurately conveyed by our simply reading or thinking of him as an
effeminate or feminine man. A telling example is in the last scene of the
third act, when Enobarbus apostrophizes Antony as he watches (what he
thinks is) Cleopatra's betrayal of Antony: "Sir, sir, thou art so leaky / That we
must leave thee to thy sinking for / Thy dearest quit thee" (3.13.63–65).

Enobarbus draws most immediately on images of Antony's navy, which is left stranded at the mercy of Caesar's fleet after Cleopatra's ships quickly turn and withdraw from the fighting. Enobarbus's description also does some deeper cultural work. Most evocatively, the subject of his little quip is not Antony's ships but Antony's body. Enobarbus takes Antony's defeated ship as a metaphor for Antony's body, which is either sinking into femininity (that is, capitulating to) or sinking (that is, dying) as Antony himself gets remade, reengendered as a woman.

Antony's body leaks. By referring to Antony's body as leaky, Enobarbus clearly intends to construct Antony as female and portray him in unkind terms. Enobarbus's metaphorical play echoes a bawdy couplet sung by the Fool in *King Lear*—"Her boat hath a leak, / And she must not speak" (3.6.26–27)—as well as a moment in the opening scene of *The Tempest*, when Gonzalo speaks from what looks like a sinking boat: "I'll warrant him for drowning, though the ship were no stronger than a nutshell, and as leaky as an unstanch'd wench" (1.1.46–48). Beyond this specific linking of the female body to a sinking ship, we may think of Lucrece's leaky body in narrative descriptions and early modern pictorials, as well as her dramatization in the overflowing body of Shakespeare's Lavinia. We may think too of Shakespeare's Lady Macbeth, whose call for the stopping up of her leaky body ends in failure and with her futile attempt to wash the "shameful stigmata" of womanness from her body. In short, the iconographic reading of the female body as leaky would be quite an accessible image for an early modern audience.

As Gail Kern Paster writes in *The Body Embarrassed*, "It was woman's normative condition to leak."[17] Antony certainly does get transmogrified, perverted, into a leaky female body. But I wish to proceed with caution before accepting the argument that Paster makes in her reading of Julius Caesar's leaky body, where she writes, "To break is to bleed shamefully, to be shamefully open, to be revealed as bearing other than patriarchal blood. Patriarchal blood in such a formulation is the blood one cannot bleed, the blood that cannot be spilled without changing its nature" (103–4). Paster's formulation is true enough and one that we have seen again and again (in Nicole Loraux, for example). Elaborating, Paster writes:

> In the organized visibility of dramatic representation, blood flowing from a wounded or dead body carries a potential narrative value.... The male body, opened and bleeding, can assume the shameful attributes of the incontinent female body as both cause of and justification for its evident vulnerability and defeat. At such moments, the bleeding male's blood comes

to differ, shamefully, from itself. . . . [W]oman is naturally grotesque—which is to say, open, permeable, effluent, leaky. Man is naturally whole, closed, opaque, self-contained. To be otherwise is both shameful and feminizing. (92)

Paster turns her argument to *Julius Caesar*, a text I wish to discuss briefly, and writes about Caesar's wounded body, which gets publicly and shamefully transformed into a female body—a transformation intended in part to separate Caesar from, as well as create, the Roman manliness of the conspirators. The Antony of *Julius Caesar* also participates in the story of Julius Caesar's shame. As Paster argues, "Even to receive Caesar's body from the conspirators as a token of political exchange and denial of hostile intents suggests Antony's acceptance of its use value as female and his own new patriarchal responsibilities to it."[18] In reference to Antony's use of Caesar's wounds, his "poor, poor, dumb mouths" (3.2.225), she argues that Antony employs them "to oppose mute femaleness to a phallicized image of speech," working ultimately to transform Antony "from part to whole, from Caesar's limb to motivated Orphic speaker" (111–12).

Although enlightening, Paster's reading of *Julius Caesar*, a reading I carry in part over into my reading of *Antony and Cleopatra*, does not interrogate far enough the issue of shame. Shame is finally not, pace Paster, an explanation but a conduit. Caesar's corpse comes into political importance less as a shameful body in itself than through a rhetoric of shame. Shame is about victory here at least as much as it is about defeat. Shame empowers, especially when we begin to think of it in terms of modesty, as opposed to a more restrictive understanding of it as reflecting some confluence of guilt and embarrassment. In his funeral oration Antony presents to his audience a modest Caesar whose body speaks of a double shame. His body may be shameful, that is, an embarrassment, because it has become female, but it is also, and more significantly, shamed because it has become a violated female body. Paster gets it right:

> Antony's oration cannot re-member Caesar or restore to his bleeding
> corpse the intact ideal maleness of the classical body. Instead, it takes up
> and redirects the political valences of the conspirator's own rhetoric of
> blood and bodily conduct, denying the conspirators exclusive rights to the
> Roman body politic. Plethoric womanly blood, however sublimated by
> Petrarchan discourse, has thus marked Caesar with the bodily sign of the
> tragic grotesque, but this marking has not achieved the conservative political results the conspirators had aimed for. (112)

Paster does not recognize the extent to which sacrifice informs the re-gendering of Caesar's corpse or the way the imaging of female sacrifice empowers Caesar's disempowered male body. Caesar's body fills in the cultural space iconographically occupied by Lucrece's sacrificial body. It is in Caesar's femaleness, in his virginal modesty, that Caesar's shame becomes most effectively a pointed issue.

To make visually emphatic the moment's cultural import Julius Caesar's sacrificial body not only competes with but outdoes Lucrece's. In the showing of the rents and tears of Caesar's mantle and in Antony's lament—

As [Brutus] pluck'd his cursed steel away,
Mark how the blood of Caesar followed it,
As rushing out of doors to be resolv'd
If Brutus so unkindly knock'd or no. (3.2.177–80)

—Caesar's body, with its multiplicity of "dumb mouths," gets dramatized as the victim of a homosexual gang rape. And Antony's oratory gives profundity to the moment by bringing the political and sexual horror of Caesar's penetrated body into presence by putting his tongue in Caesar's wounds. He performs fellatio on Caesar's wounded corpse; Antony uses Caesar's body for reasons far more political than sexual. Rather, like a self-chastising Lucrece, he publicly *retells*, that is, performs, the conspirators' rape of Caesar. His orality intends effectively and affectively to violate, to shame or embarrass a body that was once modest. As a corpse, Caesar possesses power not in his maleness but in his femaleness. Antony tries to recast Caesar's body, to transform it from a reification of male embarrassment into an emblem of female modesty, that is, from, iconographically, a nearly inconsequential picture of male weakness into the more known and rehearsed picture of a sacrificially driven female power.

In short, Antony calls on the very Romanness of Rome, its founding myths, its self-fashioning primal scene. By implicitly linking Caesar to Lucrece he asks his audience to think—indeed, he dares them to think otherwise—that Caesar was not a threat to Roman republicanism but a guarantor of it:

But were I Brutus,
And Brutus Antony, there were an Antony
Would ruffle up your spirits, and put a tongue
In every wound of Caesar, that should move
The stones of Rome to rise and mutiny. (3.2.226–30)

Antony refers here not to Decius Brutus but to Lucius Junius Brutus (from the Lucrece narrative), who is thought dumb and surprises everyone by breaking silence to stir up his fellow Romans and lead them to overthrow the tyrants. And the "stones" in Antony's gendered narrative refer synechdocically to the phalluses (that is, the swords) of Rome and hint simultaneously at the threat to them—that is, stones instead of/without penises. What we learn from Paster and *Julius Caesar* is that shame can and often does play an important role in the conventional construction of the female body, and this feminized shame can also function as a source of empowerment, lending stature to an otherwise emasculated or castrated male body.

Sacrificial Repatriation: By a Roman Vanished

Antony and Cleopatra rewrites the sacrificial virgin story of *Julius Caesar*, and it does so especially through Antony who attempts to locate himself in Rome's imperial story by refiguring his own failed male body. In *Antony and Cleopatra* Antony's body of shame, that is, of embarrassment, is his male—as well as his white, heterosexual—body. Throughout the latter scenes, Antony attempts to come into some kind of male heroism, a heroism that will presumably gain him a place in the imperial story. His body, however, has become a symbol of a failed masculinity, a masculinity marked by an "emptiness" (3.13.36), according to Enobarbus who decides by the end of the scene to desert Antony. In the latter scenes of the play Antony's manliness has been effectively compromised. His only recourse is to refigure his body as female, to refashion himself as a sacrificial virgin more generally and as the sacrificial Dido or sacrificial Lucrece more specifically. Only by refiguring himself as female can Antony write himself into Rome's imperial narrative and position himself at the birth of empire. Images of penetration, wounds, blood, marriage, orgasm, and shame inform Antony's last scenes in the play. Through these images he attempts to reshape himself as a female heroine of the empire. At the beginning of his aggressive refashioning of himself he envisions the iconographic figuring of his own body:

> If from the field I shall return once more
> To kiss these lips, I will appear in blood,
> I, and my sword, will earn our chronicle. (3.13.173–75)

According to M. R. Ridley, Kenneth Deighton and subsequent editors have pointed out that Antony alludes here to a "stag when in full vigor."[19] Here Antony partly presents himself as the stag mentioned in Caesar's Modena speech. But more than being a stag in full vigor, that is, ready to go into battle, Antony speaks of himself as being "in blood" after his return. In other words, he envisions himself here too as a sacrificial stag, a body gilded in blood and earning its place in the images of history. Moreover, the amalgam of kissing lips, blood, sword, self-proclaiming, and history bears more than a strong resemblance to Lucrece's own sacrificial story.[20]

The visual force of Antony's speech becomes even more evident a few lines later when Antony, speaking of celebrating with his "noble captains," says he will "force / The wine peep through their scars" and ends by saying, "The next time I do fight / I'll make death love me" (3.13.190–93). Two scenes later he offers an even more pointed visualization of his sacrificial corporeality: "Or I will live, / Or bathe my dying honour in the blood / Shall make it live again" (4.2.5–7). In the image here of regaining honor, of becoming rechastised, Antony evokes Lucrece's impassioned self-sacrifice. Although Antony is perhaps alluding to myths about curative blood baths,[21] the most immediate and specific echo of his speech is Lucrece, who attempts to reclaim her honor by passionately bathing herself in her own blood. Robert S. Miola misreads the direction of Antony's speech when he argues that Antony "plans a blood ritual" in order to "atone for his former indolence and effeminacy."[22] Rather, Antony attempts to empower himself, to write himself into the story of imperial heroism, by reenvisioning himself as female (and perhaps even trying to get his soldiers to do the same, but they are unable to reimagine themselves).

In all these earlier images of Antony's last scenes in the play he urgently stages his sacrificial preparations, a point that becomes emphatic in his persistent use here of the future tense. In any case, his sacrificial desires seem more discursive than not. His sacrificial self-presentation does not come into any real theatrical presence until he learns of Cleopatra's death; then he moves quickly through a series of sacrificial images that culminate in his attempt to kill himself by falling on his sword. He echoes Philo's hysterical indictment of him in the opening speech of the play: "O cleave, my sides! / Heart, once be stronger than thy continent, / Crack thy frail case!" (4.14.39–41). And not surprisingly, Antony transforms this earlier supposedly emasculating hysteria into a form of female empowerment.

A few lines later he pushes his regendering sacrificial imaging of himself even further. Speaking to an absent and presumed dead Cleopatra, he says, "I will o'ertake thee, Cleopatra, and / Weep for my pardon" (44–45). (The "weeping" helps sustain the gendering of the "frail" body in his speech a few lines earlier.) He then goes on to imagine himself in that tradition of the widow who does not wish to continue living after her husband has died: "Since Cleopatra died, / I have liv'd in such dishonour that the gods / Detest my baseness" (55–57). Between these two speeches he evokes that famous pair of lovers whose entwined story of duty and passion, of West and East, of sacrifice, is positioned as Rome's primal scene:

> Where souls do couch on flowers, we'll hand in hand,
> And with our sprightly port make the ghosts gaze:
> Dido, and her Aeneas, shall want troops,
> And all the haunt be ours. (51–54)

In pondering why Cleopatra lives so long (read "too long") after Antony or whether she kills herself for love, critics tend to miss Antony's more explicit self-inscription into the very narrative into which they wish to write Cleopatra. In his claims of overtaking Cleopatra and of having lived so long after her presumed death, Antony regenders himself and positions himself as the sacrificial spouse, the "good and faithful wife" who submits herself after her husband's death to suttee (*sati* in Hindu and Urdu), that is, to widow-burning,[23] a sacrificial death. (Gertrude's lack of suttee, her desire to keep living, is of course one of the things that appalls the men in her life and certainly makes richer Hamlet's already poignant remark that "funeral bak'd-meats / Did coldly furnish forth the marriage tables" [1.2.180–81].)

Antony envisions sacrificing himself on Cleopatra's altar. Accepting Robert S. Miola's argument that Antony attempts to emulate Aeneas,[24] I am arguing that once Antony understands his failed *virtus*, his failure to be Aeneas, he then tries to emulate Dido. His evocation of Dido and Aeneas signifies neither Shakespeare's forgetfulness about Dido's rejection of Aeneas in Hades nor Shakespeare's romantic refusal to uncouple such a famous pair. Antony sees himself as Dido and attempts to give himself to Aeneas. Dido is, after all, the suttee prototype in Western imperial fictions, and once Antony thinks Cleopatra is dead, Dido certainly becomes a logical imperial figure to emulate. By evoking the image of a Dido who does not reject Aeneas, that is, of a Dido who does not renege on the symbolic significance of her sacrifice, Antony gives himself to his Aeneas, despite his thinking that Cleopatra has betrayed him. (His hearing about Cleopatra's death does not convince him that Cleopatra has not betrayed him, an observation that may be inferred from his response to Mardian, who brings him the news of Cleopatra's death and her last word, "Antony": "That thou depart'st hence safe / Does pay thy labour richly; go" [4.14.36–37].) Part of Antony's emulation of the sacrificial Dido is that he envisions himself remaining sacrificially true even in Hades.

And the Western inversion here, a white man dying on the altar of a black woman, intends too (from Antony's perspective) to underscore the full force of his sacrifice, his rewriting of Aeneas's white story of the founding and establishing of Rome.

Part of what Antony wants to do is save his death from inconsequentiality by dying with Cleopatra, and part of the problem here in Antony's last scenes is the fact that Cleopatra must by definition die alone. What potentially erases the sacrificial force of Dido's death is that when she dies Aeneas is far away, nowhere in sight. Antony desires to catch up with Cleopatra's orgasmic/sacrificial death. "Eros!—I come, my queen:—Eros!—Stay for me" (4.14.50) and "Come, Eros, Eros!" (54). Unlike the very sacrificially deliberate Cleopatra, Antony finds himself bungling through a kind of sacrificial emergency, trying to catch up to what he presumes is a dead, that is, post-coital, Cleopatra. Antony's death is a sacrificial mess. Even as he plays Dido, he plays Lucrece as well, submitting his body to be violated, to be raped, by the mediatory figure Eros, while simultaneously taking control of his body within the frame of sacrificial chaste thinking: "Come then: for with a wound I must be cur'd, / Draw that thy honest sword, which thou hast worn / Most useful for thy country" and "Draw, and come" (78–80, 84).

Antony pushes the imaging of his female sacrificial self still further as he visualizes himself on the public sacrificial altar at once offering his throat (like Iphigenia perhaps) and showing his violated and soon-to-be-chastised body:

> . . . Eros,
> Wouldst thou be window'd in great Rome, and see
> Thy master thus with pleach'd arms, bending down
> His corrigible neck, his face subdued
> To penetrative shame? (4.14.71–75)

Even as Antony seems to say to Eros that he wishes Eros would kill him because he does not want to be shown alive in Caesar's triumph, he shrouds himself in a language from which the imaging of his body cannot be separated. Even as he offers a kind of heroic manly resistance to being female, he discursively stages his heroic female death.

Chasing after his nobility and just before falling on his sword, Antony addresses a dead Eros:

> . . . But I will be
> A bridegroom in my death, and run into't
> As to a lover's bed. Come, then; and, Eros,
> Thy master dies thy scholar. (99–102)

Of course his death cry does not work, and he fails to die literally, sexually, or sacrificially: "How, not dead? not dead?" (103). Antony's sacrificial self fails him, offering Rome's second failed sacrifice, the first being Fulvia's death: "Can Fulvia die?" (1.3.58). The images Antony has given here are quite resonant, especially so given the other images and motifs collected around them, images that serve finally to focus Antony's rush into consummation. The image of the marriage bed as a place of female death is a familiar one: the marriage bed works multiply, that is, as a generic sacrificial altar, as Dido's funeral pyre, and as Lucrece's bed. He fails finally to play a convincing Dido or Lucrece.

But even as Antony insists on a sacrificial Roman death, he offers his sacrificial death up (literally by being hoisted up) to Egypt, as is made clear through his refrain, "I am dying, Egypt, dying." By trying in his last moments to advise Cleopatra on how to negotiate her prosperity in Rome, Antony dies in a most conventional sacrificial fashion (however fanciful it turns out to be): he dies to deliver Rome (and perhaps ultimately Caesar) to Cleopatra. The iconicity of his death intends, however, to do much more. Antony attempts to radicalize the border between Egypt and Rome by insisting on both his Romanness and his orgasm. And the radicalism he affects here may partly be gleaned from the choric Cleopatra as she watches him die: "Yet come a little. . . . O, come, come, come. / And welcome, welcome! Die when thou hast liv'd" (4.15.36–38). This imperial death reverses the gender roles. The man's body is on voyeuristic display before a community of women: "O, see, my women: / The crown o'th earth doth melt" (4.14.62–63). And this radicalism is especially made theatrically powerful in the reversal of a scene always readily evoked by the imagination of Western imperialism, as the white man sacrifices himself at the feet of a black woman who has at one and the same time both loved and rejected him. As James J. Greene has argued, "If one of the seminally powerful myths in the cultural memory of our past is Aeneas' rejection of his African queen in order to go on to found the Roman empire, then it is surely significant that Shakespeare's [*sic*] . . . depicts precisely and quite deliberately the opposite course of action from that celebrated by Virgil. For Antony . . . turned his back for the sake of his African queen on that same Roman state established by Aeneas."[25]

Once dead—indeed, in the very act of dying—Antony becomes an authentic Roman. But his newfound authenticity, his newly "recovered" *virtus*, threatens to deconstruct the very cultural processes that a sacrificial Roman death should ideally stabilize. Many critics argue whether Antony's death allows him some kind of transcendence, but I am arguing that Shakespeare's play concerns less Antony's transcendence than his relationship to a narrative about transcendence, particularly of a sociopolitical kind. Ideally, Antony's death should be legible as a sign of the authenticity of Rome's imperial identity—its white, male, and heterosexual self. But his death is finally not a stable sign. He sacrifices himself at the feet of his black queen, and he dies as a violated woman and a penetrated man. Antony's death upsets the authenticity of the sacrificial virgin motif, because it fails to allow Rome to fantasize about its chaste self.

More than anything else perhaps, his death betrays the inauthenticity of Roman nostalgia. Instead of pointing toward some transcendent self, political body, or body politic, his death, at least the response to his death, makes salient how nostalgia is very much mired in the political present. To quote Susan Stewart, nostalgia speaks of "a past which has only ideological reality."[26] If nowhere else, certainly in the aftermath of Antony's death, nostalgia reveals its function in the drama of realpolitik.

Even before Antony actually dies, his self-sacrifice gets drawn into the cynical, nostalgic politics of Caesar's Rome. Shortly after Antony wounds himself, Decretas, one of Antony's followers, takes Antony's sword, hoping that it will help him secure a position with Caesar; he is concerned for himself, not for Antony: "Thy death and fortunes bid thy followers fly. / This sword but shown to Caesar with this tidings, / Shall enter me with him" (4.14.111–13). Decretas next appears in the play heroically offering his services or his life (5.1.5–12) and presenting the sword to Caesar as he delivers news of Antony's death:

He is dead, Caesar,
Not by a public minister of justice,
Nor by a hired knife, but that selfhand
Which writ his honour in the acts it did,
Hath, with the courage which the heart did lend it,
Splitted the heart. This is his sword,
I robb'd his wound of it; behold it stain'd
With his most noble blood. (5.1.19–26)

His words and the sword presentation recall Lucrece's story of honor, courage, and nobility and, of course, Brutus's heroic role in it. We learn from Caesar's Rome that Antony's body, like Lucrece's raped body, is one whose "taints and honours / Wag'd equal with him" (5.1.30–31). The stained sword, recalling the sacrificial relationship between cutting and signing (Chapter 1), works as a signature of Antony's self-chastisement of his violated body, his finally putting an end to the foreign pollution warring in his innocent Roman body. Decretas's allusion here to Lucrece may show some nostalgia for a past Roman determination, but he intends first and foremost to realign his own position in relation to the Roman polity. Antony's imperial courage and honor become a vehicle for Decretas's announcement of his own. The fact that Decretas is such a minor character, more a parody of the heroically redemptive Brutus, only further underscores the depth of the cynicism in Rome's newly made empire.

The Antony of *Antony and Cleopatra* fails to become a sacrificial woman; he falls short of occupying the sacrificial and politically empowering place realized in the other play's stripping and rescripting of Julius Caesar. Antony's picturing Julius Caesar as a victim of a gang rape turns Julius Caesar's body into the evidence of the conspirators' guilt, their treasonous act of treating the Roman male body *as though it were* a woman's body. In this instance their penetration of the male body, their homosexual trespasses, work to Caesar and Antony's advantage. Despite the physical inadequacies of Julius Caesar's body (1.2.90–131), the ideological substance of Caesar's Roman masculinity is never really a question for Caesar. If anything, the conspirators suspect him because he seems too perfectly and comfortably to embody Rome's principles of masculinity. The conspirators penetrate him again and again to mock this man who audaciously lays claim to what the proper Roman knows, retrospectively, that at least until the advent of the more epiphanic Augustan Octavius Caesar, Roman masculinity is an ideal before which men bow, humble themselves, and, like the phallus itself, not something one actually possesses. Still, in the play's ideological world Caesar is a man. The Antony of *Antony and Cleopatra* is a different story. This Antony emerges on Shakespeare's stage less as a penetrated man than as a penetrated woman. Kahn tries to recuperate Antony's masculinity by linking it with the bungled and more "manly" suicide of Cato, whose manly "voluntary death," she argues, had become a "fashionable cult" and a "much-imitated model" by Plutarch's time.[27] She insists on seeing a homosocially oriented Antony whose self-fashioned killing—"a Roman by a Roman / valiantly vanquished" (4.15.57–58)—becomes incontestable proof of his *virtus*.

But Antony's death participates in an erotics, indeed, is driven by a sexual explosiveness, not found in what may be read as Cato's more cerebrally and politically motivated suicide. The dividing line between Antony's male and female selves is never so clear as to make Antony's re-visioning himself in female terms an effective cultural and political strategy. As iterated, Antony is imagined by Rome as a male subject already overly identified with female corporeality. Ultimately, I would argue, Rome figures Antony's body as queer, that is, as an opened male body.[28] And long before Antony indulges in the wiles of Cleopatra, doing such things as exchanging clothes with her, he's already haunted by accusations of queerness. As Cicero berates him in *Philippics*:

> You assumed the *toga virilis*, which you at once turned into a woman's toga. First you were a public whore, and the price of your shame was fixed, nor was it small; but soon Curio intervened, who led you away from the prostitution business and, as if he had given you your bridal gown, established you in a steady and fixed marriage. No boy bought for the sake of lust was ever so much in the power of his master as you were in Curio's. How many times his father threw you out of his own house, how many times he posted guards to keep you from crossing the threshold! But you, with night as your ally, your lust urging you on, and your payment compelling you, were let down through the rooftiles. These shames that house could bear no longer. Don't you know I'm talking about things well known to me? Recall that time, when Curio the father was grieving, lying in bed, and his son flinging himself at my feet weeping entrusted you to me.... He himself, moreover, burning with love, affirmed that he could not bear the longing caused by your separation and would go into exile.... But now let us pass over your sex crimes and shameful acts; there are certain things which I cannot pronounce with decency; you, however, are that much freer, since you have allowed things to your discredit which you could not hear named by an enemy who had any sense of shame.[29]

Reading Antony as queer, culturally and sexually, is not lost on Shakespeare's play, in which the penetration of Antony's body is interwoven into Rome's suspicions about Antony as having been feminized by Egypt.

From the very opening we get inklings of an Antony who not only "bends" in devotion but who bends over. We hear echoes of this accusation again when Antony imagines himself "bending down" in "penetrative shame." Too, his arguing that he "dies" his student's student, conjures up and reverses the familiar language of sodomy within institutional pedagogy.[30] Antony presents himself as doubly queer, or at least as pushing the boundaries even of "proper" sodomitic relations, if Rome were capable of imagining such a thing. Caesar figures Antony in such terms when he draws an analogy between Antony's Egyptian sexual goings-on and aging boys, saying that Antony needs to be scolded "as we rate boys, who being mature in knowledge, / Pawn their experience to their present pleasure, / And so rebel to judgment" (1.4.31–33). When Caesar's depiction of these man-boys is read in the context of Caesar's most immediate subject—Antony's indulgence in sex—Caesar in effect taunts Antony not just for playing a sodomite but for playing a passive one, the one on bottom, the one who gets penetrated.

Ellis Hanson has argued that "Antony's sexual crime, like that of sodomy, is a subversion of the natural (masculine) order, accomplished by the inevitable international conflict."[31] But Antony's sexual/textual crime is not only like sodomy; sodomy is, or at least is made into, one of his many complicatedly interwoven and evidentiary crimes. Antony may be the older and more seasoned soldier, but (as said by the soothsayer [2.3.17–22]) he will always find himself second to Caesar. Unlike critics who think that Antony really is Caesar's rival competitor—a reading based largely on the way Caesar laments him in his final nostalgic reading of Antony—I would argue that part of what Caesar insists throughout is that his rivalry with Antony is not that between a man and a man. Despite Antony being older, he's Caesar's boy (for example, 2.2.207, 3.13.192, 4.1.1, 4.4.26, 4.8.22, 4.12.48). And more than this, his effort to think of himself as Caesar's competitor, as Caesar's homosocial rival, slips into a language sounding more like an offer of a homoerotic tryst:

> . . . I dare him therefore
> To lay his gay comparisons apart
> And answer me declin'd, sword against sword,
> Ourselves alone. (3.13.25–28)

There is something very right and very wrong with such arguments as the one advanced by Bruce Smith (along with others), who argue that of all Shakespeare's male pairs the least "degree of sexual feeling" belongs to "the passionless political understanding between Antony and Caesar."[32] Lucy Hughes-Hallett agrees with Smith; she argues that in Shakespeare's play "even homoeroticism is absent: none of Shakespeare's Romans love one another. The Rome of this play is a man's world, and an absolutely asexual one."[33] Although such arguments pick up quite rightly on Rome's self-fashioned lack of interest in sex of a personal sort, these same positions overlook the political and cultural usefulness of sex to Rome. For Caesar, even heterosexuality is nothing short of a distraction or a business proposition (for example,

1.4.15–25), a thing that must be strictly regulated. Such a Roman position makes more comprehensible the association in classical and early modern culture between homosexuality and a fear of excessive heterosexuality.[34] Nonetheless, for Caesar and his Rome heterosexuality is Roman; homosexuality is not. All of this—heterosexuality and homosexuality—contribute to the titillating irony of the pseudomarriage between Antony and Caesar, who come together in a homosocial and homosexual matrimony, with Octavia as the pretense between them.[35] The performance is parodic, however, only within some very real political parameters: Caesar pushes to center stage (for his audiences on- and offstage) the inconsequentiality of Antony's Roman virility. As has been noted often, Antony begins by echoing the opening of Shakespeare's Sonnet 116:

> *Ant.:* May I never
> To this good purpose, that so fairly shows,
> Dream of impediment! Let me have thy hand
> Further this act of grace: and from this hour,
> The heart of brothers govern in our loves,
> And sway our great designs! (2.2.144–49)

And Caesar solidifies the marriage between them with Lepidus as witness:

> *Cae.:* There's my hand.
> A sister I bequeath you, whom no brother
> Did ever so love so dearly. Let her live
> To join our kingdoms, and our hearts, and never
> Fly off our loves again!
> *Lep.:* Happily, amen. (2.2.149–53)

A few lines later Antony says, "Yet ere we put ourselves in arms, dispatch we / The business we have talk'd of" (2.2.165–66). It seems here that Antony and Caesar have traded places, Antony performing a Roman maleness: Antony speaks of governing and Caesar of joining. Antony's business demeanor may be read as part of his ongoing attempt to reassert his virility, his positioning himself as something other than queer. And Caesar's object here—even and especially in this moment of conjoining—is quite contrary to Antony's. Caesar's more transparently erotic language and his role as bequeather identifies him as the dominant male partner in an erotic or sexual bond with a more feminine and bending Antony. Caesar's own secured Roman *virtus* allows him to evoke a queer discourse from which the more culturally ambivalent Antony must distance himself if he is to perform masculinity convincingly and show himself capable of some kind of equitable homosocial rivalry or bonding with Caesar.

As Caesar makes clear, gender and sexuality say less about anything corporeal than they do about one's hegemonic place. Caesar remains on top. In the end Antony's sacrificial drama leaves him more vanished by the Roman Caesar than "vanquished" by his so-called Roman self. At least from Caesar's point of view, Caesar's Roman domination of Antony and Antony's failure as a sacrificial body can be seen in the mere fact that Antony possesses a sexual body (however sexualized). But finally more truly Roman, more forceful and telling, than Caesar's pragmatic view of heterosexual relations is Caesar's passionless political understanding of sodomy. A dispassionate passion informs Caesar's vision of both Antony and Rome. Caesar insists that such a stance is not only useful but fundamental to Rome, and Antony betrays himself at every turn as one filled with too much investment and passion, too much of an erotic life. Turning to the subject of race but keeping the broad issues of this section in mind, I argue in the next section of this chapter that Antony's lack of a dispassionate passion likens him to certain Englishmen who failed to secure England's interest in Ireland. And it likens Caesar to those who would challenge them and their passion, their newly composed racial selves.

The White English and the Hybrid Irish

As in William Harrison's "Bodies of the Britons," Rome's masculine anatomy (however impressive) conveys only a piece of the tale.[36] England's nostalgia for an imperial Rome also tells a racial story, and the imperial imperatives of Shakespeare's Rome also demand a narrative about Antony's lost racial whiteness. His lost whiteness reifies and textualizes Caesar's presumed natural and immutable whiteness. And of course, as I've read it on other occasions, the racial story is really always coterminous with narratives of gender and sexuality.[37] Nevertheless, whiteness eludes even by cultural definition: in its resistance to an ontology in any positivistic sense, it purports in all its nostalgic *materia* to signify an originary and chastised ur-textuality.[38] In simpler language, the defining principles of racial whiteness (with its roots in politics and not biology)[39] are predicated on a kind of textual virginity or purity. To adulterate whiteness, to narrativize it, is in effect to erase it.[40] Whiteness undergirds and evinces the substantiality of empire: it becomes an "object" of chaste thought and presumes a materiality that transcends the rituals and the bodies that create and sustain it. Within such an imperialistic frame, blackness becomes a kind of testimonial, signifying and visualizing a fall from white grace.[41]

Antony finds himself caught up in Rome's allegorical and imperial narrative about his fall. (His being hoisted up to the black Cleopatra at his death seems in part, iconographically, to mark a kind of ironic ascension of the fallen white angel.) Rome fears that Antony has gone black, gone nonwhite.[42] As Kim F. Hall has observed:

> The trope of blackness had a broad arsenal of effects in the early modern period, meaning that it is applied not only to dark-skinned Africans but to Native Americans, Indians, Spanish, and even Irish and Welsh as groups needed to be marked as "other." However ... in these instances it still draws its power from England's ongoing negotiations of African difference and from the implied color comparison therein. Thus the Irish may be called "black" and an English woman may be called "Ethiopian," but these moments always depend on a visual schema that itself relies on an idea of African difference.[43]

Egypt has presumably darkened Antony, and Rome seems (wittingly or unwittingly) to play repeatedly with Antony's newfound cultural alterity. It is emphatically barbared, if not Enobarbared (or spoken), for Rome's on- and offstage audience.[44] In the play's first Roman scene (1.4) an earnest Lepidus says that he himself must not think that there are enough evils "to darken" Antony's "goodness" and that Antony's faults "seem as the spots of heaven, / More fiery by night's blackness" (1.4.10–13). In a mixture of racial and sexual toying that turns upon the miscegenational coupling of Antony and Cleopatra, Caesar responds, "Yet must Antony / No way excuse his foils, when we do bear / So great weight in his lightness" (1.4.23–25). And, not surprisingly, even Cleopatra mocks Rome's and Antony's anxieties of hybridity when in her racialized blazon she tells the imminently departing Antony to "seek no colour"—literally, no pretense—for his going because once upon a time they had "eternity" in their lips and "bliss" in the brows of their arches, and their "parts" were not "so poor" but belonged to "a race of heaven" (1.3.32–37).

Although a certain levity moves through this kind of rhetorical playing, reproduction makes real, visible, and more permanent and serious this hybridity feared by Rome and sometimes Antony. Hybrid offspring especially unbalance the necessary dissymmetry between conqueror and conquered. A similar procreative (un)balancing looms in both *Titus Andronicus* and *Othello*, and here in *Antony and Cleopatra* this reproductive anxiety precedes Antony. Rome has already witnessed what it sees as the frightfully mesmerizing power of the hybrid-making Cleopatra: "She made great Caesar lay his sword to bed; / He plough'd her, and she cropp'd" (2.2.227–28). Antony harps on similar anxieties when he blames Cleopatra for his having left his pillow unpressed in Rome and "forborne the getting of a lawful race" (3.13.106–7). More horrific than the black body giving birth to the hybrid white body (hybrid white bodies are still "black") is the white body giving birth to the hybrid black body, betraying for the empire its tenuous hold on any myths of racial or national character. Perhaps this would explain in part why an imperial-fantasizing England, for example, seems almost obsessed with the racial (im)mutability of blackness and nearly intimidated into inarticulation about what must have been, I would venture to argue, its more pressing concern, the (im)mutability of whiteness. Nonwhite (non-Roman or non-English) progeny would by definition be unlawful; more pronounced than any disapproval of hybridity in and of itself is the national and imperial agenda and identity it hinders or at best obscures.[45]

The real and theatrical meaning and power of whiteness function in Caesar's Rome not simply as a descriptive property one happens to have but as a decree thoroughly invested in the sociopolitics of Shakespeare's Roman Empire. However so troped, the materiality of Antony's blackness—his lost whiteness—has (for Shakespeare's England) a more local habitation and a name, a cultural and racial semiotics closer to home. The blackness of Shakespeare's Antony reaches most deeply and most particularly into that blackness, that alterity associated with imprecise but exacting Irish Africanisms or African Irishisms; and Shakespeare's principal Roman players (Caesar and Enobarbus) draw a significant part of their affectivity, their legibility, from a discreetly English cultural and racial sensibility. In other terms, an Irishman is culturally and racially not an Englishman.[46] In many early modern English texts blackness seeps into Ireland through discursive trickery. And on occasion Irishness makes its way, suspiciously, into early modern English texts on Africa, sometimes to the deprecation of the former. One such example is Richard Jobson's *The Golden Trade* (1623), which provides Jobson with the opportunity to observe that Africans bury their dead "just after the same manner, as the Irish doe use, with a wonderfull noyse of cries and lamentations, . . . especially the women, running about the house, and from place to place, with their armes spread, after a lunaticke fashion."[47] He observes too that the sounds of African music have "a perfect resemblance to the Irish

Rimer."⁴⁸ And he finds occasion to argue that Irish women are further from civilization than the women who live near the Gambia River, since, unlike these women, "with cleanlinesse your Irish woman hath no acquaintance."⁴⁹ Aphra Behn similarly positions the Irishman in relationship to the African when she chooses an Irishman—"a wild Irish Man . . . a Fellow of absolute Barbarity, and fit to execute any Villany [*sic*]" (76)—to bring about the brutal punitive death of her hero, the black Caesar, who has killed his wife but toward whom Behn shows ambivalence if not outright sympathy. Such "often purely descriptive" comparisons between the Irish and the Africans were often driven by emotional overtones⁵⁰ and worked at one and the same time as a detriment to both the Africans and the Irish. The Irish, this emerging "race apart," were not only black or African through analogy or broad cultural relativism; especially from the sixteenth century forward they moved persistently toward a "real" racial inheritance,⁵¹ toward not only a discrete biological self but a firm economically racialized self as well. As Thomas Sowell has argued in regard to American slavery, in order to protect their black slave commodities, plantation owners would often hire immigrants, especially Irishmen, to do the work that would have endangered the lives of their slaves.⁵² With such comparisons in mind, I am arguing that Ireland provides a semiotics for reading Antony's lost Roman self and provides the reason why Egyptianness, like Irishness, must be sacrificed, cut off from Rome (or England) in the pursuit of an already known national and imperial character. Playing through Hall's visual schema, the English were proving themselves white in the very gesture of proving the Irish black and, therefore, in need of chastisement.

As the sixteenth century wore on, the English were less driven by a wish for any nebulous and diplomatic transformation of Ireland into England (something that had already been and was still being tried) than by the precise and almost surgical act of excision. Philip Sidney would advocate such stringency, for example, following his brief visit to Ireland in 1576. To the argument "that lenity were better to be used then severe meanes," he responds:

> Truly the generall nature of all contreys not fully conquered is plainly
> against it. For untill by tyme they fynde the sweetenes of dew subjection, it
> is impossible that any gentle meanes shoolde putt owt the freshe remem-
> brance of their loste lyberty. And that the Irishe man is that way as obstinate
> as any nation, with whome no other passion can prevaile but feare besides
> their storye whiche plainly painte it owt, their manner of lyfe wherein they
> choose rather all filthines then any law, and their owne consciences who

beste know their owne natures, give sufficient proofe of. For under the son [*sic*] there is not a nation, whiche live more tiranniously then they doe one over the other.[53]

To cut the Irishness out of the Irish would presumably reconstitute them as English, turn their land into "mearely a West England" (as one contemporary document put it).[54] There is already a shared prehistory, and the English find themselves able to cast deference, a certain sympathy of recognition, toward the Irish: like the Irish are still, the English were once an atavistic people before being chastised, cut off from their barbaric past.

Rome's sacrificing of the Egyptian Roman or the Irish English Antony becomes an exercise in the excising of one identity from the other, the symbolic and tangible act of cutting the primitive out of a newfound national and imperial civility. The cutting of white primitivism from white civility provides the founding sacrificial act of an ideological whiteness. Antony remains an important part of the dominant cultural project, particularly the *loss* of a Roman or English Antony. Although it is important that Shakespeare's England and Rome revere Antony (the nostalgic and sacrificial narrative depends on it), this same England and Rome must, in their performative discourses, accept with mourning and regret their difference from him. After all, in the new imperial order whiteness has (by definition) abandoned its primitive inheritance. According to this logic, Rome did to England what has now become imperative for England to do to (and for) Ireland: the Romans eradicated the barbarism from the English, and the English must expurgate the Irishness from the Irish.

To further this discussion it is more than a matter of convenience or expedience that I turn to Edmund Spenser's 1596 *A View of the State of Ireland*. Spenser readily admits that "the English were, at first, as stout and war like a people as were the Irish, and yet ye see are now brought to that civillity, that no nation in the world excelleth them in all godly conversation, and all the studies of knowledge and humanity" (28 [Ware's text reads "goodly," 21]).[55] Any immediate relationship between Spenser's text and Shakespeare's is not my concern here; rather, I offer Spenser's text as a demonstration of a broader and exemplary semiotics of the racialization of the Irish that began in earnest in Gerald of Wales's twelfth-century *History and Topography of Ireland* (1185) and found its most poignant and pragmatic realization in the sixteenth-century Spenser.[56] Moreover, *A View* is, as Andrew Hadfield and Willy Maley have written, "arguably the most sustained and sophisticated treatment of Renaissance concepts of race and identity by a major canonical author."⁵⁷ For example, in response to Eudoxus's question about the Spanish inheritance of the Irish—a "naked conjecture" Spenser exploits more than he attempts to clarify—Irenius calls the Spanish "the most mingled, most uncertain, most bastardlie" nation under heaven (75 [50]) and stresses that they are notably marked by their invaders from Africa. And speaking of the nations that came to inhabit Ireland, Irenius offers by way of emphatic clarity, "Who whether they were native Spaniards, or Gaules, or Affricans, or Goathes, or some of those Northerne Nations which did over-spred all Christendome, it is impossible to affirme, onlie some naked conjectures may be gathered, but that out of Spaine certenlie they came, that doe all the Irishe Cronicles agree" (67 [45–46]).⁵⁸ The Irish's having been left with no pure Spanish, Roman, or Scythian blood becomes one of the most damning and dense charges Spenser can levy against them. Such a move can almost be anticipated and surely comes as no surprise from a nation that comes increasingly through the sixteenth century to define itself against especially the Spanish, African, and the Gaelic Irish. Much historiographical, geographical, and dramatic energy would go toward proving that England was, after all, after everything, "The fairest Nation Man yet euer saw."⁵⁹

For the English, the Irish (the Gaelic Irish) were not simply barbarians but were, if only through "naked conjecture," always exhibiting barbarism in the making, adding a particular urgency to England's need to conquer, redress, and civilize them once and for all. Almost by some kind of natural impulse, the Irish had become a people to be ethnographically discovered. In the words of Gerald of Wales, "For just as the marvels of the East have through the work of certain authors come to the light of public notice, so the marvels of the West [here, of Ireland] which, so far, have remained hidden away and almost unknown, may eventually find in me one to make them known even in these later days" (57). In helping to make Ireland legible Spenser writes how the study of ancient authors, especially it seems Roman ones, helps "open a wyndow of greate light unto the rest, that is yet unsene" (68 [46]). And in reading the Irish chronicles with circumspection, Spenser argues that "there appeareth amongest them some Reliques of the true antiquitie, though disguised, which a well eyed man may happilie discover and finde out" (69 [47]). Such ocular penetration participates in what Patricia Parker has read in her discussion of *Othello* and Leo Africanus as the single ideological act of invading foreign lands and women's bodies;⁶⁰ it's as though the "well eyed *man*" may peer into and (through undressing and closely reading her) uncover the privacy of Lady Ireland. It is an act familiar too from early modern rape narratives concentrating especially on the visual penetration of Lucrece's body. Not surprisingly, in the true ethnographic spirit of the scripting and stripping of an Other people, writers from Gerald of Wales to Spenser could draw indifferently from earlier times and contemporary ones,[61] creating the sense that the Irish were as hopelessly mired in their atavism as they were dangerously perambulatory with respect to English rule.[62] Not surprisingly, in 1594 Elizabeth could (and would) issue a single edict ordering both the deportation from England of all Irish persons not recognized by the Crown and the arrest of all other vagabonds. According to the edict, together they constituted that "great multitude of wandering persons" haunting the streets of London and the environs near her majesty's court.[63] As Spenser points out, the Irish were, after all, a people "more auncyent then most that I know in this ende of the worlde" (64 [43]). Their ancientness is particularly a hallmark of their barbarity, their earning of the appellation of the "wild Irish"—an epithet whose frequent occurrence makes emphatic that the Irish are not simply incidentally or occasionally uncivilized but constitutively so. They were considered "an idle, libidinous, violent, and godless" people[64]—like the Africans.

In classic ethnographic form, their incivility becomes largely the product of a rugged (that is, mountainous) terrain, an unstable climate, and a misguided or simply false religious fervor. Writing early on in his tract, for example, of Henry II's imposing English laws on Ireland, Spenser argues that those laws were ineffective because the Irish fled to the deserts and mountains, "leaving the wide country to the conqueror," and after the division of the houses of Lancaster and York, those Irish—"banished into the mountaynes, where they lived onlie uppon white meates, as it is recorded: seeing nowe there so dispeopled land weakened"—came out of the mountains and reclaimed the land that they still possess, having successfully expelled the English (30–31 [22–23]). Even so, Ireland is "yett a most bewtifull and sweete Country as any is under heaven, seamed throughout with many godlie rivers, replenished with all sortes of fishe most aboundantlie" (38 [27]). The problem is with the Irish people who seem to find more advantage in the mountains than they do in the "sweet land." Later in his narrative Spenser writes that "corners nigh the wodes and mountaynes" serve especially as hiding places for those Irish who are more distinctly roguish than your common Irish person (157 [99]).

The climate is made no less suspect in Spenser's tract, even though Spenser himself praises its temperance. Such climatic calm simply makes it all the more lamentable for Spenser that Ireland (and here he speaks not about

Ireland's weather) is "miserablie tossed and turmoiled with theis variable stormes of afflictions" and "such tempestes" that the land has so "wretchedlie ben wracked" (39 [28]). Spenser continues his conceit, arguing how Ireland had at one point been left "like a shipp in a storme amiddst all the raginge surges" (39 [28]). It is a tempestuous Ireland, threatening even Spenser's ability to narrate it: "now (if it please you) lett us return agayne unto our first course" (40 [28]), says Irenius, as Spenser's argument seems repeatedly to lose its direction. Like the peregrinations of the Irish that Elizabeth's 1594 edict presumably wrestled to control, Spenser's straightforward narrative (so goes the performance) would find itself in a narrative contest with its very subject.

And religiously not only are the Irish superstitious (like all barbarians), and not only do they presumably and vividly evoke for Spenser images of drunkenness, disease, harlotry, darkness, death, and hell (133–35); but they are "soe blindlie and brutishlie informed, for the moste parte, as that you would rather thincke them Atheists or Infidelles" (132 [85]).[65] Being Catholic (like Spaniards?) they might as well be infidels (like Africans?). Spenser's text flaunts its sophistication and its argument that the Irish, under a cool, meticulous, and suspect imperial eye, are already (and have always been) a fully explorable and exploitable ethnographic classic, a rich and perverse text of otherness.

Although Spenser may exploit through tropes and discourse such geopolitical and cultural outsiders as the Spanish, Africans, Scythians, and Gaelic Irish in the context of an emerging national and imperial self-fashioning,[66] his most sustained, frequent, and poignant critiques are made not against these outside outsiders but against those outside insiders, the Old English, to whom they become textually, culturally, and racially linked. The Old English, as they were called in the sixteenth century, made their home in Ireland and were "the descendants of the Anglo-Norman families who had conquered and settled Ireland in the twelfth century."[67] They insisted on seeing themselves as the representatives of the English Crown, not only the spokespersons for but the virtual embodiment—incorporation (to recall a word from *Titus Andronicus*)—of its legal and civil codes. Throughout the centuries their Englishness presumably guaranteed their moral and legislative superiority, their maintenance of themselves as a culture and race apart from the "mere Irish" (as the Gaelic Irish were pejoratively called). Still, Fynes Moryson articulates in his *Itinerary* (1617) a rhetoric yoking Anglo-Irish persons with beasts and to the agrarian, to the plow:

But as horses Cowes and sheepe transported out of England into Ireland, doe each race and breeding declyne worse and worse, till in fewe yeares they nothing differ from the races and breeds of the Irish horses and Cattle. So the posterities of the English planted in Ireland, doe each discent, growe more and more Irish, in nature manners and customes, so as wee founde in the last Rebellion diuers of the most ancient English Familyes planted of old in Ireland, to be turned as rude and barbarous as any of the meere Irish lords.[68]

From the fourteenth to the sixteenth century Parliament passed numerous acts designed to keep apart the Irish and those transplanted English.[69] Nevertheless, by the later 1500s much "fostering and marrying" (109 [71]) had created an English community that was for those inside insiders more culturally and racially hybrid than pure. These hybrid Irish especially showed a tendency to stray away from nature, indeed to be unnatural (an accusation that punctuates Spenser's text); indeed, Eudoxus argues that "the English-Irish there should bee worse then the wild Irishe: O Lord, howe quickly doth that country alter mens natures!" (229 [143]). And he questions the kind of hysteria that comes to characterize the picturing, the framing, of a forgetful Antony: "Is it possible that any should soe farr growe out of frame that they should in soe short space, quite forgett ther Country and ther owne names? That is a most dangerous Lethargie" (104 [68]).

Spenser underscores the physical manifestation of such hybridity when he calls fostering and marrying between the English and Irish the "two most dangerous infections" (109 [71]):

For first the child that sucketh the milke of the nurse, must of necesssity learne his first speach of her, the which being the first that is enured to his tongue, is after most plesing unto him, insomuch as though he afterwards be taught English, yet the smacke of the first will always abide with him; and not only of the speach, but of the manners and condicions. For besydes the yonge children be like apes, which affect and Imitate what they have seen done before them ... moreover they drawe into themselves, together with their sucke, even the nature and disposition of their norses. (109 [71])

(The way here in which the physical act of suckling physically [that is, organically] marks the child's disposition follows a logic similar to that found in those rape narratives where the "aping" act of rape seems to reconstitute the woman morally and "genetically" [not that these two are seen today or were seen in Spenser's day as mutually exclusive].) And about the "infinite many evil[s]" of cross-cultural marriage—of miscegenation—Spenser queries, "And indeed how can such matching but bring forth an evill race, seeing that comonly the child taketh most of his nature of the mother" (110 [71]).[70] (Interestingly, one of the couples for whom cross-cultural reproduction is good between "greate ones" and "their vassales" was Julius Caesar and Cleopatra, 109.)

The Old English seem to be a very suspect (if not an all-out treacherous) race. As Spenser, through Eudoxus, offers them up for his audience to contemplate and perhaps to sacrifice, he attempts to move the English nation-empire beyond this Girardian crisis: "It semeth strang to me that the English should take more delight to speake that language then ther owne, wheras they should (me thinkes) rather take scorne to acquainte ther tonges therto: for it hath always bene the use of the conqueror to dispose the language of the conquered" (108 [70]).[71] (Shakespeare underscores this point of course at the end of *Henry V*, when Henry V abandons his French and tacitly forces the French Katherine to learn his English. His performative attempt at French seems to argue that he knows enough French to control France but not enough French to implicate himself or his England further into French mores.) Spenser's model, not fortuitously, is Rome: "So did the Romains alwayes use, insomuch that ther is almost not a nacion in the world, but is sprinkled with their language" (108 [70]). England fancies itself both a part of a historical continuum and a claimant to Rome's national and imperial ambitions. Rome conquered and civilized England, and now England is dutifully bound to conquer and civilize Ireland—its language, people, and land. There were those Old English who did not commingle with the Gaelic Irish and lived in isolated communities in the Pale and port towns, but for all their Englishness they too seem to have become marked with traces of Irishness,[72] not least among them Catholic sympathies. And it is toward these English, as well as toward the Old English in general, that Spenser directs his aggression when he excuses somewhat the Catholic sentiments of the Gaelic Irish because they have really remained untutored in the truths of Protestantism (132–40 [84–88], 242–46 [153–55]). Those—such as the Old English—who profess allegiance to and identification with England should know better. It is almost as though the Irish become a mere afterthought in Spenser's performative text: at a minimum the suffering they must endure is only exacerbated by the presence of the Old English.

Spenser himself belonged to that group who self-identified as the New English, those civil servants and military English persons who transplanted themselves to Ireland in order to take up positions more prestigious than any available to them at home and to acquire more land and wealth than they could almost dare dream of at home. The New English would realize their ambitions in Ireland with aggressive policies that could compel rather than invite the Irish to submit to an English hegemony. Unlike the Old English they were defiantly Protestant and unequivocally English. But to realize these ambitions the New English had to convince the English at home that a significant part of the Irish problem was not the Gaelic Irish but the Old English, those who seemed—and only *seemed*—to be English. The New English argued that the removal of this bastardized race would make more definitive and more nationalistically effective the difference between England and Ireland. What England needed most urgently to understand was how these claimants of Englishness had adulterated the purity and sanctity of an English identity by mixing it with Irish, Spanish, Scythian, and African blood.[73] In other words, England needed to grant the rule of Ireland to the New English, who were supposedly culturally, nationally, and racially pure and understood that the task at hand was not to fraternize with the Irish but to conquer them, to subjugate them once and for all to English rule.

Nevertheless, it is important to note, as Anne Fogarty argues, that Spenser (as well as other New English) functions as a subject in both senses of the term. Although he presumes to speak as a mere servant (that is, subject) for the glory of the Crown and the English nation, his authoritative and chastising voice also claims a space for self-identity and self-empowerment.[74] Spenser's subject self, however defined, is as substantial as the England he incorporates into himself. In other words, the New English right to subdue Ireland can (through the rhetorical trickery of self-fashioning) only be limited by whatever limits England would impose on its own identity, its own vision, the expansiveness of which we saw Richard Hakluyt insisting on in this book's introduction. In the nationalistic and imperial fervor of Spenser and his cohorts there are no limits—territorially, morally, legally, militarily, or otherwise. England is. Ultimately the rhetoric seems to dare the English back home (almost in Henry V's St. Crispin fashion [4.3.18–67]) to be less English than they are, than at least they should be. Spenser toys with the kind of imperial challenge later delivered more matter-of-factly by Harrington: "To ask whether it be lawful for a commonwealth to aspire unto the empire of the world is to ask whether it be lawful for her to do her duty, or to put the world into a better condition than it was before."[75]

A significant aspect of Spenser's Englishness would be a recognition of England's masculinity, a masculinity that some would argue has been called into question by the presence of a female ruler. Masculinization and nationalization are concomitant projects, and Spenser, as Highley has recently argued, comes increasingly "to imagine Ireland as a female-free zone, the site of a New English homosocial community" (5). The English may have read Ireland as being driven by the masculine arts of warfare and domination,[76] as evinced by the vast number of sixteenth-century English illustrations of the Irish, which presented them as kerns and lackeys, citizens of war.[77] (They were also popularly portrayed as beggars and barbarians or some combination of all these.) It is not however that Ireland was itself seen as some admirable bastion of masculinity or homosociality but that the English (and the New English) could go to the wild warring land of Ireland and remember, (re)discover their lost masculinity by conquering the untamed masculinity of Ireland with the more civilized and civilizing masculinity of England.[78] In short, rather than being feminized or driven to masculine (barbaric) excess by Ireland, England could through conquering Ireland demonstrate both English masculinity and English masculine temperament, in short, English civility. Ireland, with its putative barbaric and ethnographic proclivities—its ancientness, hybridity, femininity, and exaggerated masculinity—betrays *materia* demonstratively outside the ideological realm of Englishness. Returning to Kim F. Hall's assessment of the trope of blackness, the Irish (and the Old English), with their suspect link to things Spanish and African, were adulterated (black) by association; in short, they were *not* white. The English (the New English especially) were: they were as white and civilized as the Irish were black and wild.

I am not particularly interested here in a topical analysis that seeks to sustain a link between Shakespeare's play and Spenser's text or between Shakespeare's text and Ireland more generally. Neither is my point that Shakespeare's Rome in *Antony and Cleopatra* is really a disguised Ireland, although such a reading is not out of the question. Rather, I am putting Ireland forward as a text whose cultural and racial complexities and density bring materiality to Shakespeare's Rome and its sacrificing of Antony. Nonetheless, Shakespeare's and Spenser's texts do share some commonalities: each text begins in medias res, with characters bemoaning the loss (the missed opportunity) of a conquered realm, Egypt and Ireland respectively; and each text in effect laments an unrealized imperialistic potential, of Rome and of England respectively. And what the audience comes to discover in both instances, more immediately perhaps in Shakespeare's than in Spenser's text, is that the imperial subject who has assimilated too much into the culture he is supposed to control poses a threat more significant than that of the subjugated culture itself (even though these foreign subjects are of course by no

means innocent players). In this comparative scheme, the New English Caesar sacrificially offers up the Old English Antony whose cultural and racial
ambivalence risks erasing any definitive and defensive hegemonic relationship between Rome and Egypt. Both Antony and the Old English can make
manifest the need for more stringent governing policies and can through
their being sacrificed assist in bringing to realization an always already
known English and Roman empire. And for reasons symbolic and tangible
Rome needs to pull Egypt into its empire as much as England needs to pull
Ireland into its ambit.

Apheton Zoon: *The Tendencies of Realpolitik Nostalgia*

The Rome of *Antony and Cleopatra* is rooted in nostalgic (re)constructions,
an argument more than carefully and ably plotted by a number of critics including, recently, Michael Neill, who has rightly ascribed nostalgia to the
play's imaginative vision, concluding that "at best Roman nostalgia may represent nothing more than a self-indulgent regret for what the mourner has
happily seen destroyed."[79] Nonetheless, "self-indulgent" seems to attribute
too little performative and political import to Rome's nostalgia. Perhaps
closer to home would be what Renato Rosaldo and James Clifford have
identified in other contexts as an "imperialist nostalgia," in Rosaldo's words,
a longing for what "one has destroyed as a form of mystification."[80] But
more than as regret or mystification nostalgia circulates in Shakespeare's play
as a reifier of loss.[81] Rather than a response to what the imperialist has destroyed, nostalgia becomes the principal strategy for making palpable a space
or subject that can now (in its palpability) be reclaimed—nostalgia becomes
a political, military, and social call to action. In other words, this realpolitik
nostalgia would itself provide Rome, especially Caesar, with the impetus
and justification for recovering a lost Rome, a Rome that Augustan ideology and literature emphatically insisted was always Rome's destiny and
birthright. Rome's imperial claims seem to rest at one and the same time on
its past and its future. Such a nostalgia operates not only in Augustan Rome
but in Shakespeare's Rome and not only there but in Shakespeare's England
as well. This nostalgia is especially active in England's relationship to Ireland,
this place that has a way of conjuring up an England that has "but even the
other daye . . . grewe civill." With regard to its Irish neighbors, England is
only respecting its imperial/colonial destiny, its own nostalgic heritage.

As argued, Shakespeare's nostalgic narrative focuses on Antony, and the
first act has two important nostalgic recollections of him, both coming from

the seemingly disembodied voice of Rome itself: the opening gambit delivered by Philo, whose "loving" sentiment toward Rome—"loving" is of
course *philos* in Greek—occasions and characterizes the speech by this once-
appearing and effectively anonymous player; the other, the Modena speech,
presented by Caesar, who here and throughout performs such a totalizing
identification with Rome and the eponymous Caesar that his character
(ad)dresses itself, too, in a Roman anonymity and begs, like Spenser and the
other New English, to be read in terms of a doubly defined subjectivity, self-
fashioning him at once as servant and self-server.[82]

Philo's nostalgic complaint mourns the putative loss of Antony's Romanness, his *virtus*, by effectively transmogrifying his anatomy into something
culturally foreign and female, monstrously Egyptian:

> Nay, but this dotage of our general's
> O'erflows the measure. Those his goodly eyes
> That o'er the files and musters of the war
> Have glowed like plated Mars, now bend, now turn
> The office and devotion of their view
> Upon a tawny front. His captain's heart,
> Which in the scuffles of great fights hath burst
> The buckles on his breast, reneges all temper
> And is become the bellows and the fan
> To cool a gipsy's lust. (1.1.1–10)

Janet Adelman has noted that "the Roman valor associated with Antony's
past and the Egypt of overflow are both equally excessive and equally inimical to the measured Rome of the present."[83] Implicit in Philo's description
is not so particularly an overflowing Nile but an excessive Egyptianness or
foreignness as in Gerald of Wales's seemingly digressive observation in his
Irish topography that "the well of poisons brim over in the East" (56). Philo's
verbiage adds a note of panic as he prepares the audience to witness the
overflowing, bending, turning, and even bursting of a newly gendered and
culturally identified Antony. Although Antony's hystericized anatomy presumably comes from his gender-bending toward the Egyptian Cleopatra—
his temper has been cooled and effeminized—Philo's discursive choices cast
doubt on the existence as well, if not more important, of any earlier Antony
with the proper amount of Roman *virtus*. The long *o* of Antony's overflowing dotage seeps too easily into the recall of an Antony whose past martial-
ness finally finds itself transformed into the "bellows" of Philo's narrative
present. An effeminizing music or dance—"o'erflow[ing] the *measure*"—

displaces the galloping music of war that (visually) has "*glowed* like *plated* Mars." Not coincidentally, Antony comes with the kind of effeminate fullness and musicality found in Harrison's description of non-English bodies, bodies at once weighted down with their "*pregnancie* of wit" and made too light and dance-like in their "*nimblenesse* of limmes."⁸⁴ Too, Philo subjects Antony to a more conventional reading of the female anatomy when he blazons not just Antony's body but his martial (that is, manly) body—"his goodly eyes . . . his captain's heart . . . his breast"—discursively performing the instability of Antony's *virtus* and a kind of always present symbiosis between Antony's Roman masculinity and his Egyptian femininity that is present even before his first encounter with Egypt. Philo presents a blazoned and hystericized Antony, who, with or without Cleopatra, comes "short of that great property / Which still should go with Antony" (1.1.58–59) and who, not very well phallicly endowed, never does partake of Caesar's more authentic and substantial *virtus*. Philo's transmogrified picture of Antony is only the first instance of a cross-dressed, cross-cultural Antony, whose tendencies to wear Cleopatra's clothes, her Egyptian ones, mark a site where gender and national transgression become part of a single gesture. As much is found too in Spenser's text, where Irenius the punster sets the stage for Eudoxus the pundit when he argues that the Irish think the "precisenes in reformacon of apparell not to be soe materiall":

> Yet surely but it is; for mens apparell is commonly made accordinge to theire condicons, and theire condicons are oftentymes governed by theire garments. . . . Therefore it is wrytten by Aristotle, then when Cyrus had overcome the Lydeans that were a warlike nacon, [and] devised to bringe them to a more peacable life, he chaunged theire apparrell and musicke, and in steade of theire shorte warlike coate, clothed them in longe garmentes like wyves, and in steade of theire warlike musicke, appointed to them certen lascyvious layes, and loos gigges, by which in sorte space theire mindes were [so] mollified and abated, that they forgot theire former feircenes, and became most tender and effeminate. (111–12 [72–73])

Furthermore, and finally, in the kind of balancing act familiar too in early modern England's masculine maneuverings, Philo laments not simply Antony's loss of *virtus* but Antony's excessive *civitas*. Egypt has in a sense civilized him to a fault, an observation Enobarbus makes when he speaks of Antony's "being barber'd ten time o'er" (2.2.224), a barbering that depends on the ironic interplay between Antony's being quite well groomed and his getting "barbared," that is, his capitulating to barbarism or being made into a barbarian.[85] His physical cleanliness points to his being culturally sullied, and the tenfold nature of his barbering underscores the framing of him and the racial Other more generally as a figure of excessive *civitas*—as a caricature or mimic—if it has any civility at all.[86]

The Modena speech, one of the play's most vivid and sophisticated moments of realpolitik nostalgia, seems apostrophizingly to reminisce about an earlier and more manly Antony, an Antony, who, "though daintily brought up," is able to adapt his culinary skills to the exigencies of his new and more brutal environment:

> Leave thy lascivious wassails. When thou once
> Was beaten from Modena, where thou slew'st
> Hirtius and Pansa, consuls, at thy heel
> Did famine follow, whom thou fought'st against,
> Though daintily brought up, with patience more
> Than savages could suffer. Thou didst drink
> The stale of horses, and the gilded puddle
> Which beasts would cough at: thy palate then did deign
> The roughest berry, on the rudest hedge;
> Yea, like the stag, when snow the pasture sheets,
> The barks of trees thou browsed. On the Alps
> It is reported thou didst eat strange flesh,
> Which some did die to look on: and all this—
> It wounds thine honour that I speak it now—
> Was borne so like a soldier, that thy cheek
> So much as lank'd not. (1.4.56–71)

Caesar seems to be recalling an Antony properly ensconced in both a Roman *virtus* and a Roman *civitas*. But, as is the case with Philo's speech, Caesar's apostrophic lament is less descriptive than performative: Antony is, after all, already constitutively an absent/lost/nomadic/non-Roman. It makes evidentiary sense that a Roman would speak to a nonpresent Antony.

Caesar's speech is less a heroic lament than a formal condemnation,[87] literally exposing the earlier Antony to be not some recognizable anthropomorphic incorporation of Roman ideals but rather a wild animal, some kind of *apheton zoon*—as Debora Shuger has described this beast—an animal chosen in Greek society (often a stag) and encouraged to wander freely without a master, *libre sine custode*, before being recaptured and sacrificially reclaimed, that is, killed.[88] Antony's escape into the mountains is all too appropriate,[89] and just as Rome's imperial destiny coerces a relenting Caesar to speak here, this same inalienable destiny forces him to recapture and ritualistically slaughter the wild Antony, whose own words seem to return and indict him: "Our dungy earth alike / Feeds beast as man" (1.1.35–36). Or, later:

> O that I were
> Upon the hill of Basan, to outroar
> The horned herd, for I have savage cause,
> And to proclaim it civilly, were like
> A halter'd neck, which does the hangman thank
> For being yare about him. (3.13.126–31)

A theatrically tuned Caesar hesitates but finds himself duty-bound to reveal in a kind of monstrous *ekphrasis* that Antony has not recently gone primitive but has always been so. In the narrative grit of Caesar's realpolitik nostalgic performance the way Antony is "like a soldier" becomes fungible with the way Antony is "like a stag"—an *apheton zoon*.

In being allowed to run free without a master, without the civilizing principles of the Roman imperium, Antony betrays himself to exude too much *virtus*, not unlike a warring wild African or Irishman. Antony's problem is that he has too much manliness, overreaching in the narrative of Shakespeare's Caesar the more exemplary and aphoristic recount found in North's 1579 translation of Plutarch, presumably Shakespeare's main source for the speech and for much of the play: "It was a wonderfull example to the souldiers, to see Antonius that was brought vp in all finenes and superfluitie, so easily to drinke puddle water, and to eate wild frutes and rootes: and moreouer it is reported, that euen as they passed the Alpes, they did eate the barcks of trees, and such beasts, as neuer man tasted of their flesh before" (407). The narrative of Shakespeare's Caesar transmogrifies Plutarch's landscape into a nearly fantastical horrific one: the exigent and collective carnivorism in Plutarch's text becomes Antony's singular cannibalistic indulgence, as Antony's own army (which is presumably not starving) gazes on Antony's horrific theatrical body. Equally significant, if not more so, is Caesar's conjuration of that famous stage "barbarous Moore," Muly Mahamet, in George Peele's *The Battle of Alcazar*, who is "chased from his dignitie and his diademe, / And liues forlorne among the mountaine shrubs, / And makes his food the flesh of sauage beasts" (2.1.341–43). Modena, this northern Italian locale, begins to sound like some place no less fantastical in the unfamiliar lands of North America, Africa, or Ireland.[90]

Caesar's Modena speech instantiates the doubly self-fashioning rhetoric discussed earlier and perhaps ultimately says as much about Caesar as it does about Antony, if not more. Caesar is more of a wounding "I" than his speech lets on. Although he remains a kind of anonymous, disinterested, and distanced chronicler in his Shakespeare Modena recount, Plutarch tells quite a different story, one that has Caesar very much at its center. According to Plutarch, having as their aim to drive Antonius out of Italy, Hirtius and Pansa "together with Caesar, who also had an armye, went against Antonius that beseeged the citie of Modena, and there ouerthrew him in battell." This battle, which ended with "Antonius flying vpon his ouerthrowe [and falling] into great miserie . . . of faminne," was only the latest example of Caesar's aggressive campaign against Antony.[91] The aim was to turn Antony into an enemy of Rome. What may at first seem ironic—that it is Caesar who defeats Antony in Modena—speaks to the point: Caesar's self-erasure is in many respects his greatest cachet. Far be it from Caesar to boast when he is only Rome's servant. Nevertheless, his victory over Antony should not go unnoticed: Caesar's realpolitik nostalgia begs for the return of an Antony who has been and who will again be defeated by the powers of Caesar. Antony may have the raw *materia* of *virtus*, even an admirable abundance of it, but he lacks the *civitas*, the discipline, that gives it shape and invincibility. However much Caesar speaks about Antony, the end point of this monstrous *ekphrasis* is the contrasting classical body that sets this grotesque portrait before the audience. The proof is in the body. Caesar promotes himself even as he argues that he has no self that exists literally or figuratively outside of Rome. He *is* Rome.

But he is not Shakespeare's play, and Caesar's realpolitik nostalgia reaches beyond him—associating him with and implicating him in another memorable picture of famine and cannibalism—and provides the play's most visually suggestive link to Irish matters. If, as I have set out, Antony's character takes a significant part of its legibility from the Old English, those Irish sympathizers who are in the throes of creating an even more bastardized race, then Caesar's character draws proportionately on the New English, those English purists (such as Lord Gray, Spenser, and Spenser's Irenius) who supported starvation tactics as a way of controlling the Irish. Especially the New English advocated famine as a way to crush the Irish, who were also allegedly known for their ability to withstand hunger.[92] The centerpiece of this story is the infamous "late wars of Mounster" of the early 1580s, which turned a more critical gaze (both at home and abroad) on England's policies toward Ireland. Spenser's Irenius describes the horrors of the wars:

The proof whereof I saw sufficientlye ensampled in those late warrs in Mounster; for notwithstandinge that the same was a most ritch and plenty-full countrye, full of corne and cattell, that you would have thought they would have beene hable to stand longe, yett eare one yeare and a half they weare brought to such wretchednes, as that anye stonye herte would have rewed the same. Out of everye corner of the woode and glenns they came creepeinge forth upon theire handes, for theire legges could not beare them; they looked Anatomies [of] death, they spake like ghostes, crying out of theire graves; they did eate of the carrions, happye wheare they could find them, yea, and one another soone after, in soe much as the verye car-casses they spared not to scrape out of theire graves; and if they found a plott as of water-cresses or shamrockes, theyr they flocked as to a feast for the time, yett not able long there were none almost left, and a most popu-lous and plentyfull countrye suddenly left voyde of man or beast: yett sure in all that warr, there perished not manye by the sworde, but all by the ex-treamytie of famyne which they themselves hadd wrought. (161–62) [101–2][93]

Both Spenser's and Caesar's narratives stage arresting spectacles, "anato-mies of death," however much Caesar may protest his own voyeuristic agency.

Most revealing of the ideological underpinnings of these two narratives is how the perpetrators of these acts of starvation—Caesar in one case and the English in the other—*forget* themselves, *chastise* themselves from their own creation of these sacrificial spectacles. Culturally, Antony seems to have more than a passing resemblance to the kind of wild, half-human cannibalistic an-imal (probably in reality an alpaca) being bridled and tamed in the anti-Irish (or anti-Anglo-Irish) print *The Irish Monster*, published in Hamburg in 1690 (figure 10). Although smaller than his captive monstrosity, the civilized cap-tor (who, according to the text beneath the engraving, will display his bri-dled prize in England, Holland, and Germany) proves more effective than the overwhelming physical bruteness of this monster springing from the land (the Catholic land) of Ireland. This engraving, complete with the skele-tal remains of a devoured horse in the foreground, presents too a land in the process of being stripped, a land of starvation. However read, this image draws for its affectivity on an image of Ireland (available from at least the twelfth century onward) as barbaric, bestial, cannibalistic, and starving. Shakespeare's Caesar does not laud Antony's resilience.[94] He shows Antony—rather, lets Antony picture himself—to be even more bestial than the wild Irish. And given Antony's status as one who still has "dainty" pretenses of Romanness,

10. *The Irish Monster* (1690). British Museum.

a hybrid and wild Antony makes a much more notable and horrific spectacle than one who is merely and expectantly a wild Irishman. The topos of
the starving Irishman, which at once shapes and betrays Caesar's narrative,
makes more legible the kind of sacrificial spectacle necessary in the pursuit
of a "universal peace" in Caesar's Rome (4.6.5) or an "eternall peace" in the
imperialistic utopian vision of Spenser's Irenius (212 [133]). It also makes
more legible the strategy Caesar deploys to found and make more tangible
the racial distinction between a truly white Roman and one who is merely
a white impostor. However much Shakespeare's Caesar may claim a classical
body for himself and Rome, his implication in Irish matters would at a minimum in Shakespeare's play lend a cautious aesthetic to Rome's imperial
project.

Caesar is Rome's most active and invisible political agent; he silently positions himself to become Rome's primal father, the guarantor of its phallic
self. In such a capacity Caesar presumes to become the perfect subject: his
personal ambitions are the same as Rome's imperial ones. Ultimately, he, as
authentic Roman, and not the leaking, hybrid, and culturally splintered
body of Antony, figures as Rome's real sacrificial anatomy. Caesar says as

much himself, when he offers his encomium on receiving news of Antony's death:

> But yet let me lament
> With tears as sovereign as the blood of hearts,
> That thou my brother, my competitor,
> In top of all design; my mate in empire,
> Friend and companion in the front of war,
> The arm of mine own body, and the heart
> Where mine his thoughts did kindle;—that our stars,
> Unreconciliable, should divide
> Our equalness to this. Hear me, good friends. (5.1.40–48)

In effectively killing Antony (Decretas is right to bring Caesar Antony's dagger), in cutting him off ("launching" him), Caesar argues that he himself has accepted the self-defying logic of the sacrificial challenge:[95] he has in essence committed *sparagmos*, that is, dismemberment, on his own body. In castrating, that is, chastising, his own body he provides the definitive and evidentiary proof of a formidable and stable Roman imperium. He is Rome: its *virtus* and its *civitas*.

(Re)Posing with Cleopatra

In one of his more Roman moments and in a fashion too conspicuously quick and precise, Antony describes the Egyptian crocodile for his compatriots: "It is shap'd, sir, like itself, and it is as broad as it hath breadth: it is just so high as it is, and moves with it[s] own organs. It lives by that which nourisheth it, and the elements once out of it, it transmigrates . . . Of it[s] own colour too" (2.7.41–46). Lepidus's response is succinct and culturally indicting: " 'Tis a strange serpent" (47), and his drunkenness (however much it may color his response) is profoundly beside the point. Anything Egyptian will smack of strangeness. As an epistemological moment, the crocodile becomes "strange" even though Antony of course has said nothing about it. Egypt's strangeness, its profound legible illegibility, always precedes and shapes any particulars a Western audience may happen to discover about it. It is not really necessary for Antony to say anything, since the specifics of the crocodile's color, size, and shape are immaterial. Like Antony's description of the crocodile, Orientalism points to a truth that is already known, already determined. As Edward Said, the foremost critic of Orientalism, has argued, "[Orientalism] shares with magic and with mythology the self-containing, self-reinforcing character of a closed system, in which objects are what they are *because* they are what they are, for once, for all time, for ontological reasons that no empirical material can either dislodge or alter. . . . [I]t is frequently enough to use the copula *is*."[1] Rome's Orientalizing discourse has already fixed the crocodile, determined and recognized its strangeness. For Homi K. Bhabha and Said, the term *fixing* describes the consequence of whatever cultural acts work to secure the Other's inescapable entrapment in otherness.[2] Although the fixing of the Other must remain flexible enough to ensure "its repeatability in changing historical and discursive conjunctures," as says Bhabha, it must also remain limiting and unchangeable enough to earn the stigma of always being decisively different in its essence.[3]

In other terms, then, Antony's crocodile is fixed in a "radical realism," a realism whose strangeness exists separate from any details of color, size, shape, or comportment. And although "radical realism" remains a particularly fruitful language for postcolonialism, the language does appear in other critical discourses as well, such as Susan Stewart's study of objects and narration:

> An adequate description is always a socially adequate description. It has
> articulated no more and no less than is necessary to the membership of the
> sign. Independent of this social organization of detail, description must
> threaten infinity, an infinity which stretches beyond the time of speech in a
> gesture which points to the speech's helplessness when bereft of hierarchy.
> To describe more than is socially adequate or to describe in a way which
> interrupts the everyday hierarchical organization of detail is to increase not
> realism but *the unreal effect of the real*.[4]

In either instance, I argue that Shakespeare's Rome persists, particularly through Enobarbus, Shakespeare's wisest Orientalist, in pushing a reading of Egypt that has as its goal the fixing of Egypt in a radical reality, a world that is perceived as different and threatening because it is so different from Rome's own more quotidian and pedestrian reality.

Shakespeare's *Antony and Cleopatra* is very much about Rome's Other-fashioning and self-fashioning realism. Critics have generally agreed that "Shakespeare's Cleopatra rules over a world of poetic vision more than a geographical empire."[5] But it is worth asking to what extent is this poetic reenvisioning of Egypt finally a violent reinvention of a "real" Egypt as a piece of imaginative geography. After all, one way to conceptually depopulate a country is to transform it into a poetic object, a radically real one.[6] Cleopatra is also of course part of Rome's imperial re-visioning of Egypt. As Michael Neill writes (perhaps with a different understanding of *radical*), "From the Roman point of view these things [that is, Cleopatra's bounty and boundlessness] are the sign of Cleopatra's radical otherness."[7] Rome's poetic vision isn't trying to be poetic, that is, imaginative, as an end in itself; rather, I insist, Rome narrates and parades the strange reality, the strange realness of this Other space. Egypt is poetic only to the extent that it is strange, excessive, radically real. In other words, Shakespeare's imperially directed Rome reads Cleopatra and Egypt as pieces of a poetic ethnography. Rome shapes its Egyptian imperial struggle most visually around the contours of Cleopatra's sexualized and racialized black body—most explicitly her "tawny front," her "gipsy's lust," and her licentious climatic genealogy, "with Phoebus' amorous pinches black" (1.1.6, 10, and 1.5.28).[8] And when Rome does not explicitly reference her racial blackness, it affects still as part of a more imperious and broader cultural code of alterity as Rome conjures her up as non-Roman, nonwoman, black woman, witch, slut, serpent, bitch, Egyptian, African. I argue, particularly with an eye toward Cleopatra's sacrificial death, that Shakespeare's Cleopatra challenges Rome's radical reinvention of Egypt and offers a radical reading of her own. In her sacrificial and deliberate poly-morphous perversity Cleopatra at once partakes of the iconography of Eve, the Virgin Mary, and Lucrece, as she does, for example, in a sixteenth-century Flemish engraving (figure 11). Shakespeare's play takes advantage of Cleopatra's legibly illegible indeterminate sacrificial body. Through her Shakespeare offers what I argue is his most radical reading of England's own fanciful and imperial theater.[9] Shakespeare's Cleopatra poses, repictures, and repositions herself, straining if not upsetting the realness of an imperial nar-rative that strives to fix her, radicalize her, in Rome and England's racial and sexual story.

Behind the Pornographic and Ethnographic Scene

Behind the scene but very much at the center of Rome's Egyptian vision—from imagining Cleopatra in the throes of sexual orgasm to imagining her invitingly stretched out on her barge—is Enobarbus, the writer, Rome's most explicit and articulate porno-*grapher* and ethno-*grapher*. It is his role, his imperial duty, to bring fixity and definition to Cleopatra's cultural and racial otherness. In the true spirit of the imperialist scribe, his writing about har-lots (that is, *pornographos*) and an Other people (that is, *ethnographos*) move all too seamlessly from merely de-scribing Egypt's putative harlotry and alterity to becoming itself the evidentiary performance of Egypt's pornographic and ethnographic habits.[10] Not surprisingly, Cleopatra is Enobarbus's most natu-rally unnatural pornographic and ethnographic "wonderful piece of work," which "left unseen" would presumably "have discredited [Antony's] travel" (1.2.151–53). Enobarbus's narratives argue that Romans must not under-mine or misread Egypt and Cleopatra's power to seduce pornographically and ethnographically. And through himself he offers a performative persua-sion as his witnesses watch him wrestle with narrative control as he tries to explain Egypt—a ploy that is supposed to make Egypt (or in a different travel account, Africa or Ireland) all the more immediate and dangerous. At-tempting to discern or objectify the salacious habits of women can, for ex-ample, itself lead to, transmogrify into, a salacious text—in effect destroy Rome's self-proclaimed habits of chaste thinking.[11] Similarly, his description

11. A sixteenth-century Flemish engraving of Cleopatra. Warburg Institute.

of Cleopatra's passions not only evokes from him a climatic response (Spenser of course puts the climate to affective use in *A View*, as does any number of accounts of Other cultures) but conjures up weather that bursts through the bounds of empirical documentation: "We cannot call her winds and waters sighs and tears; they are greater storms and tempests than almanacs can report" (1.2.145–47). Like the female body or lands of alterity, the Other is always naturally prone and even solicitous of the pornographic or ethnographic narratives that characterize "them" and threaten to mesmerize or consume "us."

Enobarbus's Orientalist role and Cleopatra's eventual response, not only to him but also to Rome, rehearse, too, the very real inseparability of pornography and ethnography. Christian Hansen, Catherine Needham, and Bill Nichols have collectively identified the discursive patterns shared by pornography and ethnography[12] and elaborate on their claim that both pornography and ethnography are impulses born out of the twin desires of knowing and possessing:

> Pornography is part of a larger discourse of sexuality and the organization of pleasure, and ethnography is part of a larger discourse of science and the organization of knowledge. But our culture makes ethnography (science) licit knowledge and pornography (sexuality) illicit, carnal knowledge. Ethnography is a kind of legitimated pornography, a pornography of knowledge, giving us the pleasure of knowing what had seemed incomprehensible. Pornography is a strange, "unnatural" form of ethnography, salvaging orgasmic bliss from the seclusion of the bedroom.[13]

However imperfectly these terms may fit a sixteenth- and seventeenth-century culture that is not "our" culture, Shakespeare's Rome (through Enobarbus) argues that it merely dutifully and objectively narrates the pornographic and ethnographic culture that *is* Egypt. Ultimately, pornography and ethnography do more than share structural patterns but are implicated in each other's construction. As much may be gleaned from Enobarbus's first significant speech in the play (and his most significant speech outside his Cydnus description), where he voices the possibility that the imperial cause may indeed call for the death, that is, the sexual and mortal death, of women:

> Under a compelling occasion let women die: it
> were pity to cast them away for nothing, though
> between them and a great cause, they should be
> esteemed nothing. Cleopatra catching but the least

noise of this, dies instantly. I have seen her die
twenty times upon far poorer moment: I do think
there is mettle in death, which commits some
loving act upon her, she hath such a celerity in
dying. (1.2.134–42)

His words—*under, compelling, pity, nothing, between*, and *dies* especially—make
clear the sexual thrust of his speech, made all the more terrifying in his bold
mix of levity and violence. Even though his rape narrative here does not explicitly include Cleopatra (he is after all speaking to Antony), he manages
still to pull her into it through a rhetorical and visual trickery that allows
for "under a compelling occasion" to slide into "commits some loving act
upon." Cleopatra, whom he has seen "die twenty times," is one of the bodies he fancies will be strewn on Rome's imperial and rape-laden battlefield.

   Most obliquely, Enobarbus isn't talking about all women (or any women),
when he calls for Roman men to serve Rome's "great cause" as rapists. His
imperatively driven narrative especially advocates a hegemonic imperial re-
visioning of what may be termed Rome's most foundational and sacrificial
communal law, the *merum imperium*, that is, the state's absolute right over the
life, the death, and, for Enobarbus, the sexual death of its subjects. Enobarbus
may be a "man's man" (as Norman Holland has dubbed him),[14] but his real
and "compelling" rhetorical skill and power depend on sifting his crude
masculinity through the more imperially orchestrated racial story of Shakespeare's Rome and England. He begs the question that if Roman men have
in the past gone to war to defend the honor of their raped women, is it any
less a Roman act for them to compel, that is, rape, foreign women. His
"compelling" conjures up a sense of cultural rectitude, arguing for Rome's
"moral necessity" or "rightful claim" ("compel," *OED* definition 2b) to the
bodies of these foreign women and, in a much more limited way, to the
bodies of all women. If a black—read foreign—man raping a white woman
encapsulates an iconographic truth (conjuring up a cultural picture of at
least a thousand words) of the dominant society's sexual, racial, national, and
imperial fears (see Chapter 2), a white man raping a black woman becomes
the evidentiary playing out of the dominant society's fantasies of its self-
assured and cool stranglehold over these representative foreign bodies. And
just as a white man may be said to lose his status as a *white* man by raping a
white woman (see Chapter 1), his raping a black woman becomes one way
that *he* may be initiated into whiteness. (By falling in love with Cleopatra,
Antony proves himself both a failed imperialist [see Chapter 3] and a failed

rapist.) Enobarbus in effect turns the sacrificially driven classical rape narrative inside out. Egypt figures only as a perverse picture of Rome's chaste self, since a woman dying in Egypt does not conjure up a picture of a woman sacrificially laying claim to her essence, her invisible *integritas*, but of a woman luxuriating in her highly visible and experienced sexual body. Here and elsewhere Enobarbus insists on Rome's imperial right, indeed its duty, to discover and violate Egypt—to script and strip it, ethnographically and pornographically.

His most elaborate and richly poetic yoking of pornography and ethnography comes in his Cydnus description, the narrative most responsible for those alluring critical readings of Cleopatra. But Enobarbus's own words betray this as *his* narrative, his writing, "I will tell you" (2.2.190):

> The barge she sat in, like a burnish'd throne
> Burn'd on the water: the poop was beaten gold;
> Purple the sails, and so perfumed that
> The winds were love-sick with them; the oars were silver,
> Which to the tune of flutes kept stroke, and made
> The water which they beat to follow faster,
> As amorous of their strokes. For her own person,
> It beggar'd all description: she did lie
> In her pavilion—cloth of gold, of tissue—
> O'er-picturing that Venus where we see
> The fancy outwork nature. On each side her,
> Stood pretty dimpled boys, like smiling Cupids,
> With divers-colour'd fans, whose wind did seem
> To glow the delicate cheeks which they did cool,
> And what they undid did.
>
> Her gentlewomen, like the Nereides,
> So many mermaids, tended her i'the eyes.
>
> A seeming mermaid steers: the silken tackle
> Swell with the touches of those flower-soft hands,
> That yarely frame the office. From the barge
> A strange invisible perfume hits the sense
> Of the adjacent wharfs.
>
> [And] but for vacancy, [the air]
> Had gone to gaze on Cleopatra too,
> And made a gap in nature. (2.2.191–205, 206–7, 209–13, 216–18)

A cruel irony, a passive aggression, courses through Enobarbus's speech as he conjures up the scene of Cleopatra on her barge, floating toward Antony, moving in for the seduction, if not the kill. Enobarbus's description of Cleopatra on her barge amounts to nothing less than Cleopatra's sexual seduction of the West and what would presumably become Antony's traumatic and primal sexual encounter with the East. Nothing drives this point home more crudely and, ironically, quickly than this narrative in which Cleopatra's barge transmogrifies into a primal bed pushed slowly and mesmerizingly before Antony's unprepared and childlike eyes. In effect, she becomes Antony's rapist, his conqueror—one of those favored inverted hegemonic moves of colonial discourse; the audience has already heard a self-reclaiming Antony say, "These strong Egyptian fetters I must break, / Or lose myself in dotage" (1.2.113–14). Enobarbus's overly romanticized and carefully plotted primal scene narrative of this first contact between Cleopatra's Egypt and Antony's Rome toys, too, with another enduring Augustan picture of Cleopatra, that is, her final Roman encounter—a defeated Cleopatra fleeing Actium in her burning ship. Hence, Enobarbus's paronomastic slide from "burnish'd" to "burn'd." As the Augustan-propagating Horace would recall,

> Sed minuit furorem
> vix una sospes navis ab ignibus;
> mentemque lymphatam Mareotico
> redegit in veros timores
> Caesar, ab Italia volantem
> remis adurgens. (12–17)

> [But the escape of scarce a single ship from burning sobered her fury, and Caesar changed the wild delusions bred by Mareotic wine to the stern reality of terror, chasing her with his oars, as she sped away from Italy.][15]

In his imaging of Cleopatra in her burning ship, Enobarbus recalls England's famous defeat of the Spanish Armada in 1588 (echoing, for example, a commemorative portrait of Elizabeth in which the left window shows a defeated Spanish fleet). His burning ship also mocks a sacrificial and heroic Cleopatra, one who has submitted herself to what the English would see as the exotic ritual of sati.[16] Throughout, his pornographic and ethnographic scripts and visualizations of Egypt move in at least two directions, allowing him (in the ambivalent ways of colonialism) to mask inimical relations with amiable ones.

His description offers a virtual pornographic *ekphrasis*, this despite the fact that there's nothing static or fixed about Enobarbus's narrative. It moves more like a pornographic film, replete with a pan-eroticism, as it repeats (plays out) both the actions and words of "beating" and "stroking." Cleopatra herself shifts (or is made to shift) from sitting in her barge to lying in it, evoking a comparison between her and some commonly drawn pictures of Venus. And his Cleopatra surpasses the venery of those Venuses: she takes her voyeurs beyond Rome's own more pedestrian pornography. As Rosalie L. Colie has noted: "[His words] seem almost to crowd out other meanings, to stop the action and the plot, to force attention on . . . [its] resonances alone. . . . Enobarbus' giving way to grandiloquence seems an almost sexual abandon before her; the cynical and experienced Roman soldier, suspicious of Egypt and its ways, cannot and will not contain his climactic praise of the Queen."[17] To put Colie's observations in other terms, Enobarbus's Cleopatra does signify an unattainable Western *jouissance*[18] but not one simply circulating in the domain of sexual pleasure. Enobarbus works to make Cleopatra not only more sexually enticing but also more sexually dangerous. It is this cannibalistic siren Cleopatra, using Enobarbus merely as an intermediary, who brings Enobarbus's Roman audience to a standstill.[19]

Enobarbus may seem narratively tested and overworked by the overwrought details of Egypt, but this cynical and experienced Roman soldier finally abandons himself no more here in this ethnographic picture than he does in his account of Egypt's sexual mores. And although his description of Cleopatra seems to anticipate what Laura Brown argues is "the cultural obsession with the connection of female adornment and trade, exploitation, and empire" in eighteenth-century culture, Cleopatra is one piece among many, and, furthermore, a piece whose sexual distractions are no match for the more imperially trained Enobarbus.[20] However much Cleopatra exposes herself (and this is part of the game for Enobarbus), she merely tries to cover up what is truly enticing about Egypt. But Enobarbus is not to be fooled as he goes on in his very determined narrative to enumerate the riches of Egypt—its gold, silver, silk, perfumes, and young male and female sexual and laboring bodies. His narrative performatively strains to conjure up, to make comprehensible, Egypt's infinite wealth. And if Egypt's resources are beyond simple reality—beyond Enobarbus's ability to describe them, they are also beyond Egypt's ability to control. As Alexander Leggatt notes, "Where a sensible shipbuilder would use wood and rope we have silver and silk. Instead of real sailors there are women with 'flower-soft hands.' "[21] But Enobarbus does more than adhere to a fundamental or Roman realism. Rather, as Chris

Tiffin and Alan Lawson have said in their study of the written empire, "Inscribing the natives as primitive and unable to make use of the natural resources around them allowed first the biblical parable of the ten talents, and then the Darwinian theory of natural selection to justify their dispossession as part of the plan of Destiny."[22] Enobarbus argues that waddling somewhere between infantilism and atavism, Egypt doesn't quite know what to do with its human or its raw materials and could benefit from Rome's intervention, however nonbeneficent.

Egypt becomes Enobarbus's own ethnographic text of the Other's "infinite variety" (2.2.236), as he competes, for example, with the likes of George Best in Richard Hakluyt's *Principall Navigations, Voyages, and Discoveries of the English Nation* (1589, 1598–1600). Best begins by listing twelve "commodities and instructions [that] may be reaped by diligent [sic] reading this Discourse." In the seventh item he writes about "how dangerous it is to attempt new Discoveries" because of "new and unaccustomed Elements and ayres, strange and unsavoury meates, danger of theeves and robbers, fiercenesse of wilde beastes and fishes ... dread of tempestes ... and infinite others." In the eighth, however, he proclaims "How pleasant and profitable it is to attempt new Discoveries, either for the sundry sights and shapes of strange beastes and fishes, the wonderfull workes of nature ... the sight of strange trees, fruite, foules, and beastes, the infinite treasure of Pearle, Golde and Silver."[23] And to return for a moment to the interplay between Ireland and Shakespeare's Egypt (see Chapter 3), David Quinn has noted, "In scores of ... papers, mostly unpublished but circulated at the time, are ... comments on the fertility of Ireland, the fine quality of its timber, its rivers swarming with fish, its fields with game, its climate mild, its people (only) savage. But these eulogies are almost wholly to be found in propagandist tracts devoted to setting out the attractions of Ireland for English settlers."[24] Spenser performs his own exhaustion around describing the details of Ireland. In Spenser's *View*, "To accounte the particuler faultes of private men, should be a worke infinite," or "too infinite" in Ware's edition (140–41 [88]). However so, Spenser's text begins with Eudoxus musing, "But if that country of Ireland ... be so goodly and commodious a soyle as you report, I wounder that no course is taken for the tourning therof to good uses, and reducing that salvage nation to better government and civility" (13 [11]). And later Irenius will enumerate these details more lavishly:

> Suer it is yett a most bewtifull and sweete Country as any is under heaven, seamed thoroughout with many godlie rivers, replenished with all sortes of

fishe most aboundantlie: sprinkled with verie many sweete ilandes and
goodlie lakes, like litle inland seas, that will carrie even shippes uppon theire
waters, adorned with goodlie woodes, fitt for buildinge of houses and
shipes, so comodiouslie, as that if some princes in the world had them,
they would soone hope to be lordes of all the seas, and er longe of all the
worlde: also full of verie good portes and havens openinge uppõ England
[and] (*sic*) Scotland, as invitinge us to come unto them, to see what excellent comodities that Countrie can afforde, besides the soyle it selfe most fertile, fitt to yelde all kynde of fruit that shalbe comitted there unto. (38 [27])

In Enobarbus's ethnographic text Egypt awaits the real arrival of Rome, and
Rome must seize it, not luxuriate in it as the wayward Antony has done.

Finally, Enobarbus's narrative isn't about Egypt per se—"*I* will tell you"—
but Enobarbus's efforts to convince his listeners of Egypt's pornographic and
ethnographic otherness; and the more his listeners are convinced, the more
easily Egypt may be subsumed by Rome's imperial project. The manly Enobarbus doesn't really compete with Cleopatra's supposedly mesmerizing
powers but with other writers—other pornographers and ethnographers.
Throughout his Cydnus description, his most conspicuous competitor is
Plutarch, Enobarbus's main written source: he continuously strives to push
his version of Egypt's radical realism beyond Plutarch's. He insists on his observer self—on himself as imperial traveler, as witness to cultural otherness.
His theatrical *presence* argues that he, unlike Plutarch, is no mere chronicler;
rather, he provides a true and immediate performance, representing and
re-presenting what he has himself seen, like the best of them, for example,
Herodotus, Pliny, George Best, Leo Africanus, and, perhaps, Spenser.[25] In the
end he offers a vision of an Egypt filled with storms, drunkenness, wild boars,
strange smells, and monstrous matter. And his account of the meeting on the
river of Cydnus is finally as much an aggressive creation and rejection of
Cleopatra as it is an indictment of Antony, who has failed to read Egypt's
pornographic and ethnographic possibilities. In Enobarbus's text Cleopatra
may be Egypt's most symbolic pornographic body, but she is certainly not its
most real or valuable ethnographic prize.

The Realpolitik of Metatheatrical Space

However much Enobarbus may compete with other ethnographic and pornographic writers and not with Cleopatra, Shakespeare's play belongs to
Enobarbus no more than it does to the always seemingly politically fraught

Caesar, whose narrative attempts to wrestle Rome away from Antony were examined in Chapter 3. Shakespeare's drama produces a less univocal response and one that is finally more driven by the immediacy and constantly flowing and fluctuating theatrical energy as it may be momentarily apprehended in the recitations and physical movements of his players. More so than in any other Shakespeare play, the characters' battle over political and sexual space becomes one with their battle for theatrical space. *Antony and Cleopatra* becomes Shakespeare's most studied metatheatrical piece, staging a war waged between competing performers. No Shakespeare text exemplifies more than *Antony and Cleopatra* Herbert Blau's observation that "the erotic capacity of theater is not of secondary importance. It is right there, in the bodies."[26] And although Antony may be blazonly anatomized by his Roman enemies before finally putting his own sacrificial body on display, and although Caesar, with his usually removed body, may later stage his as symbolically self-mutilating, the linchpin of Shakespeare's erotic theater is Cleopatra, who is narratively transformed into an ethnographic and pornographic wonder. And although Enobarbus arduously theatricalizes Egypt, turns it into an Oriental theater of sorts,[27] Cleopatra counters by repeatedly calling attention to Rome's supposedly nonperformative seriousness—"Good now, play one scene / Of excellent dissembling, and let it look / Like perfect honour" (1.3.78–80)—and, concomitantly, by outplaying Rome by becoming herself a consummate actress, a consummate actor.

Through Cleopatra Shakespeare offers a metatheatrical critique of realpolitik: all the world may be a stage, but the dominant culture is only made an ethnographic and pornographic witness to the theatrical world of the Other; its own theatrical antics need not get witnessed. When it recognizes the Other's theatricality, it also performs a gesture of chaste thought, choosing not to contextualize the realpolitik of the performing Other. The Other gets cut off from the exigencies of the sociopolitical matrix, and suddenly and almost magically the performing Other becomes a mere jester—or Cleopatra a frivolous and comic queen. However playful and improvisational Cleopatra may seem—"If you find him sad, / Say I am dancing; if in mirth, report / That I am sudden sick" (1.3.3–5)—her theater is finally as purposeful as Rome's. If Rome can act its way into claiming Egypt, she will do her best to act its dispossession of it. And if the fate of Egypt is a foregone conclusion, the same cannot be said for Egypt's theatrical space. Shakespeare's play provides Cleopatra with a forum for her last great performance, and I mean it more analytically than prescriptively when I argue that her performance, her metaperformance, must be all-absorbing. She must call attention to her own entrapment in performativity, in Rome and England's theater. She must perform as though her and Egypt's future depends on it, and it does. As she moves about the stage acting—playing sartorial games, displaying her royal self, pretending histrionics, and rehearsing ways to die sacrificially—she challenges Rome's attempt to fix her ethnographically and pornographically. There is finally no frivolous or politically irresponsible queen in Shakespeare's play. Throughout, she poses her theatrical body against Rome's inevitable conquest of Egypt.

Her purposefulness, her Egyptian seriousness, is especially evident when she and Antony first appear on stage:

> *Cleopatra:*   If it be love indeed, tell me how much.
> *Antony:*   There's beggary in the love that can be
>   reckon'd.
> *Cleopatra:*   I'll set a bourn how far to be belov'd.
> *Antony:*   Then must thou find out new heaven, new
>   earth. (1.1.14–17)

The moment not only invites the audience into a metatheatrical occasion conjured up by the stage-directing Philo—"Behold and see" (1.1.13)—but, given the aura that always precedes any particular representation of Cleopatra in Shakespeare's day or our own, it also conveys the distinct sense that Cleopatra herself is by nature a theatrical event. After all, she says herself she will play the fool she is not (1.1.42). (This aura helps explain why this scene is so often misread as signaling Cleopatra's frivolity, her "absolute excess," even though Cleopatra talks here about setting boundaries.)[28] This scene seems to offer no surprises and seems very much the product of a classic Cleopatra. The audience may very well surmise that Cleopatra and not Antony spearheads this sexual banter, since, pre-textually, Antony is a Roman (even if he is not always a very convincing one) and the Egyptian Cleopatra a near catchphrase for bawdiness. Their banter indulges in wordplay as the adverbial *indeed* comes to specify the sex act, the deed. (A similar joke is made later when the eunuch Mardian responds to Cleopatra's question, "Indeed?" by saying, "Not in deed, madam, for I can do nothing / But what indeed is honest to be done" [1.5.14–16].) William Harrison's "Bodies of the Britons" (see Chapter 3) strains toward a similar doubled *indeed* when he argues that those peoples residing closer to the sun are "fearfull by nature, blacker in colour, & some so blacke in deed as anie crow or rauen."[29] Along with the deed of sex, the pre-textually known emasculating Cleopatra tries to quantify—hence, telling and reckoning—(if not shorten or cut off) the length of Antony's penis. Antony protests, insisting that his sexual equipment is beyond measurement. It's just like a man, of course, to overstate the size of his penis. But more at issue for Antony is its immeasurable potential—it is a phallus not a penis[30]—and the claims it gives him not only on manliness in general but on Roman masculinity in particular. And Roman (or English) masculinity, as discussed in the preceding chapter, signifies far beyond the domain of gender.

I want to argue that however much Antony and Cleopatra compete with each other through thinly veiled obscenities, this first discussion, this opening gambit between them, is of a far weightier matter and that Cleopatra enters the play on a rather skeptical and cautionary note. Indisputably, sex ignites their speech, but they do not talk about sex as much as they play with it, use it, as they playfully and competitively engage each other *through* it. Theirs is a conversation of national, imperial, and theatrical import into which they pull their eroticized bodies, to recall Blau, or Andrew Parker and others, who have argued, "Whenever the power of the nation is invoked . . . we are more likely than not to find it couched as a *love of country:* an eroticized nationalism."[31] If Antony speaks of love (or sex) at all, it is a love thoroughly implicated in an orgasmic love for imperial things. His and Cleopatra's repartee lies most heavily on the words *in deed*, with *deed* referring less poignantly to their sexual antics than to an entitlement bond, a deed of property. Regan makes a similar and quite sinister pun in *King Lear*, when she, competing with her sister Goneril for Lear's love and land, says, "I find she names my very deed of love" (1.1.71). What Cleopatra (who is no fool) really wants to know is how much land will Antony's "love" cost Egypt. Cleopatra wants Antony's love restricted to herself and does not want it getting refigured as Antony and Rome's penetration of Egypt. As Antony tries to merge bodies and land into a single rhetorical and ideological vision, she struggles to keep a real distinction between corporeal and territorial matters. She fears quite rightly that Antony's deed extends not only (or even primarily) to her sexual space but to her geographical space as well.

Antony's response is quite foreboding. According to Plutarch and a host of other Augustan apologists, Rome's claiming Egyptian space as part of its empire has always been a fait accompli. So when Shakespeare's Caesar announces before his decisive victory that "the time of universal peace is near" (4.6.5), for example, he speaks of a peace that may now be near but has always been imminent. At least retrospectively, Antony's "beggary" seems too close to Enobarbus's "beggar'd" in the latter's imperial narrative pursuit. Moreover and most caustic for Egypt (and ironically for Antony himself it turns out) is Antony's echo of Virgil's Jupiter, who declares, "I set no limits to their fortunes and / no time; I give them empire without end . . . [and make the Romans] masters / Of all things"; prophesying too that Octavius Caesar's "empire's boundary shall be the Ocean; / the only border to his fame, the stars" (*Aeneid*, 1:389–403). To put a final stamp on this argument, Antony's evocation of Virgil here merely repeats what had become at least by the early seventeenth century a kind of imperial signature text, as is evident too by Richard Knolles's use of it in his 1603 deprecation of the Ottoman Empire in his *The Generall Historie of the Turkes:* "Preferring to it selfe no other limits than the vttermost bounds of the earth, from the rising of the Sunne unto the going downe of the same."[32] Long before the battle of Actium the war between Rome and Egypt is already fully evident in Antony and Cleopatra's eroticized negotiation of sexual, territorial, and theatrical space.

The Divine Politics of White Culture

Cleopatra most earnestly challenges at the level of representation Rome's imperial fixing and picturing of her as heathen and black whore. Rome, of course, signifies as Egypt's constructive opposite, portraying itself as everything Egypt is not. And perhaps what needs more critical attention here is the extent to which Caesar's Rome, especially for Shakespeare's early modern audience, would not only anticipate a Christian Rome but have germinations of it indelibly scripted into its history, its very foundation. In this instance Caesar's imminently approaching "universal peace" (4.6.5) would point to Caesar's Roman Empire as well as to the coming of Christ. Rome functions as part of a Christian topology, its *Pax Romana* serving as a prototype and placeholder for the catholic vision of Christ. But it is not only Shakespeare's audience who could or would perceive Christ as part of Caesar's character. It is perhaps not enough to say that Caesar seems to assume a kind of Christlike air in Shakespeare's play; nonetheless, Cleopatra reads him in such terms as she mocks him and casts suspicions on the too-intimate connection between Caesar's materially imperial universe and the Christological spirituality within which he cloaks himself. Caesar's Christ-fashioning is made explicitly evident in the first part of the last scene, when Proculeius, one of Caesar's party, advises the defeated Cleopatra:

> Y'are fall'n into a *princely hand, fear nothing,*
> Make your full reference freely to my *lord,*

Who is so *full of grace*, that it *flows* over
On all that need. Let me report to him
Your sweet dependency, and you shall find
A conqueror that will *pray* in aid for kindness,
Where he for *grace* is *kneel'd* to. (5.2.22–28, italics mine)

This new Rome becomes a palimpsest, effectively displacing, erasing, or flooding over with biblical texts the ominous fullness of the flowing Nile,[33] especially with texts such as the Psalms focusing on fear and overflowing (Psalms 23:4 and 27:1) and Hebrews on grace ("Let us therefore go boldely unto ye throne of grace, that we may receive mercie, & find grace to helpe in time of nede," 4:16). Cleopatra turns Rome's praying back onto its material and not-so-mystical self:

Pray you, tell him
I am his fortune's vassal, and I send him
The *greatness* he has got. I hourly learn
A *doctrine of obedience*, and would gladly
Look him i'the face. (5.2.28–32, italics mine)

Rome's greatness—its "graceness" (as Cleopatra puns)—is predicated on its confiscation of Egyptian properties and bodies, not on any kind of divine gift.[34] Her critique of Rome's religiosity disturbs the cultural topology that will rewrite Rome's material goals in Christian spiritual terms.

Just as Shakespeare's Rome promotes Caesar as a premonition of Christ, it also pushes Rome to read Cleopatra as the Virgin Mary's opposite: the Madonna white and virginal, Cleopatra black and whorish. Already, in the opening lines of the play, the Roman Philo presents an idolatrous Cleopatra before whose dark face, Antony "bend[s]" in his "office and devotion" (1.1.4–5), that is, before whose picture (whose pose) he both prays and strays.[35] As we may expect, Cleopatra challenges this image of herself as a perverse Madonna. Most irreverently when she demands the Roman messenger "ram [his] fruitful tidings in [her] ears, / That long time have been barren" (2.5.24–25), recalling in sexually graphic terms the angel Gabriel bringing news to the Virgin Mary that she will give birth to Jesus (Luke 1:26–38). Most seriously in her sacrificial death, when, nurturing her asp, she scripts herself as the *Madonna lactans*: "Dost thou not see my baby at my breast, / That sucks the nurse asleep?" (5.2.308–9).[36] However much Augustan apologists or Shakespeare's Romans may insist on seeing her as the black whore, as *atrum venenum* (black poison), she pushes herself right up

12. *Cleopatra with the Asp*, by Guido Reni (c. 1638). The Royal Collection ©
2000. Her Majesty Queen Elizabeth II.

against the picture that will eventually replace her, not emphasizing simply
her and the Madonna's differences but their radical causal affinities, an argument Guido Reni seems to make in his painting of a Mariological Cleopatra (figure 12). She too gives birth to Christianity.

Her challenge to Rome's imperial positioning and picturing of her extends, too, to Shakespeare's England, to Queen Elizabeth I herself. Given the

play's debut only a short time after Elizabeth's death, it would seem nearly impossible for Shakespeare's original audience not to draw associations between these two queens.[37] Fulke Greville thought so; he destroyed his own play, written (while Elizabeth was still alive) on the "irregular passions" of Antony and Cleopatra, fearing that it may "be construed, or strained to a personating of vices in the present Governors," that is, Elizabeth and the earl of Essex, and cause him to be put to death.[38] Both queens are known for their sharp intelligence, quick temper, fluency in many languages, and command on the battlefield, as well as for their insistence on maintaining real demarcations between their land and their bodies when it comes to suitors. They are both also theatrically hyperconscious, given to similar scenes of ostentation and public display, such as Cleopatra's floating in her barge and Elizabeth's arriving at St. Paul's in her chariot throne; Elizabeth also travels several times between Whitehall and London in her own royal barge complete with tapestries, gold cushions, and music. For a reading of Shakespeare's play, similarities are especially noteworthy between Shakespeare's Cleopatra's questioning of the messenger about the physical details of Octavia (2.5 and 3.3) and Elizabeth's 1564 detaining of Sir James Melville, Mary Queen of Scots's emissary, in order to interrogate him about Mary's features. (This particular connection tells more than most, since Plutarch neither mentions nor alludes to such a moment in his account of Cleopatra; the moment seems wholly to belong to Shakespeare.) Although Elizabeth most audaciously claims her iconographic power by arrogating the aura of and essentially reposing as the Virgin Mary, replacing the Virgin's spiritual body with her political one, the historical Cleopatra does much the same with her Egyptian goddess Isis. And even though Isis was most commonly known as the goddess of fertility, she was also addressed as "the Great Virgin." And the Greeks did liken her to their Artemis, the chaste goddess of childbirth.[39] When all comparisons are done, however, Shakespeare's Cleopatra isn't just similar to Elizabeth; she offers a more aggressive mimicry and challenge. Reading the relationship between these two queens in too topical or realistic a fashion compromises the very vital and immediate temporal and theatrical energies of Shakespeare's drama. Cleopatra plays Elizabeth, conjures her up as the quintessential imperial poser, as someone who has made much theatrical use of virginity. Cleopatra positions herself, too, right up against, if not in, Elizabeth's whiteness.

Elizabeth's whiteness is an integral part of Elizabeth's own ideological self-fashioning. Melville, Mary's emissary, writes about Elizabeth's detaining him and of her trying to find out details about Mary, especially who is the fairer of the two queens: "I answered, The fairness of them both was not their worst faults. But she was earnest with me to declare which of them I judged fairest. I said, She was the fairest Queen in England, and mine the fairest Queen in Scotland. Yet she appeared earnest. I answered, They were both the fairest ladies in their countries; that her Majesty was whiter, but my Queen was very lovely."[40] Roy Strong, the most astute critic of the cult of Elizabeth, has noted that "in the last years of her reign white—the colour of purity and chastity—was widely adopted at court in deference to the Queen."[41] And as Peter Erickson has argued about blackness in early modern England: "[It was] played out against the background of a spectacle of whiteness, most prominently figured in the cosmetically enhanced and poetically celebrated version presented by Queen Elizabeth I. The cult of Elizabeth is a cult of whiteness. . . . The royal iconography of whiteness is established through the mutual reinforcement of official portraiture and the orchestrated live displays of her own person."[42] Elizabeth's pursuit of whiteness symbolizes more than her almost belligerently unwavering purity, her palisaded virginity; if her pursuit works arduously to picture a fortified anything, it is her discrete, superior, and constitutive place in an emerging imperial hegemony. Portraits of Elizabeth make this emphatically evident: the "Darnley" (1575), "Ermine" (1585), "Ditchley" (1592), and "Rainbow" (1600–1603) portraits, for example, participate in the evincing of Cleopatra's white, imperial, and corporeal *integritas*.[43] However much whiteness seems to communicate an authentic cultural sense of purity, divinity, and power, it remains a theatrical device. And in the metatheatrical world of Shakespeare's play, Elizabeth precedes Cleopatra, who offers an aggression for an aggression, a Cleopatra performative gesture for an Elizabeth one. Shakespeare's Cleopatra argues that Elizabeth's whiteness is no less a narrative fiction, a cultural pose, than Cleopatra's Orientalized blackness.

Despite the very conspicuous theatricality of Cleopatra's suicide, she is understood by her Western admirers to come at her death into a more noble and authentic self. (Perhaps without irony, she uses the word *noble* four times to describe her self-slaughter [4.15 and 5.2]; Caesar also uses the term to describe her death [5.2.342].) She poses her performative body against and draws out Caesar's own imperial theater. One of Caesar's followers pleads with her after thwarting her effort to stab herself:

> Do not abuse my master's bounty, by
> The undoing of yourself: *let the world see*
> *His nobleness well acted*, which your death
> Will never let come forth. (5.2.43–46, italics mine)

She challenges Rome's more presumptively authentic theater. Her only option in the end (and really throughout) is to mimic and, through her mimicry, to deconstruct Rome's more naturally real presentation of itself. Her most triumphant moment of mimicry, her coup de theatre, is of course her self-sacrifice: "And then, what's brave, what's noble, / Let's do it after the high Roman fashion, / And make death proud to take us" (4.15.86–88), a noble resolution that leads her to put on her robe and crown before enacting her sacrificial performance.

Her suicide responds to Rome's imperial framing of her. As Clare Kinney has argued, "In dying thus she not only escapes the actual bonds that Octavius would place upon her, but (in acting in a manner that assorts with *his* codes) prevents him from fixing her nature by reducing her to his 'Egyptian puppet.' She does not, moreover, slavishly imitate the 'high Roman fashion' of death but rather appropriates it and remakes it in her own image."[44] To insist that Cleopatra transforms here into a chaste or virginal sacrificial Roman woman would be an oversimplification. As Judith Butler has argued about gender (but a statement whose cultural implications may be further generalized), "The task is not whether to repeat, but how to repeat or, indeed, to repeat and, through a radical proliferation of gender, *to displace* the very gender norms that enable the repetition itself."[45] Cleopatra's rehearsal of a Roman way of dying breaks through Rome's constriction of her to what purports to be its naturally sanctioned (though imperially driven) narrative. In the end the Roman way of dying is only a "fashion."

A kind of cultural chaste thinking occurs when Cleopatra, and not just Shakespeare's, kills herself. According to Lucy Hughes-Hallett, for example, the Christian apologist Tertullian (c. A.D. 155–220) "blithely overlooked Cleopatra's fabled promiscuity when he proposed her as a model of courage and honourable behaviour." He sets her up as one of the models for a group of persecuted and imprisoned Christians, who should do the right thing by becoming martyrs.[46] Her conversion from a licentious woman to a nearly divine one has become a literary commonplace, though not necessarily uncontested. From Tertullian to Chaucer to John Gower to John Lydgate, and a host of other writers and thinkers from the fourteenth through the sixteenth century, her suicide teeters on the borders of martyrology.[47] Chaucer gives her top billing in *The Legend of Good Women*, for example: "*Incipit Legenda Cleopatrie, martiris, Egipti regine*" (Here begins the legend of Cleopatra, martyr, queen of Egypt [line 580]). Her inclusion not only among but at the head of these women is neither surprising nor ironic,[48] and, not coincidentally, about a third of Chaucer's poem focuses on her death. In short, she enters English literature not only as a good woman but, quite relatedly, as a dead one, a self-chastising one.[49]

The cultural implications of her suicide have certainly not been lost on commentators, whose readings have wittingly and unwittingly marked the categories from which and to which Cleopatra converts. Speaking of Shakespeare's Cleopatra, some earlier critical voices make the conventional position quite clear: "Now for the first time she is a woman—and not Woman." Or, "Repudiating a dream of Roman rule she achieves a Roman nobility: casting off her unnatural world she dies a more than natural heroine."[50] More recently Lorraine Helms has argued that "Cleopatra's suicide is an achieved rite of passage through eroticism into marriage."[51] Jack D'Amico gives the most vividly succinct of recent responses: "Shakespeare transforms the very image of her tawny front; for being honorably true to her dark nature he allows us to see how she can move not only toward darkness and death but also toward light and life. She who sees herself blackened by excessive life confounds beauty and ugliness, youth and age, pleasure and pain, promiscuity and faithfulness, life and death."[52] Throughout these varied critical assessments there also seems to be a consensus that Cleopatra experiences a cultural transformation: she moves from the dark and unnatural world of sex and Egyptianness to the more natural world of domesticity and Romanness. Her sacrificial act most consistently signifies or hints at a racial and sexual conversion. The act of killing herself converts her from black to white, from harlotry to virginity. Her racial conversion is not an anomaly among black and blackened women in the early modern imagination. Given that women, especially black women, are already seen as having a dangerously mutable racial identity, it should not be surprising that there exists a popular tradition in early modern England of converting black women and blackened women to white. It should also not be surprising given the black woman's tenuous hold on a "real" identity—that is, an identity other than a radical one. Sharing a race with *black* men and a gender with white *women*, she always lacks a real signifying (natural and dominant) identity.[53] The cultural argument that men are racially less susceptible to change than women would perhaps explain why the Restoration stage would allow English actors but not English actresses to appear in blackface.[54] Kim F. Hall has noted a similar convention in early modern sonneteering: "Positing a mistress as dark allows the poet to turn her white, to re-fashion her into an acceptable object of Platonic love and admiration."[55]

But Cleopatra and these women belong more particularly to a tradition of black and blackened women whose conversions to whiteness are accomplished with nothing less than their sacrificial or pseudosacrificial deaths. The seventeenth century dramatizes increasingly these women who become white on the sacrificial altar. And perhaps as a consequence of New World and English slavery, through the seventeenth century their racial blackness becomes more and more ethnographically real and less an easily discardable or transmutable allegorical garb. Shakespeare's Cleopatra participates in a tradition shaping both black and white women, even though the dominant discourse invests differently in black and white women. Examples of this tradition may be found in Shakespeare's repertoire. The self-slaughter of his Lucrece purges her blackened blood, and Lavinia's sacrificial death finally closes her body off from Gothic and African racial contamination (Chapter 1). The sacrifice of the racially transgressive Desdemona "returns" her to an angelic whiteness (Chapter 2). In Shakespeare's *Much Ado About Nothing*, Hero is accused by her fiancé Claudio of fornicating; she faints. And as her father stands over her body and eulogizes her, he imagines her to be a proverbial Ethiope:

> O, she is fall'n
> Into a pit of ink, that the wide sea
> Hath drops too few to wash her clean again,
> And salt too little which may season give
> To her foul tainted flesh! (4.1.139–43)

The friar insists that Hero is innocent and speaks of her "angel whiteness" (4.1.161). Hero is declared dead and kept concealed until the deception can be discovered and her innocence and life restored. Nonetheless, her pseudo-sacrificial death works to prove her innocence. Moreover, when her father presents Claudio with what Claudio thinks is a substitute bride, Claudio says, "I'll hold my mind were she an Ethiope" (5.4.38). Claudio's little quip works because Hero is supposedly quite the antithesis of an Ethiope. Within the racialized cultural imagination, the black Hero has sacrificed herself and has been reborn as the white heroine. Cleopatra is Shakespeare's black female response to his racially altering white sacrificial heroines.

There are telling non-Shakespearean examples of black women being sacrificially transformed into white women. The black women in Ben Jonson's *Masque of Blackness* willingly die to their father Niger and to their African homeland in order to become white British women. In William Heminge's *The Fatal Contract*, the Blackamoor eunuch, Castrato, surprises the audience both on- and offstage, when he unmasks himself, revealing that he is really Crotilda, the white woman who has been raped prior to the play. But, significantly, Crotilda only reveals herself once she has forgiven the king (the rapist), who has fatally stabbed her in a dual and with whom she has now fallen in love. In John Crowne's masque *Calisto*, two black nymphs agree to die in place of two white nymphs who have been condemned to die. The black nymphs agree to sacrifice themselves not just to save the white nymphs but so they may become (according to a divine deal they have made) stars, that is, *white* stars, shining in the dark sky. This opportune sacrifice offers them a chance to counter the proverbial lore of washing the Ethiope white. And for another example still, in Aphra Behn's novella, *Oroonoko, or the Royal Slave* (1688), the black Imoinda is sacrificially killed by her husband so that she, Lucrece-like, may not be "ravished by every Brute": "All that Love could say in such cases, being ended, and all the intermitting Irresolutions being adjusted, the lovely, young and ador'd Victim lays her self down before the Sacrificer; while he, with a hand resolved, and a heart-breaking within gave the fatal Stroke, first cutting her Throat, and then severing her yet smiling Face from that delicate Body, pregnant as it was with the Fruits of tenderest Love."[56] Even though Behn clearly creates Imoinda as a black African, Imoinda's racial identity has not proven very stable. Her highly romanticized sacrificial death reads very much like a white sacrificial story, and her Africanness has not stopped some critics from seeing her as Native American "at the least."[57] Adding to this, Thomas Southerne would make Imoinda white in his 1695 stage version of Behn's novella. More than any other aspect of her character, I would argue, her sacrificial death makes her white. To the point is the 1735 frontispiece to Southerne's play, a frontispiece especially reminiscent of some paintings and drawings of Tarquin's rape of Lucrece and Othello's murder of Desdemona (figure 13). In Southerne's frontispiece the black Oroonoko reluctantly aims his dagger at the body of the white Imoinda, whose arms are open to welcome the blade. And not surprisingly, this frontispiece has found its way onto the cover of the 1973 Norton edition of Behn's novella.

The mutability of women, particularly of these black female characters, provides a representational and iconographic basis for the popular "tragic mulatta," whose proper history extends from the eighteenth century through at least the early years of the twentieth century. I offer two brief examples. In Dion Boucicault's play, *The Octoroon; or, Life in Louisiana* (1859), Zoe, the octoroon, kills herself by drinking poison:

166

13. Frontispiece from Thomas Southerne's *Oroonoko* (London, 1735). William
Andrews Clark Memorial Library, University of California, Los Angeles.

George:	Zoe, you are suffering—your lips are white—your cheeks are flushed.
Pete:	'Taint no faint; she's a dying.
Dora:	Her eyes have changed color.
Pete:	Dat's what her soul's gwine to do. It's going up dar, whar dere's no line atween folks.
George:	Have I then prompted you to this?
Zoe:	No; but I loved you so, I could not bear my fate.... [She dies.][58]

Of course, as Pete knows, deracialized souls default to an originary racial whiteness. In any event, as Joseph Roach argues about Boucicault's eponymous octoroon, by way of expurgating Zoe of "her own traces of African blood," Boucicault has "her die by her own hand and then—miraculously turn white" (Roach, *Cities*, 224). And George L. Aiken's *Uncle Tom's Cabin: Or, Life Among the Lowly* (1852), closes with the following stage directions for its mixed-race heroine: "Gorgeous clouds, tinted with sunlight; Eva, robed in white, is discovered on the back of a milk-white dove, with expanded wings, as if just soaring upward. Her hands are extended in benediction over St. Clare and Uncle Tom who are kneeling and gazing up to her" (6.7).

Almost by definition, Cleopatra, who is so dangerous because she is so culturally and racially unfixed, emerges from among these women as the quintessential, imperially read woman. Even though Shakespeare's Cleopatra would be the only black Cleopatra to grace the pages of early modern drama, she nonetheless remains no racial anomaly in early modern English literature, where, for example, Robert Greene's *Ciceronis Amor* (1589), Aemilia Lanyer's *Salve Deus Rex Judaeorum* (1610), and Thomas Dekker's *The Wonder of a Kingdom* (1631) refer to her as black; George Gascoigne's "In Praise of a Gentlewoman" (1575) as "nutbrowne"; and Samuel Brandon's *The Virtuous Octavia* (1598) as "sunne-burnt" (1341). Sometimes this racially othered Cleopatra adeptly occupies a number of cultural and racial positions in a single text, as she does in Elizabeth Cary's *Tragedy of Mariam* (1613), where she is variously described as brown, black, Egyptian, and Ethiopian.[59] But her tendency toward cultural and racial polymorphous perversity extends, too, to white Cleopatras, who are no less secure in their cultural and racial positions and often seem just a step away from the cultural/racial border or having about them at least a hint of color.[60] White Cleopatras dominated the early modern stage, most notably the countess of Pembroke's *The Tragedy of Antony* (1590; translation of a play by Robert Garnier), Samuel Daniel's *The Tragedy of Cleopatra* (1594), John Fletcher's *The False One* (1620), and Thomas May's *The Tragedy of Cleopatra, Queen of Egypt* (1626). However so, Achillas in Beaumont and Fletcher's play immediately qualifies his reference to Cleopatra's fairness by noting it as "an attribute not frequent to the climate" (1.1). The chorus in Daniel's play indicts its Greek Cleopatra for betraying her racial nobility (1663–64) by overly indulging in Egypt's "poyson"—its "sumptuous treasure," its "pleasures so delightfull" (1247–54). Daniel's racialization only continues a classical tradition found as early as Horace's Ode 37, which at once praises and casts aspersions on his presumably Greek Cleopatra, whom it describes as *"fortis et asperas / tractare serpentes, ut atrum / corpore combiberet venenum"* (Courageous enough to handle asps so that she might swallow black poison into her body). While *atrum* (black) and *venenum* (poison) come together in Horace's poetic design as end rhymes, the word teasingly and incriminatingly following *atrum* is *corpore* (body). Given the more intensified sense of drinking, of consuming, in the word *combiberet*, Horace in short and emphatic form accuses his Greek Cleopatra not simply of imbibing blackness into her body but of pulling it into herself, of metamorphosing into it. The ascription of blackness to or the association of blackness with these white Cleopatras exists to do more than provide them with some superficial hints of local coloring; rather, it points to the profound cultural and racial instability of Cleopatra, whether she is primarily figured as white or black: by legendary definition, she is always culturally and racially passing and, therefore, culturally and racially dangerous. And although Shakespeare images his Cleopatra as racially black, she too partakes of this representational ambivalence. As if by cultural or sacrificial fiat, Shakespeare's dark queen also sports a "white hand"—of course it's a hand (see Chapter 1)—with "bluest veins" (3.13.138 and 2.5.29, respectively). However so, she does not passively participate in this ambivalence but is made a reader of it. In fact, she rewrites herself—re-poses, repositions Rome's depiction of her body in its imperial picture.

　　Given the polymorphous perversity of Cleopatra's cultural and racial identity and history, the possibility of the transformation of Shakespeare's Cleopatra from black to white is always in textual play. Still, her racial conversion is not directed toward an authentication of a sacrificial whiteness. Her transformative sacrificial act becomes a way of responding to Rome's ongoing attempts to fix her in its narrative as the dark cultural Other. Cleopatra attempts to radicalize Rome, its textual self-fashioning, by exposing the performativity of Rome's *integritas*—its natural and immutable (and naturally immutable) whiteness and virginity. Cleopatra herself comes into a new radical self. Her sacrificial death becomes, like Lucrece's, a *mori pudicam*, a recovery of chastity in death.[61] She converts from whoredom to virginity. If Rome's premiere and primary performance of textual/corporeal chastisement really works for Lucrece's *integritas*, Cleopatra opens up a space to both mimic and interrogate this narrative on which Rome's symbolic, if not also its real, identity depends. As she stirs from having fainted at Antony's death, and shortly before her own death, she imagines herself as a milkmaid, "a figure of essentialized, chaste femininity, the idealized lower-class virgin of pastoral convention, quite literally allied with the whiteness of milk."[62]

This newfound virginity gets reinforced in the last scene, when she speaks of herself as having "nothing / Of woman in me: now from head to foot / I am marble-constant: now the fleeting moon / No planet is of mine" (5.2.237–40). No longer like the grotesque Nile with its overflow and seasonal mutability, she now envisions herself as a Roman statue, a classical Bakhtinian body.[63] As she imagines her sacrificial self emptied of her woman's blood, she figures herself most demonstratively as re-becoming a *parthenos*, that is, a virgin, the girl/woman who does not yet bleed, who will become the *aparthenos*, the wife, "Husband, I come" (5.2.286), as the asp devirginates her hymeneal self, "O, break! O, break!" (309). Like the body of a proper sacrificial virgin, her body gets marked too with the sign of her ritual offering, "a vent of blood" on her breast (346–47). Here Cleopatra comes into the fullness of her own name, "the glory of her country/father," as she, like Lucrece, sacrifices herself on her bed. Cleopatra's sacrificial death converts her from black to white. She does not simply repeat Rome's whiteness; the fact that Rome's whiteness can get repeated or mimicked provides the foundation for her deconstruction of it.

Most saliently she mocks the iconographical scene of the white sacrificial Lucrece. In her death Cleopatra not only plays Lucrece but plays with the culture's serious investment in Lucrece's self-sacrifice. Although I am arguing that Shakespeare's Cleopatra mocks Roman fixity by performing in Lucretian fashion, the association between her death and Lucrece's is not only in Shakespeare. Both of these self-slaughtering women are included, for example, in Chaucer's *Legend*, as well as in several other such lists in early literature.[64] Moreover, there are explicit iconographic links between Cleopatra and Lucrece. Mary D. Garrard has cogently argued that early modern European artists found a similar visual affectivity in both suicides and have sometimes "presented them as nearly interchangeable characters."[65] One very telling example is a drawing of Cleopatra by Giacomo Francia, which at once recalls Lucrece in the act of resisting her rapist, Tarquin (who figures here in the form of a serpent), and Lucrece's suicide (figure 14). Another example is Guido Reni's painting of a self-wounding Cleopatra (1638–39), a near replica of his painting of a sacrificial Lucrece (1635–40), both paintings modeling the same woman no less.[66]

And Hughes-Hallett's observation that in painting after painting in early modern Europe Cleopatra is "not only the object of the viewer's salacious scrutiny, but of a metaphorical ravishment" certainly resonates with my remarks (in Chapter 1) about early modern European paintings of Lucrece.[67] As Garrard also argues in her more explicit comparative study of Cleopatra and Lucrece, "The naked woman assaulting her own body, frequently the breasts, with a conspicuously phallic object as her instrument, undoubtedly had an additional appeal to some viewers, on a grosser sadopornographic level."[68] Too, the pornographically known Cleopatra exposes the officially unseen and unknown pornographic imaging of Lucrece. Especially at this moment in Shakespeare's play we should not forget that the salacious scrutiny directed toward Shakespeare's Cleopatra is quite explicitly aimed at his boy actor. He does not simply perform *her* but mounts a theatrical mockery of the Orientalism and homoeroticism of the white male who gazes on her.[69]

As far as I have been able to tell, early modern artists present Cleopatra exclusively as white, but like many early modern writers, they do racialize or exoticize her nonsacrificial history, surrounding her with bits and pieces of otherness—including, on occasion, black male bodies. Her self-sacrifice, like Lucrece's, however, is most decisively a virginal white experience; as I argue throughout this book, the woman who dies sacrificially is understood, quite unequivocally, to die as a white woman, if not, indeed, in the very name of whiteness. To put all this over-schematically (even though my essential point remains), black Cleopatras seduce; white ones kill themselves. In Shakespeare's play Cleopatra's performance of whiteness cannot be separated from her performance of Lucrece. Neither can her performance of whiteness be separated from her performance of the Madonna or Elizabeth I.

Queering the Empire

Although the historical Cleopatra's death may be construed as her most authenticating moment, her most successful act of Roman mimicry, it remains

14. *Cleopatra*, by Giacomo Francia (sixteenth century). Art Museum, Princeton University.

more than a passing argument that Shakespeare's Cleopatra confronts rather than adopts this authenticity, this Roman way of being white, female, and real. Between her call for her death in "high Roman fashion" and the execution of the deed, Shakespeare's most illustrious queen unfixes herself and interrupts her most anticipated and authorizing (signature) scene. However much Cleopatra's suicide thwarts Caesar's plans to parade her through Roman streets, her culturally transformative death, her repositioning herself as a sacrificial woman, Madonna or milkmaid, still allows Rome to absorb her into its imperial narrative. For her to die so full of, as Caesar says, a "strong toil of grace" (5.2.346) would mean that in the end Cleopatra has proven, like so many culturally mutable women, that she is after all a real (Roman) white woman. But, I wish to argue, finally, that by seeming to abandon her radical nature and take on a more domestic one, she offers her most radical gesture yet. Like her intensely performative language at her death and throughout the play, her calling attention to herself as a boy actor "serves as a reminder that this is a pageant acted out against the play's own ruthless questioning of theatrical display."[70] Rather than evoking a theater that she can transcend (or one that she even desires to transcend), she conjures up the theatrical space qua theatrical space so that she may wallow in it. The "historical" Cleopatra slips off Shakespeare's stage and deconstructs her historical realness, even if Western imperial eyes refuse to acknowledge her absence. She forces the theater itself to disrupt what has nonetheless succeeded as, arguably, the most celebrated, authentic act of self-sacrifice in English drama. By *re*-repositioning herself, she locates herself only tenuously in Rome's putative pedestrian realism but most firmly in the radical poetics and politics of England's metaculture: all the world's a stage, indeed:

> The quick comedians
> Extemporally will stage us, and present
> Our Alexandrian revels: Antony
> Shall be brought drunken forth, and I shall see
> Some squeaking Cleopatra boy my greatness
> I'the posture of a whore. (5.2.215–20)

She confronts Shakespeare's theater in the immediate moment, the real present, revealing the boy beneath the costume and offering what is arguably the most celebrated scene of transvestism on the early modern English stage, a kind of transvestic coup de theatre. The speech provides more than a temporary threat to the dramatic illusion;[71] it creates a fissure that remains a vital and complex piece of Cleopatra's representation. It insists on making a space for—perhaps a cultural narrative to elucidate—the illusiveness of the dramatic illusion. There are other seductive bodies onstage besides the "historical" Cleopatra's. The white boy actor challenges his audience to see him as cross-gendered and cross-racialized, exposing the underpinnings of a theater that traffics not only in women's bodies but in black bodies as well. It is an endlessly and dangerously refractive theater because Cleopatra lays bare a theater that traffics, too, in the bodies, the tenderly eroticized bodies, of white boys. Shakespeare's audience finds itself entangled in Cleopatra's own infinite play with masks, as the boy Cleopatra engages in his own "theater of war," that is (as I understand Bhabha's use of the term), a struggle between the authorizing and de-authorizing powers of colonial and imperial representation.[72]

Throughout, but at this moment in particular, Shakespeare's boy Cleopatra strikes a pose: in queer parlance, he "camps." Cleopatra exposes England (at least the English stage) as a jungle, as "a place where hoboes camp," in ways more than one (see Introduction). *Camp* connotes at once wit and a military sense of fighting. David Bergman argues that "the drag performance is the essential act of the camp."[73] And as George Chauncey so aptly defines it:

> Camp was at once a cultural *style* and a cultural *strategy*, for it helped gay men make sense of, respond to, and undermine the social categories of gender and sexuality that served to marginalize them. . . . [C]amp was a style of interaction and display that used irony, incongruity, theatricality, and humor to highlight the artifice of social convention, sometimes exaggerating convention to the point of burlesquing it, sometimes inverting it to achieve the same end. The drag queen thus epitomized camp. . . . Such a realization had highly subversive implications at a time when the social order represented itself as natural and preordained, for it allowed gay men to question the very premise of their marginalization. The social order denounced gay men as "unnatural"; through camp banter gay men highlighted the unnaturalness of the social order itself.[74]

Shakespeare's Cleopatra may seem to threaten the undoing of herself by calling attention to her cross-dressed nature, but Cleopatra indulges in much more here than theatrical play. We do well to recall Claire Sponsler's argument (partly referenced in Chapter 2) that "drag and blackface" in mummings and morris dances were not simply some form of disguising but an ingress "to powerful sites of cultural alterity."[75] They were also a way of exercising "control over subversive cultural forms (women and blackamoors) while also invoking the power associated with such forms."[76] By playing white and female, what Shakespeare's *black boy* Cleopatra does, I insist, is make densely problematic (if not paralyzingly schizophrenic) England's assumptions of its self-assured and cool control over cultural alterity.

As I have iterated throughout this chapter, only by foregrounding the theatricality of the cultural text does Cleopatra have a chance of unfixing herself from Rome's imperial narrative. As Cleopatra faints, studies, and plays with death, she knows that her audience is anxiously waiting to watch her die. Throughout, she mocks her own self-sacrifice. None of this is to detract from the seriousness of Cleopatra's suicide. Quite the opposite. As Cleopatra plays the milkmaid, as she plays the sacrificial virgin, she attempts to give the performance of her life, literally. It is the most aggressive of responses to Rome's national-imperial fictions. The boy Cleopatra offers a moment of "authentic" theater, an authentic death scene. It is, finally, the "high seriousness" of Cleopatra's frivolity that gives her moment of "high Roman fashion" the appeal of "high camp"—that is, camp imbued with an authentic, a nonparodic, sensibility.[77]

Carol-Anne Tyler has done a convincing job of showing similarities between mimicry and camping, arguing that in both "one 'does' ideology in order to undo it."[78] And when Butler writes that "there is a subversive laughter in the pastiche-effect of parodic practices in which the original, the authentic, and the real are themselves constituted as effects,"[79] she speaks too to what I am arguing in Shakespeare's play is Cleopatra's challenge to the invisible status of Roman performativity. At its most effective, camp deconstructs the seemingly seamless and unseen performativity of "our" authenticity. Again, "we" are only made witness to the performativity of cultural Others.

The theater does squeak too much. Most ostensibly, perhaps, Cleopatra alludes to and mocks the boy in the throes of a changing voice; like the boymen in Caesar's earlier apostrophic scolding of Antony (1.4.31–33), the maturing boy actor occupies a dangerous liminal zone that pushes Antony and Cleopatra's relationship into a homoerotic space. Leggatt does only a partial reading when he argues that "the Romans become dirty old men, their view of Antony and Cleopatra a vulgar play of a drunk and a whore."[80] Cleopatra pictures the primal sexual encounter between East and West as a sex scene between a drunken Antony and a squeaking Cleopatra boy. Gordon Williams, in his dictionary of early modern sexual language and imagery, defines *squeak* as "the sound expected of a modest woman when sexually molested." Williams's numerous examples show more than an incidental or occasional link between squeaking and rape, if not more simply, aggressive sexual braggadocio. Two examples closest to the date of Shakespeare's text are from John Marston's *The Malcontent* (1600–1604), where a count "will put the beauties to the squeak most hideously" (5.3), and John Day's *Ile of Gulls* (1606): "We olde Courtiers can hunt a Cony and put her to the squeak & make her cry out like a young married wife of the first night.'"[81] When Cleopatra refers to herself as a squeaking Cleopatra, she inscribes herself into the language of the raped modest or virginal woman. Enobarbus's highly romanticized meeting between East and West becomes in effect the rape, the overpowering, of Egypt by Rome.

Shakespeare's boy Cleopatra calls attention to the real stage presence of these most famous of cross-cultural lovers by foregrounding the very conventions of the theater that seeks to exoticize and colonize her. Through her squeaking boy, Cleopatra betrays the English representation of the primal sexual encounter between East and West, between Cleopatra and Antony, as a sex scene between an inebriated man and a "posturing" boy posing as and assuming the sexual position of a whore, the position of *retrosum* (the posterior pose), common with both harlots and sodomites.[82] Shakespeare's boy Cleopatra lays bare early modern England theater's own open secret, its own "preposterous" conventions. And in the truly rigorous and unrelenting militancy of camp, he critiques and offers his body up, sacrifices it, for the audience's seduction through the very language used both to identify him (name his kind) and vehemently weigh in against him. His "posture" plays in paronomastic fashion with the "preposterous," signaling the corporeality, the fleshiness, of sodomy, of the whore, as in Thersites' diatribe against Achilles and Patroclus in Shakespeare's *Troilus and Cressida*: "Why, his masculine whore. Now the rotten diseases of the south, the guts-griping, ruptures, [catarrhs,] loads a'gravel in the back, lethargies, cold palsies, raw eyes, dirt-rotten livers, whissing lungs, bladders full of imposthume, sciaticas, lime-kills i'th palm, incurable bone-ache, and the rivell'd fee-simple of the tetter, take and take again such preposterous discoveries!" (5.1.17–24). Furthermore, as Parker has noted, the word *preposterous* pervades those antitheatrical tracts speaking against a transvestite theater.[83] Phillip Stubbes refers in his *Anatomy of Abuses* (1583), for example, to the "preposterous geare" of England's transvestite theater.[84] Shakespeare's Cleopatra insists there is no easy erasure here of the performing boy, as she pushes for a more textured reading of this early modern stage convention. Shakespeare's boy Cleopatra evokes an entire polemics of theatrical transvestism: accepting the heteronormative claims made by those early modern defenders of this theatrical practice while opening himself up to its homo*erotic* possibilities and remembering and testifying to its horrific ones.[85] The squeaking and posturing boy actor conjures up a not so oblique reference, too, to Antony's putative pathic homosexuality and pederasty.[86] Antony as drunkard with his Egyptian whore or as drunken man with his boy solidifies Antony's emasculation, his non-Romanness. Finally, I would argue, the theatrical unveiling of Shakespeare's Cleopatra responds to Enobarbus's pornographic, ethnographic, and culturally driven rape narratives. Reading *through* English stage convention, Shakespeare's boy Cleopatra repeats and displaces Rome's imperial project by stripping and rescripting the encounter between East and West, not as a romanticized or poeticized meeting but as a brutal rape scene between a man and a boy. He speaks less passionately about Cleopatra's fate in Rome than he does about his *vulnerable* posture, his being forced to parade his *vulnus*—that is, his wound—in front of the dirty old men in England's theater. Shakespeare's sacrificial virgin turns Rome's radical reading back on itself. Perhaps as Cleopatra dies she does finally find her signifying gestures swallowed up within the strictures of Roman and English conventions, but the boy actor who embodies her leaves behind a theater that seems quite improper in its proprieties.

Afterword

A book comes with many voices, all competing and speaking to each other in a language that one can at best only pretend to understand: many of these voices resonate with some semblance of one's own; many of them do not. As I finish this book, I dwell for a final time (at least for a final time here) on my larger vision of it as a project on Shakespeare, as a project on the triad of race, rape, and sacrifice. I hope the broader critical designs of this project bring some degree of materiality, of visibility, to early modern processes of chaste thinking, especially with regard to this triad. I also fantasize that this project will or can have implications beyond the boundaries of its more discrete historical parameters.

The course of writing this book has been a powerful journey for me, especially with respect to issues of race: not to disavow myself of agency, this book did not begin as an exploration of race, but race found it. For whatever critical dangers that may pose themselves when we begin with a more cautious but more liberal interchange between us "now" and them "then," there is also much to be gained by locating and contextualizing our intellectual and professional purpose in these early days of the twenty-first century. Perhaps I am predisposed to such thinking, to such critical pursuits, because I, like many gay academics and academics of color, have spent my life—at least an inordinate part of it—witnessing a variety of dominant discourses working hard to relegate me to the category of a "them." Such binary social relations, whether part of a diachronic construct or a synchronic one, always need interrogation.

I have also been haunted by numerous images, numerous dramatizations, over the course of writing this book. I think it more than fitting to close by bringing to the critical table the three most recent scenes that may seem different from the images I have examined here but that do speak nevertheless to the cultural fictions on which this book has taken much of its theoretical and critical energy. Coming at me through the print media, the television, and the cyberworld at a speed almost too fast to make them comprehensible are images of bodies in strange and complicated shapes trapped in even more strange and complicated conversations with this triad of race, rape, and sacrifice. June 1998: The African American William Byrd Jr. tied to a pickup truck in Jasper, Texas, and dragged to his death by two white men. October 1998: Matthew Shepard, a small-framed gay college student in Laramie, Wyoming, tied to a fence, bludgeoned and left to die—which he does a few days later in a hospital. February 1999: The purchasing of sixteen-thousand dollars' worth of the memorabilia of O. J. Simpson, former football star and former American hero, and then in the name of a morality supposedly counterbalancing the lack of a morality in Simpson, we witness these "pieces" of him being publicly burned, significantly, on the steps of the Los Angeles County Courthouse before a group of enthusiastic witnesses, to say nothing of this incident's repeated replay in the media. (This is the city where I live.) The cultural and racial memories of lynchings, slave markets, and burnings are too vivid, too present; hence, the paronomastic, captivating, and castrating title of a national news item: "O. J. Simpson's Belongings on the Auction Block."[1] And I watch and I write as various media and outraged voices try to recuperate these bodies—the bodies of Simpson's wife, Nicole Brown Simpson, and her friend Ronald Goldman in the case of Simpson—into their proper place in the sacrificial story of a liberal humanism. In *all* these instances, which evince our all-encompassing communal health, we delude only ourselves, deny ourselves critical access to our own wound culture, as we rescript such terrifying murders as sacrifices of a realpolitik kind.

Reference Matter

Notes

Introduction

1. Leonard Tennenhouse, *Power on Display*, 116. For an excellent discussion of women in tragedy, see Nicole Loraux, *Tragic Ways of Killing a Woman*. Her study focuses on Greek tragedy, but her critical acumen, as well as the perspicuity of her argument, makes her study quite suggestive for those interested in early modern tragedy. Her book has been of fundamental importance to this project. For one example of Loraux at work in early modern dramatic studies, see Lorraine Helms, " 'The High Roman Fashion.' "

2. Debora K. Shuger, *Renaissance Bible*, 129. As found in Shuger's text, the dates in parentheses are the first translations of these plays into Latin or into a vernacular language.

3. Shuger, *Renaissance Bible*, 129.

4. René Girard, *Violence and the Sacred*, 141–42.

5. Nancy Jay, *Throughout Your Generations Forever*, xxiii. Jay discusses gender throughout her book. For a good feminist critique of René Girard and Walter Burkert, see her chapter, "Theories of Sacrifice" (128–46). See also Mihoko Suzuki's discussion of Girard and Burkert among others in the introduction to *Metamorphoses of Helen* (5–7). For Mieke Bal's sacrificial reading of the Book of Judges see *Death and Dissymmetry*. For some provocative essays on the relationship between women and death, see part 2, "Death and Gender," in Goodwin and Bronfen, *Death and Representation*. See also Judy Maloof, *Over Her Dead Body*.

6. Susan Griffin, *Pornography and Silence*, 79.

7. Helen King, "Sacrificial Blood," 119, 123.

8. Helkiah Crooke, *Body of Man*, 260–61.

9. Girard, *Violence and the Sacred*, 168, also 143–68. We may also consider Girard's argument (that ritual is always already representational of an originary act of violence) in order to suggest that tragedy functions as metaritual. Tragedy does, in fact, do what many sacrificial theorists argue ritual does: it creates diversions from and masks the force and determinations of its sacrificial

objectives. See Max Horkheimer and Theodor W. Adorno, *Dialectic of Enlightenment*, 50–52, who discuss sacrifice as deceitful; and Mihoko Suzuki, *Metamorphoses of Helen*, 7–9, who calls the narrative workings of sacrifice a hoax.

    10. See, for example, Eva C. Keuls, "Brides of Death, in More Ways Than One," in *Reign of the Phallus*, 129–52.

    11. Griffin, *Pornography and Silence*, 159. See also Kim F. Hall's reference to Griffin's passage in Hall's discussion of Caliban. Hall, *Things of Darkness*, 142–43.

    12. Ania Loomba, *Gender, Race, Renaissance Drama*, 149.

    13. See also Elliot H. Tokson, *The Popular Image of the Black Man*, 100.

    14. James Clifford, "On Ethnographic Allegory," 99.

    15. Stephanie H. Jed, *Chaste Thinking*, 4–5, 51, but see also 126–31.

    16. Clifford, "On Ethnographic Allegory," 101.

    17. Homi K. Bhabha, *Location of Culture*, 79.

    18. Black women were also allowed to participate in the rape or attempted rape of white women by helping white male villains procure access to the black woman's mistress. See, for example, the black serving woman, Zanthia, in Marston's *Wonder of Women, Sophonisba* (1606), who joins forces with Syphax, who desires to rape Sophonisba. See also Zanthia, another black serving woman, in Beaumont and Fletcher's *The Knight of Malta* (1618–19), who actively participates in Lord Mountferrat's efforts to rape her mistress, Oriana. Both Zanthias do so for what they hope will be their sexual rewards from these white rapists.

    19. See Hall, *Things of Darkness*, 14–15, 259–60; and Patricia Parker, *Shakespeare from the Margins*, 11–14. For more extended critique of new historicism and some of its working assumptions see the introductions to Richard Halpern, *Primitive Accumulation*, 1–15, and Albert H. Tricomi, *Reading Tudor-Stuart Texts*, 1–22.

    20. Neil L. Whitehead, introduction to Sir Walter Ralegh, *Empyre of Guiana*, 34 (emphasis mine). For further discussion of the (a)politics of new historicism, see Hugh Grady, *The Modernist Shakespeare*, 231–32; and Simon Barker, "Re-Loading the Canon," 53.

    21. See John Guillory, *Cultural Capital*, who discusses Shakespeare here and there throughout his study. A good summary of his position on Shakespeare appears late in his chapter, "The Discourse of Value":

> If Shakespeare's plays . . . can be received or "used" as moral exempla for adolescent schoolchildren, as monuments of nationalist pride, as the cultural capital of the educated classes, they are only capable of these "nonaesthetic" uses because they are classified as (canonical) works of art. . . . [T]he possibility of a sociology of art depends upon this complexity of consumption, the fact that "uses" are not simply chosen from amongst a potentially infinite number of equal possibilities (aesthetic, political, moral, hedonic)

but are complexly articulated in nested hierarchies according to the relation between the specific domains of the social named by such categories as the aesthetic, the political, the moral, the hedonic. (295)

22. Stephen Greenblatt, *Learning to Curse*, 163.

23. P. Parker, *Shakespeare from the Margins*, 3.

24. Clifford, "On Ethnographic Allegory," 110.

25. Louis Althusser, "Ideology," 165–71. Quoted in Nancy Sorkin Rabinowitz, *Anxiety Veiled*, 10–11. See her discussion there of Althusser and gender.

26. See especially the first chapter of Jed, *Chaste Thinking*.

27. Rabinowitz, *Anxiety Veiled*, 48.

28. Although I am not directly addressing Catherine Belsey's still wonderfully provocative book on the status of the subject in early modern tragedy, I do have in mind here a quote from the introduction of that book:

Signifying practice is never static, and meanings are neither single nor fixed. Meaning is perpetually deferred by its existence as difference within a specific discourse; it is perpetually displaced by the trace of alterity within the identity which is no more than an effect of difference.... Alternative discourses propose alternative knowledges, alternative meanings.... Since meaning is plural, to be able to speak is to be able to take part in the contest for meaning which issues in the production of new subject-positions, new determinations of what it is possible to be. Belsey, *The Subject of Tragedy*, 6.

29. Here I am agreeing with Martin Orkin and Ania Loomba in the introduction to their jointly edited collection, *Post-Colonial Shakespeares*, 1.

30. Baldwin, "Autobiographical Notes," 7–8.

31. Cf. the popularization of our present-day political slogan "Take Back the Night," referring to women mobilizing to reclaim their bodies, to take back their bodies, from the hands of rapists.

32. I stand by this statement even though the move here is not to make new historicism univocal. For a few of the important and variant voices of new historicism, see Patricia Fumerton, Leah Marcus, Louis Montrose, and Karen Newman. For a few examples of the more "urgent" Shakespeare voices found outside England and the United States, I have found especially illuminating Ania Loomba on India, Michael Neill on Australia and New Zealand, Avraham Oz on Israel, and Martin Orkin on South Africa.

33. Loomba, *Gender, Race, Renaissance Drama*; Hendricks and P. Parker, eds., *Women "Race," and Writing*; Hall, *Things of Darkness*. My noting these three excellent texts is not to say that I am always in agreement with some of their conclusions, but they do have critical and theoretical vocabularies and biases that I share. Furthermore, by naming them, I do not mean to make secondary

the very informative and remarkable studies that have preceded them, that have made these later studies possible. These include Samuel Chew, *The Crescent and the Rose* (1937), on the role of Islam in early modern English society and literature; Eldred Jones, *Othello's Countrymen* (1965) and *The Elizabethan Image of Africa* (1971), two wonderful studies of the place of Africa and blacks in early modern English literature and society; Winthrop Jordan, *White over Black* (1968), especially the two chapters of part 1, examining the pre-1700 literal and imaginative presence of blacks in England and America, respectively (3–98); Leslie A. Fiedler, *The Stranger in Shakespeare* (1972), a close textual study of various cultural "strangers" in Shakespeare; Janet Adelman, *The Common Liar* (1973), a silence-breaking consideration of Cleopatra's racial blackness (appendix C, 184–88); G. K. Hunter, *Dramatic Identities and Cultural Tradition* (1978), on the language of race and the status of foreigners in the period and in the drama; Elliot H. Tokson, *The Popular Image of the Black Man in English Drama* (1982), a groundbreaking assessment of black figures in early modern drama and poetry; Anthony Barthelemy, *Black Face, Maligned Race* (1987), a well-organized study of black figures in early modern drama and masques, a very clear and concise critical introduction to the primary dramatic texts featuring black characters; and Errol Hill, *Shakespeare in Sable* (1984), a very readable history of black Shakespearean actors and their intellectual and professional choices. This is of course not an exhaustive list.

34. Toni Morrison, *Playing in the Dark*, 13.

35. Definitions are taken in order from the third edition of *The American Heritage College Dictionary* (1993).

36. Morrison, *Playing in the Dark*, 15.

37. Hakluyt earned this epitaph from J. A. Froude, whom Kenneth R. Andrews has called "the Victorian prophet of empire." Both epitaphs are found in Andrews, *Trade, Plunder, and Settlement*, 1.

38. From Richard Hakluyt's dedicatory epistle to Francis Walsingham Knight, *Principall Navigations*, 1:3.

39. Andrews, *Trade, Plunder, and Settlement*, 1. Andrews goes on to explain that "more years still were to pass before English ships began to trade in eastern seas and Englishmen began lasting plantations in the New World. Behind the glory of Elizabethan legend and nationalist propaganda lay a long and painful series of failures and disasters, only occasionally relieved by some brilliant feat such as Drake's voyage round the world, or some modest success like the opening of trade with Muscovy."

40. Queen Elizabeth I, "Licensing Casper van Senden to Deport Negroes" (1601), in Hughes and Larkin, *Tudor Royal Proclamations*, 3:221–22.

41. W. Jackson Bate, "The Crisis in English Studies," 209.

42. Notwithstanding this, it is worth noting that some studies (although not primarily new historicist) have drawn on the methods and lessons of new

historicism, using them to interrogate our very space of reading the English Renaissance. Some of the most notable recent works are Patricia Parker on philology, *Shakespeare from the Margins*; Kim F. Hall on race, *Things of Darkness*; Richard Rambuss on private religious practices, *Closet Devotions*; Richard Halpern on materiality and economics, *Primitive Accumulation*; and Jonathan Goldberg's edited volume on same-sex relations, *Queering the Renaissance*.

43. Brian Vickers, *Appropriating Shakespeare*, xii–xiii (emphases added).

44. Tzvetan Todorov, "'Race,' Writing, and Culture," 376.

45. Eve Kosofsky Sedgwick, *Epistemology of the Closet*, 51.

46. Cf. Harold Bloom's "Shakespeare's Universalism," in *Invention of the Human*, 1–17.

47. Eve Kosofsky Sedgwick's introduction to her edited volume, *Novel Gazing*, esp. 5–28. See also Judith Butler, *Excitable Speech*, esp. the introduction, "On Linguistic Vulnerability" (1–41), and chap. 3, "Contagious Word: Paranoia and 'Homosexuality' in the Military" (103–26).

Chapter 1

1. These four lines also appear at the end of the third quarto and the first folio, except in these two instances *Then* is substituted for *Than*, and in the first folio *From* is substituted for *By*. Except where otherwise specified, all Shakespeare quotations are from *Riverside Shakespeare*.

2. Aaron's ability to steal the show depends on more than the text of Edward Ravenscroft, *Titus Andronicus, or The Rape of Lavinia* (1687), in which Aaron's role had been enlarged from Shakespeare's play, or on Ravenscroft's starring actor, James Quin (as Aaron), or later on the fame of Ira Aldridge, who played Aaron and launched the only production of the play in the British Isles during the nineteenth century. See the introduction to the Oxford edition, 45–49.

3. Mieke Bal, *Reading "Rembrandt"*, 70 (Bal's emphasis). See also A. Robin Bowers, "Emblem and Rape," 93.

4. Tacitus (c. A.D. 55–120), for example, recounts in his *Annals* a scenario that epitomizes the forging of a relationship between rape and death. He refers here to the exemplary punishment of Sejanus's daughter in A.D. 31: "It is recorded by authors of the period that, as it was considered an unheard-of thing for capital punishment to be inflicted on a virgin, she was violated by the executioner with the halter beside her: they were then strangled, and their young bodies were thrown on to the Gemonian Stairs" (5.9). The pairing of rape and execution emerges as a normative Roman practice in Suetonius's (A.D. 75–160) writings about Tiberius's cruelties: "Immaturae puellae, quia more tradito nefas esset virgines, strangulari, vitiatae prius a carnifice, dein strangulatae" (Since ancient usage made it impious to strangle maidens, young

girls were first violated by the executioner and then strangled). Suetonius, "Tiberius," *Suetonius* (61.5), 380–81. See also Amy Richlin, "Reading Ovid's Rapes," 177. The interplay between rape and sacrifice has not disappeared from literature. See, for example, Charles Busch's dark comedy, *The Vampire Lesbians of Sodom* (1985), where the Girl about to be dragged to the sacrificial altar pleads with her executioners, "Break my hymen. Rape me and I'll no longer be a virgin fit for sacrifice" (50).

5. William Roper, *Lyfe of Thomas More*, 58–59. Roper wrote his father-in-law's biography c. 1558, but it was first published in 1626. The story quoted was presumably told by Thomas More.

6. Francis Beaumont and John Fletcher, *Works*, 4:1–92.

7. See Cyril Tourneur, *The Revenger's Tragedy*. The rest of the scene is invested more in the celebration of the honor of this nameless wife than in the fact that she is raped.

8. However earnest or disingenuous the countess may be, still present at least in such a national and legal forum as the Castlehaven trial is this link between rape and self-slaughter. True to early modern rape politics, the Countess Dowager of Derby, the mother of Countess Castlehaven, would not forgive her daughter or granddaughter for their having been raped until they received the king's pardon. See Gossett, "Marrying the Rapist," 313–14. This rape trial deserves comparison to the extended trial of the nobleman Burghill, the alleged rapist of Margery Evans, an illiterate fourteen-year-old serving maid. See Leah Marcus's well-argued studies of this trial: "Notes Toward a Political Reading of *Comus*," and "The Problem of Sexual Assaults."

9. William Painter, "The Second Novell," in *The Palace of Pleasure*, 24. For Painter's complete 1566 translation of the Lucrece rape narrative see "The Second Novell," 22–25. For the Latin text and translation of Livy see B. O. Foster's *Historia*, 1:197–209. For a more accessible edition of Livy (without the Latin text) I recommend Aubrey de Sélincourt's translation, *The Early History of Rome*, 97–101.

10. Coppélia Kahn, "Sexual Politics of Subjectivity." See also Bowers, "Emblem and Rape." For a brief reading of rape in Shakespeare and his more "brutal," i.e., less poetically glossed, characterization of it, see Catherine R. Stimpson, "Shakespeare and the Soil of Rape."

11. Stimpson, "Soil of Rape," 57.

12. Roy W. Battenhouse, *Shakespearean Tragedy*, 16. For a more thorough engagement with Battenhouse's masculinist reading of Lucrece, the reader may wish to consult the whole chapter, "Shakespeare's Re-Vision of Lucrece," 3–41.

13. I am, at least interpretively, comparing my argument to what Michael Camille calls "a well-developed tradition in English medieval art which according to one artist's testimony emphasizes that what we see *corporaliter*, we

are meant to interpret *spiritualiter.*" Camille, *Gothic Idol*, 204. See also Camille's note: "These are the terms used by the early-twelfth-century English artist of the *St. Albans Psalter* in an inscription of the Beatus page. See O. Pacht, F. Wormald, and C. R. Dodwell, *The St. Albans Psalter* (London, 1960), pp. 149–52 & pl. 41" (380). Cf. A. L. Meyer's reading, in Huston Diehl's *Staging Reform*, of a "purely bodily seeing" (11) common in late medieval lay culture.

14. Despite the many variants to the story, Livy's account remains fairly representative, and I use Livy's account as a basis for my own reading of the story (see note 9 above).

15. See generally Peter Brooks, "Freud's Masterplot." Brooks also speaks to the cathartic nature of plot when he says, for example, that "it is characteristic of textual energy in narrative that it should always be on the verge of premature discharge, of short-circuit" (296). The contest over the wives' virtue comes close to being a premature discharge, a secondary orgasm; the rape re-energizes the narrative, setting up the possibility of a monumental catharsis.

16. Bal, *Reading "Rembrandt"*, 76.

17. Stephanie H. Jed, *Chaste Thinking*, 150–51.

18. Ibid., 151–52.

19. Ibid., 8.

20. See also Rene Girard, *Violence and the Sacred*, 38.

21. Pseudo-Albertus Magnus, *De Secretis Mulierum*, 68.

22. Ovid, *Fasti*, 118–19.

23. Unless otherwise noted, all Chaucer citations are from *Riverside Chaucer*.

24. Bal, *Reading "Rembrandt"*, 84 (Bal's emphasis).

25. Ibid.

26. Lynda Nead, *Female Nude*, 59.

27. For a thoroughly engaging study of this portrait, see Lowell Gallagher's chapter, "The 'Siena Sieve' Portrait and Book 5 of *The Faerie Queene*: Vanishing Points, Aphasiac Readers, and the Rhetoric of the Lax Conscience," in *Medusa's Gaze*, 123–40. There are many parallels between my broader points here and those made by Gallagher. For him the English conscience officially misrecognizes what it sees. See also Roy C. Strong, *Splendour at Court*, 111–12. (Strong says the painting is attributed to Ketel.) We could also compare what I am arguing here are Elizabeth's claims to James I's own arguments about his invisible body. See also my mention (note 28 below) of James's preface, "To the Reader," in *Basilicon Doron*.

28. The "Prohibiting Portraits" quotes are from Hughes and Larkin, *Tudor Royal Proclamations*, 2:240–41. I have added the emphases here to foreground some of the discursive moves made in Elizabeth's proclamation. This quote also reminds me of James I's claim in *Basilicon Doron*, where in his preface, "To the Reader" (4–11), he says he has been forced to publish this work, originally only meant for his son, as a way of "defacing" the "false copies" that do not

represent him the way he argues he officially and naturally should be represented. I have discussed the ideological imaging of James's body in "Absolute Bodies, Absolute Laws."

29. Simply paraphrasing, "Without permission one should not attempt to paint Elizabeth's picture." But the language of the proclamation also moves in more explicit sexual and corporeal directions. The passage argues, too, that those outside the queen's space should not attempt to break in and try to play out their temptations, that is, as I argue below, by attempting to rape her, however figuratively. When everything is very strictly stage-managed by the state, there is such a thing as proper access to the queen.

30. See especially Huston Diehl's "Bewhored Images," in her *Staging Reform*, 158–63.

31. John Stubbs, *Gaping Gulf*, 3–4.

32. Ibid. Stubbs also argues that Elizabeth is Adam.

33. Jean-Joseph Goux, "Vesta, or the Place of Being," 94.

34. Hughes and Larkin, *Tudor Royal Proclamations*, 2:240 (editor's note 1). And, of course, not all unseemly portraits can be destroyed, or even accessed. Consider, for example, Dr. Simon Forman's 1597 "dirty" dream of the queen, "a little elderly woman in a coarse white petticoat all unready." See Louis Adrian Montrose's full text and discussion of Forman's dream in "Shaping Fantasies," 65–87.

35. Battenhouse, *Shakespearean Tragedy*, 17–19. The word *awaits* here is mine. I have put it in quotation marks to indicate that my usage is cautionary. The idea it expresses, Lucrece's subconscious desire to be raped, belongs to Battenhouse, among others.

36. Nead, *Female Nude*, 57.

37. See also ibid., 7–8.

38. Bal, *Reading "Rembrandt"*, 71.

39. See Nicole Loraux, *Tragic Ways of Killing a Woman*, 39.

40. See the classic essay of pens and swords: Gilbert and Gubar's "The Queen's Looking Glass," which opens their coauthored book, *Madwoman in the Attic*, with the question, "Is a pen a metaphorical penis?" See also their discussion of the remarks made by Wolfgang Lederer, M.D., concerning "woman's own tendency to 'kill' *herself* into art in order to 'appeal to man.'" See also Lederer's *Fear of Women*, where he argues, "From the Paleolithic on, we have evidence that woman, through careful coiffure, through adornment and makeup, tried to stress the eternal type rather than the mortal self. Such makeup . . . [may reach the] somewhat estranging degree of a lifeless mask— and yet that is precisely the purpose of it: where nothing is lifelike, nothing speaks of death" (quoted in *Madwoman in the Attic*, 14–15).

41. Such an adage is common in paintings of Lucrece. It appears, too, in other evocations of Lucrece. Compare, for example, in Tourneur's *The*

Revenger's Tragedy: the nameless wife, who has been raped and has poisoned herself, dies holding a prayer book with a leaf of the book tucked up and pointing to this statement, *"Melius virtute mori, quam per dedecus vivere"* (Better to die in virtue than to live dishonored) (1.4.15–18).

42. *Webster's Third New International Dictionary* argues for a relationship between *signare* (to sign) and *secare* (to cut) (both Latin). I am particularly interested in the fourth definition of *seco* in the *Oxford Latin Dictionary*: "To make an incision in, cut, gash, etc." and "(of a surgeon) to cut open." Also, the first and second definitions of *signo*, "To mark with writing, inscribe; to inscribe, imprint (words)" and "to make, impress (a mark)." (Hence, the pun about the self-sacrificing nameless wife in Tourneur's *Revenger's Tragedy*: "She's made her name an *empress* by that act" [1.4.50, and editors' note].) For a related term see the definition for *inscriptio*. To draw an association between cutting and writing—a cutting into a tablet—is nothing new, but by working through things in a somewhat elaborate fashion, I hope to keep both concepts in the foreground.

43. The quotation is from Derrida's *La dissémination* (Paris, 1972); I have, however, taken the quotation from Gayatri Chakravorty Spivak's "Translator's Preface" to Derrida's *Of Grammatology*, lxvi, and have added the emphasis in order to underscore the position that both ontological states are real at the same time.

44. Loraux, *Tragic Ways*, 28. See her section, "The Glory of Women," 26–30, where she discusses the links between Greek tragedy's treatment of women's deaths and what she calls "norms" in classical Athens: "We should accept that tragedy constantly disturbs the norm in the interest of the deviant, but at the same time we must be aware that under the deviant the norm is often silently present" (30).

45. Quoted in Marianna Torgovnick, *Gone Primitive*, 108–9. The quote appears in Torgovnick's discussion of gender and race in Michel Leiris's ethnographic work, "The Many Obsessions of Michel Leiris" (105–18, esp. 108–11). Torgovnick is also interested in the relationship between art and pornography and spins her narrative most suggestively around Leiris's claim that "nothing seems more like a whorehouse to [him] than a museum" (111).

46. Diehl, *Staging Reform*, 63.

47. Ibid., 62.

48. Martin Hume, *Courtships of Queen Elizabeth*, 265.

49. Ian Donaldson, *Rapes of Lucretia*, 13.

50. Nancy Vickers, "Shakespeare's *Lucrece*," 105. Vickers argues that the word *color* appears more times in Shakespeare's poem than anywhere else in his work. She concludes quite suggestively that this "signals the rhetorical origins of the crime" (107). Vickers does not speak of the racial possibilities at work in these colors, even though her argument gives much note to corporeal

coloring. The "origins of the crime" can be located not only in rhetoric but in an original racial crime, that is, in the early modern mythic, criminal origins of racial difference, of a racial blackness (see Chapter 2).

51. For a more sustained comparison between the Queen Mother's speech in Thomas Dekker's *Lust's Dominion* and Lucrece's apostrophes to Night and Opportunity, see the queen's full speech, as well as her next major speech (3.1.1–20; 3.1.28–38). In Dekker's play Eleazar attempts to rape Isabella: "I'le touch you, yes, I'le taint you, see you this [his rapier], / I'le bring you to this lure" (5.1.281–82). Although I am arguing that Shakespeare's poem uses a metaphorical blackness to racialize rape, I would argue that the Queen Mother's speech offers an explicit racial reading of Shakespeare's Lucrece.

52. Beckford Sylvester, "Form in Shakespeare's *Lucrece*," 511.

53. See note 21 above.

54. William Harvey, *The Works of William Harvey*, 384–85, 480–82. The reader may also find interesting *An Anatomical Disquisition on the Motion of the Heart and Blood in Animals* (1628) and a second disquisition (1649), both included in *The Works* (1–86 and 87–141; see esp. chapter 16, where he writes about mixing of other substances in the blood [71–75]). See also Sylvester's use of Harvey in his discussion of the physical basis of Lucrece's corporeal pollution. "Form in Shakespeare's *Lucrece*," 510–11.

55. *The Countess of Montgomerie's Urania*, 541. The reader should also see Kim F. Hall's argument that white hands, like whiteness itself, very often articulate "ideologies of race, class, and gender." Hall, *Things of Darkness*, 208–10. See also Peter Erickson's discussion of the importance of white hands in the courtly love tradition. Erickson, "Representations," 521.

56. Girard, *Violence and the Sacred*, 49. The entire chapter is worth a look; see "Sacrificial Crisis," 39–67.

57. Cf. Eva C. Keuls's discussion of the relationship between marriage and rape in ancient Greek culture in *The Reign of the Phallus*, 52–57.

58. Bowers, "Emblem and Rape," 91. For a more thorough discussion of Christian sacrificial virgins, see Jane T. Schulenberg, "Heroics of Virginity."

59. Marion Wynne-Davies, "Consumed and Consuming Women," discusses the pit as a symbolic vagina; however, she does not link it to any particular body in the play. See especially 135–36.

60. Albert Charles Hamilton, *Structure of Allegory*, 69–72; and Albert H. Tricomi, "Aesthetics of Mutilation," 18.

61. See Giulia Sissa, *Greek Virginity*.

62. See Gail Kern Paster, *Body Embarrassed*, 98–99.

63. Cf. Coppélia Kahn, *Roman Shakespeare*: "Though Lavinia is 'a new-married lady' (2.2.15) when she is raped, Tamora uses the term 'deflower' (2.2.191) to describe what is done to her, thus representing her as virginal

daughter rather than chaste wife, even before her husband is murdered and she returns to her father in the daughter's position (2.2.191)" (54).

64. See esp. 4–7 of Girard's *Violence and the Sacred*, although Girard elaborates on the importance of sacrificial substitutions throughout his book.

65. Bowers, "Emblem and Rape," 13.

66. Lorraine Helms, "'High Roman Fashion,'" 558.

67. Ibid., 559; see also James L. Calderwood, *Shakespearean Metadrama*, 34–35.

68. Particularly relevant here is Nancy J. Vickers's classic reading of the blazon in "Diana Described: Scattered Women and Scattered Rhyme," which takes its impetus from Petrarch's poetic sequence *Rime sparse* (scattered rhymes). The scattering of the woman by ostensibly celebrating her body parts in effect dismembers the woman whom the poet presumably praises. Poetic scattering becomes a form of masculinist poetic revenge. Vickers points out that some cognate of *spargere* (to scatter [Italian]) appears some forty-three times in Petrarch's poetic sequence, with nineteen of these being used to describe Laura, the object of his lyrics. Here in Shakespeare's play, the scattered body of Lavinia, a body that has experienced *sparagmos*, i.e., a ritual dismemberment, betrays the violence inherent in Petrarchanism, especially for this study, the early modern Petrarchanism of Lucrece. Marcus's own discourse becomes doubly tortured because Marcus cannot find a way of describing that will allow him to separate *sparagmos* from poetic *spargere*.

69. Calderwood, *Shakespearean Metadrama*, 35.

70. See Gillian Murray Kendall, "'Lend Me Thy Hand,'" 307–8.

71. See Richlin, "Reading Ovid's Rapes."

72. Wynne-Davies, "Consumed and Consuming Women," reads this moment differently. She sees Lavinia here as taking "over the textual discourse, thereby castrating the source of male power" (146–47). We do agree, however, that Lavinia's writing moment is the play's "narrative fulcrum."

73. Marjorie Garber, *Shakespeare's Ghost Writers*, 54–55.

74. See esp. Bowers, "Emblem and Rape"; and Kahn, "Sexual Politics of Subjectivity," 156–57.

75. Katherine A. Rowe offers a highly suggestive reading of the play in her argument that it "insists on hands as the central emblem of effective political action" (301). Unlike Rowe, however, who imagines "Lavinia as a kind of anti-emblem of the Just Virgin, 'lopp'd' of the iconic hands that might hold scales and sword, and made the center of a vengeful demand for justice" (285 n), I would argue that Lavinia is lopped most significantly of the iconic hand that directs chastising demands toward her own body. In the end our readings do share some important foundational points.

76. Girard, *Violence and the Sacred*, 102–3.

77. Loraux, *Tragic Ways*, 32.

78. Ibid.

79. Jed, *Chaste Thinking*, esp. 8, 18–50; Girard, *Violence and the Sacred*, 269–73, 295–306.

80. Donaldson, *Rapes of Lucretia*, 21–39.

81. See Karen Cunningham, "Trials by Ordeal."

82. Quoted in Anthony Barthelemy, *Black Face*, 101–2.

83. Stimpson, "Soil of Rape," 57.

84. For examples see critique of this phenomenon in Leonard Tennenhouse, *Power on Display*, 106–22; also Guido Ruggiero, *Boundaries of Eros*, 89–108.

85. For a fuller text of the 1601 edict from which I take this phrase see my introductory chapter. For the complete text see Hughes and Larkin, *Tudor Royal Proclamations*, 3:221–22. I will make more explicit and implicit use of this document in Chapter 2.

86. We see this kind of racial contamination in many early modern texts. It's as though one kind of cultural or racial pollution makes possible a more dangerous kind of racial contamination. The infiltration of Jewishness can lead to the infiltration of blackness; the Anglo-Irish can open the doors to the Irish, who can in turn lead the presumably racially pure state into Spanishness and even Africanness. (See, for example, my discussion of the Irish in Chapter 3.) The bottom line of England's national-imperial project is that it can't be too careful when it comes to any kind of cultural or racial mixing.

87. For some later examples see Edward Ravenscroft's adaptation of Shakespeare's play, *Titus Andronicus, or the Rape of Lavinia* (1687), and Aphra Behn's *Abdelazer; or, The Moor's Revenge* (1677), an adaptation of Dekker's *Lust's Dominion*.

88. English plays dramatizing the possibility of interracial sex and rape are often set in Spain or Italy, and a more extensive discussion of these plays would require a deeper reading of these geographical signifiers. Spain and Italy are in important ways interim cultural spaces, floating somewhere between an English whiteness and an African blackness. See, for example, my discussion of Venice in Chapter 2.

89. I would especially like to emphasize the term *hysterical* here, since I am using it to mean something more emphatic than is immediately available in popular parlance. The notion of hysteria here signifies Crotilda's split female self, the woman divided against herself. In Mary Jacobus's reading of hysteria, Crotilda experiences "self-estrangement, fracturing into two dimensions the unity which the hysteric yearns to recreate on the site of her body." Jacobus, *Reading Woman*, 206. (For a succinct analysis of hysteria and the woman's body, see also Charles Bernheimer, "Introduction Part One," in *In Dora's Case*, 5–12.) The split between what is in effect Crotilda's chaste white self and her raped black self points, too, to the way woman (in whatever circumstance) is seen as

naturally divided against herself. For some attention to the dilemma of the hysterical woman in early modern tragedy, see my essay "'Transshaped' Women."

90. I put "tricks" in quotation marks here because although Mulymumen does ostensibly mislead Julianus into killing his daughter, I am insisting still that Julianus participates in a sacrificial economy similar to Titus's when he kills his daughter (an argument made below). Julianus's stabbing of his daughter, whom the play explicitly links to Lucrece, three times (1.1.11–12, 1.2.97–98, 4.1.99–101) presumes to shift the narrative from one of a foreign and polluting rape to a saving and protecting sacrifice. The sacrifice, the *barbarity* of sacrifice, does not (or perhaps cannot) announce itself as desired or stage-managed. In other words, sacrifice for Julianus conveniently enters textualization as a trick—as a mockery, to use Julianus's own word (5.5.181)— but it still does the sacrificial work. A sacrifice by any other name. . . .

91. Barthelemy, *Black Face*, 97.

92. See Wynne-Davies, "Consumed and Consuming Women," 138–39.

93. Helms, "'High Roman Fashion,'" 558.

94. Wynne-Davies, "Consumed and Consuming Women," 138–39.

95. For another example of Shakespeare's punning on *barber* and *barbar(ism)* see my discussion in Chapter 3 of Antony's getting barbered in Cleopatra's Egypt.

96. Unless otherwise noted, all biblical quotations are from the 1560 Geneva Bible.

97. Helen King, "Sacrificial Blood," 120.

98. *Titus Andronicus*, Oxford ed., 202.

99. Joseph R. Roach, *Cities of the Dead*, 220.

100. Calderwood, *Shakespearean Metadrama*, 42.

101. For further explanation I direct the reader to Girard's argument in *Violence and the Sacred* about the insidedness and outsidedness of the sacrificial victim (see, e.g., 11–13).

102. Calderwood, *Shakespearean Metadrama*, 45.

Chapter 2

1. Rona Goffen, *Piety and Patronage*, 139.

2. For some brief references and discussions see Daniel J. Vitkus, "Turning Turk in *Othello*," 163–64; David C. McPherson, *Myth of Venice*, 33; Virginia Vaughan, *"Othello": A Contextual History*, 16–21.

3. For more discussion of the actual and perceived relationship between these two governing bodies, as well as for a more detailed discussion of some other similarities and differences between England and Venice, see Murray J. Levith, *Shakespeare's Italian Settings*, 12–39.

4. Ibid., 14.

5. Ibid. See also Vaughan, *"Othello": A Contextual History*, 16–21.

6. John Stoye, *English Travellers Abroad, 1604–1667*, 71.

7. See also Martin Orkin, "Civility and the English Colonial Enterprise." Orkin moves beyond the fact that one reason for Shakespeare's locating this play in Venice is that Giraldi Cinthio does so in *Hecatommithi* (published in Venice in 1566), the play's main source. Orkin elaborates on England's real and symbolic interests in Venetian culture, particularly in the area of commercial exploration. The next two chapters discuss English perceptions of Rome's cultural and racial purity and whiteness. See also Levith, *Shakespeare's Italian Settings*, 14, for a brief but informative discussion of early modern competitions and alliances among Rome, Venice, Spain, and England. For an expanded contemporary discussion see Fynes Moryson's *Itinerary* (1617): 398–470. For a convenient and diverse critical discussion see Agostino Lombardo, "The Veneto, Metatheatre and Shakespeare"; Roberta Mullini, "Streets, Squares, and Courts: Venice as a Stage in Shakespeare and Ben Jonson"; Leo Salingar, "The Idea of Venice in Shakespeare and Ben Jonson"; and Avraham Oz, "Dobbin on the Rialto: Venice and the Division of Identity. All are in part 3, "Venice: Spectacle and Polis," in Michele Marrapodi et al., eds., *Shakespeare's Italy*, 143–57, 158–70, 171–84, 185–209, respectively.

8. My use of the term *horror* here is to evoke not only the common usage of the term but also Julia Kristeva's use of it in *The Powers of Horror*, where she defines it in terms of the confusion of boundaries. See also Mary Douglas, *Purity and Danger*, esp. chapter 1, "Ritual Uncleanness," 7–29.

9. Levith, *Shakespeare's Italian Settings*, 17–18.

10. Jack D'Amico, *The Moor in English Renaissance Drama*, 163.

11. Levith, *Shakespeare's Italian Settings*, 23.

12. For another sampling of the kind of imperialistic rhetoric espoused by Portia, compare Walter Ralegh on Guiana:

> For whatsoever Prince shall possesse it, shall bee greatest, and if the king of Spayne enjoy it, he will become unresistable. Her Majesty hereby shall confirme and strengthen the opinions of al nations, as touching her great and princely actions. And where the south border of *Guiana* reacheth to the Dominion and Empire of the *Amazones*, those women shall hereby heare the name of a virgin, which is not onely able to defend her owne territories and her neighbors, but also to invade and conquere so great Empyres and so farre removed. Ralegh, *Bewtiful Empyre of Guiana*, 199.

13. In addition to the prince's going on too long in his protestations (*Merchant of Venice*, 2.1.1–12, 2.1.22–38), the proximity in the three lines referenced in my text of the words *lady, feared,* and *valiant,* and of the phrases "best-regarded virgins" and "loved it too," along with his speaking a couple of

lines earlier of cutting himself, make emphatic a cohering sexual violence seething through the prince's manner.

14. For some studies on the black presence in early modern England see James Walvin, *Black and White*; Edward Scobie, *Black Britannia*; the introduction to Kim F. Hall, *Things of Darkness*, 1–24; Jack D'Amico, *The Moor in English Renaissance Drama*, 7–40; and Winthrop Jordan, *White over Black*, 3–43.

15. Ruth Cowhig, "Blacks in English Renaissance," 7.

16. Eldred D. Jones, *Elizabethan Image*, 16–17.

17. *Acts of the Privy Council*, 36:16–17, 20–21. Also quoted in Cowhig, "Blacks in English Renaissance," 6.

18. This argument holds even while acknowledging Kim F. Hall's observation that whereas Elizabeth attempted to expel Africans, James I sought to bring them into England, especially as curiosities. For Hall, the appropriation of difference and the denial of difference are part of the same racial construct. See Hall, *Things of Darkness*, 176. See also Peter Fryer, *Staying Power*.

19. Unless otherwise noted, all *Othello* quotations are from Alvin Kernan's edition.

20. Cf. Song of Sol. 1:4: "I am blacke, O y daughters of Iierusalém, but comelie, as the frutes of Kedár, as the curtines of Salomón."

21. At an earlier stage in my own work I found Michael Neill's expression "racialist ideology" giving intellectual stimulus to my own inchoate ideas and critical purpose. See Michael Neill, "Unproper Beds," 394. Neill's work has been instrumental to my understanding of race in England's early modern era. Cf. Jacques Derrida: "Visibility should—not be visible. According to an old omnipresent logic that has reigned since Plato, that which enables us to see should remain invisible: black, blinding." Derrida, "Living On/Border Lines," 90–91.

22. Several recent essays have addressed Othello's blackness as a serious and complex trope. Emily C. Bartels argues that the Moor becomes demonized and implicated in the growing desires of England to delineate territory and establish borders between the Other and the self. Neill traces how the play and its directors, engravers, and critics have fetishized and agonized over the racially adulterated marriage bed. And, by way of the idea of cultural monsters, Karen Newman demonstrates how femininity and blackness are made to complement each other in the play's construction of horrific desires. See Bartels, "More of the Moor"; Neill, "Unproper Beds"; Newman, " 'And wash the Ethiop white.' " I also recommend Ania Loomba's *Gender, Race, Renaissance Drama* for a more general discussion of Othello's blackness.

23. I am alluding in part to Edward W. Said, *Orientalism*, especially his chapter "Knowing the Oriental" (31–49). Said is interested in exploring how European cultures (especially in the nineteenth century) come to *know* the "Oriental" as Other. He argues that "knowledge gives power, more power

requires more knowledge, and so on in an increasingly profitable dialectic of information and control" (36). Said also writes about how Europeans came to believe that their representations of the Oriental could actually lead to their discovery of the Oriental's "Platonic essence" (38).

24. Said writes, "Knowledge of the Orient, because generated out of strength, in a sense *creates* the Orient, the Oriental, and his world" (40). Derrida has also written about racism as "a memory in advance." See Jacques Derrida, "Racism's Last Word," esp. 291.

25. My point extends Neill's argument, which focuses on the offstage audience as being turned into voyeurs by the play. See Neill, "Unproper Beds." The voyeuristic dimension, the early modern period's ethnographic experiencing, of staged Others more generally is still largely undertheorized. One of the underlying arguments of this chapter is that the metatheatrical workings of Other characters, particularly black ones, inform the myriad ways they signify on the early modern stage.

26. Cf. the Queen Mother's response to the mischievous plottings of the Moor Eleazar in Thomas Dekker's *Lust's Dominion*: "What shape will this prodigious womb bring forth, / Which groans with such strange labour" (4.4.2604–5).

27. Cf. the prince of Morocco in *The Merchant of Venice*: "Mislike me not for my complexion, / The shadowed livery of the burnished sun, / To whom I am a neighbor and near bred" (2.1.1–3).

28. Ben Jonson, *The Masque of Blackness*, in *The Complete Masques*, 47–60, lines 136–42.

29. John Crowne, *Calisto*, in *The Dramatic Works*, 219–342, esp. 321.

30. See Barbara J. Shapiro, *Probability and Certainty*, esp. 119–62. Shapiro argues that during the sixteenth century, history, which had been situated somewhere between literature and science, began to shift toward the scientific. On the "scientific" philology of the sixteenth century, see also Richard Halpern, *Poetics of Primitive Accumulation*, 176–214.

31. Quoted in Newman, "'And wash the Ethiop white,'" 146–47.

32. Thomas Browne, *Pseudodoxia Epidemica*, in *The Works*, 2:367–95, esp. 380. For all his empiricism, Browne offers explanatory images that do not seem far removed from the images associated with Phaeton. See Browne's two chapters on "the Blackness of Negroes" and his chapter on the color black more generally. Quite interestingly, Browne argues against those who find blackness a "curse of deformity." He writes that beauty is not in one's color but in "a comely commensurability of the whole unto the parts, and the parts between themselves." Blacks, he emphasizes, are "not excluded from beauty" (383–84).

33. Ambroise Paré, *On Monsters and Marvels*, 38–39. Paré also tells of a "gentle beast" called Thanacth, which has the face of a "well-formed man" and

the hind legs of a tiger but is covered in black body hair and has "head hair slightly black and kinky just like the Moors whom one sees in Africa" (146–47). He tells of another African animal called Haiit, whose "face and hands are almost like those of a child" (147). In short, black persons are shown to be inextricably linked to reproductive perversities and to the wild animal kingdom.

34. Newman, "'And wash the Ethiop white,'" 148. Derrida's argument about the discursive manipulation of race underscores my argument here: "The point is not that acts of racial violence are only words but rather that they have to have a word. Even though it offers the excuse of blood, color, birth—or rather *because* it uses this naturalist and sometimes creationist discourse—racism always betrays the perversion of man, the 'talking animal.'" Derrida, "Racism's Last Word," 292.

35. Bartels refers to this attempt to define blacks as a "double vision." She argues, "For the discovery of both positive and negative extremes within this other world serves not to neutralize the negative but to destabilize the positive, to suggest that at any moment the civil might devolve into the savage, its darker and truer underside." *Spectacles of Strangeness*, 31. See also Neill, "Unproper Beds," 394, 399, 412, for some excellent attention to the interplay and usefulness of the "natural" and "unnatural" in shaping what he sees as the emerging imperialistic and racial discourse of Shakespeare's play.

36. John Bulwer, *Anthropometamorphosis*, 468–69; quoted in Hall, *Things of Darkness*, 88. Browne also poses such an explanation in his *Pseudodoxia Epidemica* (6.10, 377).

37. "Othello's Colour," in *Othello*, ed. Horace Furness, 395.

38. Orkin maintains that "the possibility of racism" is "only one element in the unfolding of Othello's crisis" ("Othello and the 'Plain Face,'" esp. 175). Orkin argues that the play is actually an affirmation of Othello's blackness. Although Orkin's essay includes a comprehensive survey of sixteenth- and seventeenth-century English writings on the subject of blacks, his conclusions do not sufficiently respond to the uneasy depths of Shakespeare's cultural interrogation.

39. I am thinking here of the number of times particular words occur in the text. The bed and sheets are mentioned twenty-five times and the handkerchief twenty-eight, versus only eleven mentions of blackness.

40. Neill, "Unproper Beds"; Boose, "Othello's Handkerchief," esp. 370.

41. Stanley Cavell, "Epistemology and Tragedy," esp. 14.

42. Neill, "Unproper Beds," 402.

43. A discussion of *Historie* and the handkerchief is in T. G. A. Nelson and Charles Haines, "Othello's Unconsummated Marriage," esp. 8. Africanus's *Historie* was in circulation from 1550 onward—available mainly in Latin, but also in Italian and French, and translated into English by John Pory in 1600.

For a comparison of Africanus's *Historie* and Shakespeare's play, see Rosalind Johnson, "African Presence in Shakespearean Drama." See also Bartels, "More of the Moor," esp. 435–38, who emphasizes and then theorizes the differences between these two texts.

44. Quoted in Nelson and Haines, "Othello's Unconsummated Marriage," 8.

45. Lynda Boose, "Othello's Handkerchief," 361.

46. Peter L. Rudnytsky is one of the few critics who take seriously not only the handkerchief but its absence. Although his reading concurs with mine to the extent that he links the cloth to the primal scene, for him the primal scene is ultimately the "maternal penis," this "always absent thing." Rudnytsky, "The Purloined Handkerchief in *Othello*," 185. Such a reading risks ascribing to the napkin a real objectness. See also Susan Gubar, "'The Blank Page,'" where Gubar discusses concepts of absence/presence and (in)visibility with regard to blood-stained nuptial bed sheets.

47. For more bibliography, as well as for further discussion of the breast, penis, nipples, glans, and some of the other corporeal objects critics have associated with the cloth and its design, see Boose, "Othello's Handkerchief," 371.

48. The ongoing interplay between response and creation is what I mean more broadly by the "primal scene." More specifically, I am using "primal scene" as it derives from psychoanalysis, which is generally interested in the relationship between response and creation and which therefore provides a conceptual field for thinking through the ways this relationship manifests itself in Shakespeare's play. Since Freud, who first identified the primal scene (the *Urszene*), the concept has become more interdisciplinarily and critically applied and implied in the work of theoretical critics such as Ned Lukacher and William Beatty Warner. The primal scene denotes the moment when a child imagines or (by accident) actually sees his or her parents engaged in sexual intercourse. The child attempts to repress this moment, but it becomes known and seen through his or her repeated effort to hide it. It manifests itself in representations that are never exact, never literal, but always distorted. Because of this distortion, the primal scene does not point to a first scene so much as to the absence of the originary one, whose prior existence is evinced by some present scene. And because of a range of accidental associations of time, place, experience, and fantasy, the primal scene is forever figured and disfigured by this moment. As Warner says, the scene "has a decisive effect upon the person, his neurotic symptoms, his relationships with others, his style of thinking and feeling—in other words, it is a contributing factor in much of what we take an individual person to be." Warner, *Chance and the Text of Experience*, 47. The primal scene is both real and fantastical, both literal and metaphorical. It is also, like Othello's blackness, something that the onlooker both responds to (i.e., represses) and creates (i.e., repeats). And Othello's blackness, like the primal scene, remains from beginning to end a site of

interplay between the literal and the metaphorical. As Lukacher has argued, in the primal scene "every disclosure [is] also a concealment, and every literal truth a figural lie." The primal scene, writes Lukacher, exists in the constant enfolding of "historical memory and imaginative construction." Lukacher, *Primal Scenes*, 23–24; in the language of my chapter, it exists in the always present relationship between pre-text (memory) and pretext (construction), or between response and creation. Also see my essay, "'An Essence That's Not Seen.'" In revisiting this essay in this chapter, I am trying to shift that work's earlier psychoanalytic frame to a cultural and historical one.

49. Boose, "Othello's Handkerchief," 367.

50. Rudnytsky, "Purloined Handkerchief," 184–85. Rudnytsky thinks of the "primal scene" as the scene of Desdemona and Cassio. Understanding the primal scene to signify the originary moment of the ocular crisis, I am arguing that the primal scene is the scene of Othello and Desdemona. It should be noted, however, that the *meaning* of the primal scene depends on the ultimate inseparability of these two scenes.

51. Rudnytsky's reading ("Purloined Handkerchief," 184) is similar to that of Kenneth Burke, who according to Boose, thought of the strawberried cloth as "some sort of displaced genital symbol of Desdemona" ("Othello's Handkerchief," 371).

52. Stephen Greenblatt, *Renaissance Self-Fashioning*, 234. For more discussion about the issue of probability and improbability in *Othello* (especially as it is treated by critics from Thomas Rymer through Harley Granville-Barker), see Joel Altman, "'Preposterous Conclusions.'"

53. Samuel Purchas, *Hakluytus Posthumus*, 1:39.

54. Jean Bodin, *Method for the Easy Comprehension of History*, 105. See also Winthrop D. Jordan, *White over Black*, where Jordan discusses early modern England's yoking of blackness, beasts, and sex, esp. 28–38. Looking ahead, the reader may also wish to see my discussion of the Irish in Chapter 3. We are certainly not immune from such yokings in the late-twentieth-century West. Nothing has made this clearer than some of the rumors circulating in the West about the beginnings of AIDS, especially the belief that AIDS began with Africans having sex with apes. For a very accessible and informed discussion of the cultural play between AIDS and Africa, see Simon Watney, "Missionary Positions: AIDS, 'Africa', and Race," in his *Practices of Freedom*, 103–20, esp. his discussion of "monstrous passions," 114–16.

55. Keith Vivian Thomas, *Man and the Natural World*, 39–40, 135. See also Linda Woodbridge's discussion of anthropological pollution and social boundaries in early modern culture, "Palisading the Body Politic," 289–91.

56. See, for example, Boose's more extensive discussion of pornography in *Othello* in "'Let it be hid.'" Her essay examines the assumptions of our voyeuristic compliance in the play, as well as those imperatives that, through-

out, command the visual attention of the audience on- and offstage. Her observation that the "forbidden" gets repeatedly eroticized is suggestive of the primal-scene claims of my argument.

57. For a diverse group of readings with regard to Iago's evocation of homosexuality here see the following critics, even though these critics and the critical tradition don't really explore the relationship between Iago and homosexuality unless Iago himself is being figured as homosexual: Rudnytsky, "Purloined Handkerchief," 184; Randolph Splitter, "Sexual Conflict," 24; Bruce Smith, *Homosexual Desire*, 61–64; and Jonathan Dollimore, *Sexual Dissidence*, section entitled, "Forget Iago's Homosexuality," 157–62.

58. In his study of homosexuality in the Renaissance, Alan Bray discusses the intertextual associations among such terms or concepts as bestiality, whoredom, rape, adultery, and incest and emphasizes how an act of homosexuality quite frequently figures as the culmination of these "perversions." Paraphrasing Du Bartas, Bray writes, "through rape, adultery and incest they came at last—'glutted with all granted loves'—to homosexuality." Bray, *Homosexuality in Renaissance England*, 14–15. See also Du Bartas's chapter entitled "The Vocation" in his *Suite de la Second Semaine* (1603), where Du Bartas revels in the punishment of the "homosexual," the most profane of sinners (repr. in Snyder, *The Divine Weeks*, lines 1189–320). Excluding overt incest, *Othello* is quite thoroughly implicated in this particular construction of homosexuality. Nevertheless, Bray is surprisingly silent about *Othello* and about homosexuality in Shakespeare more generally. On the subject of homosexuality and its association with bestiality, see also B. Smith, *Homosexual Desire*, esp. 174–80.

59. For the English, not least among Venetian and Italian proclivities was their fascination with homosexuality. See John Stoye's *English Travellers Abroad, 1604–1667*, 71; and Levith, *Shakespeare's Italian Settings*, 38. See also Guido Ruggiero's chapter "Sodom and Venice" for a better grasp of the homosexual subculture (and some of its legal entanglements) in fourteenth- and fifteenth-century Venice, 109–45.

60. Knocking in Shakespeare works most dramatically as a way of suddenly forcing characters into recognition. Cf. knocking in *Henry IV* (Part 1) and *Macbeth*. Also, James I would refer to knocking as signifying one's move into moral consciousness.

61. For a more elaborate explanation of the word *fixity*, see Chapter 4.

62. For discussions of the issue of Othello and Desdemona's sexual consummation, see, by way of examples, Nelson and Haines, "Othello's Unconsummated Marriage," 1–18; Norman Nathan, "Othello's Marriage is Consummated," 79–82; and my essay "'An Essence That's Not Seen,'" 320–21.

63. Maria, who marries the Moor Eleazar, in Dekker's *Lust's Dominion* comes close to being such a white woman, but although she comes close to

Desdemona in racial sentiment, she does not in actual prominence. The lascivious Queen Mother commands a much more significant place in the drama.

64. For more on the racial blackness of Shakespeare's Cleopatra see Chapter 4.

65. John Atkins, *A Voyage to Guinea, Brasil and the West Indies*, 108. See discussion of Atkins in Jordan, *White over Black*, 31–32. Jordan also writes about the Western belief that "apes were inclined wantonly to attack Negro women," 31.

66. Loomba, *Gender*, 150.

67. See Patricia Parker's discussion of the interlingual pun on *cause, case, chose,* and *thing.* P. Parker, *Shakespeare from the Margins*, 250–52.

68. In a problematic marriage and consummation, Hymen, the god of marriage, focuses his energies on blood as opposed to the unity of disembodied souls. These problematic instances seem to expose the woman's hymeneal self, her blood. In a proper marriage and consummation, on the other hand, Hymen deflects attention away from the hymen and toward the unity of souls. For exemplification of these observations see Ben Jonson, *Hymenaei, or the Solemnities of Masque and Barriers at a Masque* (1606) in *The Complete Masques*, esp. lines 1–25. See also Thomas Kyd's *The Spanish Tragedy*, where Revenge explains a dumb show to the ghost of Andrea:

The two first, the nuptial torches bore,
As brightly burning as the mid-day's sun:
But after them doth Hymen hie as fast,
Clothed in sable, and a saffron robe,
And blows them out and quencheth them with blood,
As discontent that things continue so. (3.15.30–35)

See also my discussion of hymeneal imagery in Thomas Middleton and William Rowley's *The Changeling* (1622). Little, "'Transshaped' Women," 34.

69. Kahn, "Sexual Politics of Subjectivity," 146. Cf. my discussion of the cult of Vesta (Chapter 1), which suggests that Othello's desire here to put out the light may also reflect his desire not to see Desdemona, particularly if seeing her itself signals a sexual violation: Jean-Joseph Goux, "Vesta," 94.

70. Reno Thomas Simone has noted (without elaboration) that "in *Othello* the sexual preoccupation and the setting of the final emblematic scene in Desdemona's bedchamber link closely with [Shakespeare's] *Lucrece*." Simone, *Shakespeare and "Lucrece"*, 191. Neill comes to a related conclusion in his reading of critical responses to this closing scene. He quotes, for example, a nineteenth-century Russian writer who comments on the portrayal of Othello by Ira Aldridge, the first black actor to perform the role: "That savage

flesh did its fleshly work." Neill remarks that in this commentator's account
"the play exhibits nothing less than the symbolic rape of the European 'spirit'
by the 'savage, wild flesh' of black otherness." Neill, "Unproper Beds," 391.

71. For some other fairly accessible depictions of this scene, in addition to
the ones reproduced in my book, see the frontispieces to the Rowe (1709) and
Bell (1785) editions of the play. I also recommend a print by H. Hoffman (early
eighteenth century?), in which Othello stands over a rather peaceful and
angelic Desdemona; he holds a knife in one hand, and protruding from his
cloak is a large, dark hilt that is unmistakably figured as a giant phallus. For
reprints of the Rowe and Bell frontispieces see *Shakespearean Criticism*, Vol. 4,
Harris, ed., 393 and 426, respectively. Some additional images may be found in
Neill, "Unproper Beds," 386–89, and Paul H. D. Kaplan, "The Earliest Images
of Othello," *Shakespeare Quarterly*, 39 (1988), 173–74.

72. This "daring" social critique particularly springs from Shakespeare's
putting a black protagonist at the center of his play. And even though under-
cuttings of Shakespeare's critique (focused mainly on Othello's race) continue
through most of the twentieth century, a diverse and rather vituperative
articulation of what is at stake may be found in the appendix on "Othello's
Colour" in Horace Howard Furness's New Variorum edition of the play,
389–96. See, for example, J. E. Taylor's comments on the play in the introduction to his translation of Cinthio's *Gili Hecatommithi*, Shakespeare's main
source. He defends Shakespeare from the accidental stuff of textuality. He
argues that Othello's blackness "is an instructive instance of the fact that artistic
truth may consist with accidental errors which lie beyond the pale of art; the
character of Othello may be in itself perfect, faultless; and yet, when a nation-
ality is affixed to it, it may violate the physical and moral laws of nature
displayed in the distinction of the races" (*Othello*, ed. Furness, 394). Moreover,
Taylor's "violation" cannot be separated from the play's sexual drama. Cf.
M. R. Ridley's Arden edition of the play (London: Methuen, 1958), li.

73. See Michael D. Bristol's chapter, "Race and the Comedy of Abjection
in *Othello*," 175–202, in his *Big-Time Shakespeare*, 201.

74. Errol Hill, *Shakespeare in Sable*, 9. What in effect makes Othello's blackness a critical and theatrical problem is in fact the emergence of a theater that
would increasingly demand naturalistic performances and performers. As far as
concerns Shakespeare's play, the stage would demand a naturally black actor,
undermining that dramatic space that called for the white actor to negotiate,
to enter into cultural dialogue with (as it were) his black character. As we have
recognized increasingly with boys staging women's bodies, much useful work
can and remains to be done on the *theatricality* (the cross-dressedness) of
nonwhite bodies on the early modern English stage.

75. Hill, *Shakespeare in Sable*, 9.

76. For a more developed reading of the terms *fixity*, *radical*, and *performativity*, see Chapter 4.

77. Laurence Olivier, *On Acting*, 152–59. I wish to thank Christopher Thinnes for first alerting me to Olivier's monograph.

78. Donald Spoto, *Laurence Olivier: A Biography*, 330.

79. For a more detailed introduction to Ira Aldridge and Paul Robeson, see Hill, *Shakespeare in Sable*, 17–27, 120–30, respectively.

80. Vaughan, *"Othello": A Contextual History*, 181.

81. For a fairly informed discussion of Othello and white and black actors, see Vaughan, *"Othello": A Contextual History*, esp. 181–98.

82. Of course I am in no way suggesting that a white actor should now play Othello. In the "real" world in which we live, it strains my imagination, my social knowledge and experience, to see someone other than a "black" man (potentially a rather broad category) assuming the role of Othello.

83. Claire Sponsler, "Outlaw Masculinities," 340.

84. Sponsler, "Outlaw Masculinities," 322. See also Eric Lott, "White Like Me," esp. 476; and Sponsler and Clark, "Othered Bodies."

85. Vitkus, "Turning Turk," 160.

86. My reference here to a "fly" intends in part to allude to the association made in Shakespeare between the black human body and this flying insect. Iago, telling Roderigo to rouse Brabantio and tell him about Desdemona's marriage to Othello, says,

And though he in a fertile climate dwell,
Plague him with flies; though that his joy be joy,
Yet throw such chanes of vexation on't
As it may lose some color. (1.1.67–70).

Compare Marcus's line in *Titus Andronicus*: "Pardon me, sir; it was a black ill-favoured fly" (3.2.66).

Chapter 3

1. Coppélia Kahn, *Roman Shakespeare*, 2, 14–15.

2. See Raphael Holinshed, *Chronicles*, chap. 20, 192. William Harrison's essay "Of the Generall Constitution of the Bodies of the Britons" was first published in 1577 as *An Historical Description of the Island of Britain*. It appears in Holinshed under the title, *The Description of England*.

3. For one such reference to Gregory I's having presumably said this see *The Oxford Companion to English Literature* (1981 [1932]), s.v. Gregory I.

4. Quotation from Winthrop Jordan, *White over Black*, 41. See also my discussion in Chapter 2 of early modern theories about the origins of black people.

5. William Camden, *Britain, or a Chorographicall Description*, 2.66. See also Debora Shuger's discussion of this and other passages from Camden in her "Other White Barbarians," 496–97, which she in part uses contextually to soften Edmund Spenser's advocation of solving the Irish crisis through deployment of military forces. She uses it too to register her own shock at Rosalind Jones and Peter Stallybrass's shock that Spenser would seek such a violent means of bringing to rest England's conflicts with Ireland. See Jones and Stallybrass, "Dismantling Irena," 160. See the subsection of this chapter, "The White English and the Hybrid Irish," where I argue that although Spenser by no means offers a unique solution to the Irish issue, his plans of violence and starvation were certainly capable of being profoundly disturbing to some early modern folk.

6. James Harrington, *Commonwealth of Oceana*, 48.

7. Shuger, "Other White Barbarians," 514–15. Unlike Shuger's, my argument is not that "civility" in English tracts is necessarily more "bourgeois" than the "civility" found in classical Roman texts, but that the English are as concerned with pursuing *civitas* as they are with pursuing *virtus*. The goal (as I argue below) is how to portray an unequivocal masculinity without becoming excessive, i.e., barbaric, about it.

8. Harrison, "Bodies of the Britons," 194.

9. See Kahn, *Roman Shakespeare*, 110–12; E. W. Waith, *The Herculean Hero*, 113–20; and Janet Adelman, *The Common Liar*, 132–39.

10. See Adelman, *The Common Liar*, appendix C, where Adelman discusses the complex relationship in early modern England and Shakespeare's play between Egypt and Africa.

11. For example, Ania Loomba argues in her study of the play that "all Egyptians, represented and symbolised by their queen, are associated with feminine and primitive attributes"; she also stresses that the femininity of Egypt has as much (if not more) to do with Rome's construction of its own masculinity. Loomba, *Gender*, 78–79.

12. Unless otherwise noted, all quotations from Shakespeare's *Antony and Cleopatra* are from Ridley's edition.

13. My reading differs from the richly informed argument advanced by Kahn in *Roman Shakespeare*. Kahn reads Antony's wound as a masculine sign. Her argument that Shakespeare's Antony actually lays claim to *virtus* differs from mine, which reads Rome's *virtus* as being realized through Rome's insistence and promotion that Antony has lost it (or has too much of it). Hence my investment in this chapter in nostalgia.

14. Dollimore's observation that Antony tries throughout the play "to reassert his virility, not only to Cleopatra but also to Caesar, his principal male competitor" remains viable, but I want to argue that ultimately Antony must negotiate virility rather than simply assert or reassert it. See Jonathan

Dollimore, *Radical Tragedy*, 210. See also Valerie Traub, who insists that Antony has too much masculinity. Traub, *Desire and Anxiety*, 48, 134.

15. See Traub, *Desire and Anxiety*, esp. 94, 97, 142, for the relationship between femininity and homosexuality.

16. Paster, *Body Embarrassed*, 94; Nancy Vickers, "Shakespeare's *Lucrece*."

17. Paster, *Body Embarrassed*, 105.

18. *Ibid.*, esp. 110, where Paster discusses women as objects of exchange.

19. See Ridley's annotation for this line in his edition of the play.

20. Cf. Robert S. Miola, *Shakespeare's Rome*, 143–44, on Antony's speech.

21. See Ridley's annotation for this line in his edition of the play.

22. Miola, *Shakespeare's Rome*, 144.

23. Lucy Hughes-Hallett, *Cleopatra*, 121–22.

24. Miola, *Shakespeare's Rome*, 123.

25. James J. Greene, "Birth and Death of Androgyny," 38.

26. Susan Stewart, *On Longing*, 23.

27. See Kahn, *Roman Shakespeare*, 123–27.

28. For a more thorough and theoretical discussion of "queer," see Jonathan Goldberg's introduction to his recent collection, *Queering the Renaissance*. See also Alexander Doty, *Making Things Perfectly Queer*, esp. the introduction and 1–38, even though the reader may find his reading more particular in its nuance to late-twentieth-century American popular culture.

29. Cicero, *Philippics*, 2.44–47. The translated quotation is from Amy Richlin, *Garden of Priapus*, 14–15. For the complete work and an earlier translation see Cicero, *Philippics*, Loeb Classics, esp. 108–10. Interestingly enough, writing about this passage, Richlin offers a critique of Cicero's rhetorical style similar to my critique of the style of Caesar's Modena speech in Shakespeare's play: "In the *Philippics* Cicero leaves little unsaid about Antony's alleged depravities, while always using formal language and professing his own reluctance to state the full truth." Richlin, *Garden of Priapus*, 14.

30. Cf. Alan Bray, *Homosexuality in Renaissance England*, and Elizabeth Pittenger, "'To Serve the Queere.'"

31. Ellis Hanson, "Sodomy and Kingcraft," 147.

32. Bruce R. Smith, *Homosexual Desire*, 67.

33. Hughes-Hallett, *Cleopatra*, 142.

34. Richlin, *Priapus*, esp. 222. See also note 15 above.

35. For a general theoretical point see Eve Kosofsky Sedgwick's highly suggestive study, *Between Men*. Carol Thomas Neely has read this moment as a parodic betrothal ceremony. See Neely, *Broken Nuptials*, 143.

36. See discussion of Harrison at the beginning of this chapter.

37. As Lynda E. Boose has quite rightly argued, white racism cannot be separated from the patriarchal system that generates it. See Boose, "Racial Discourse," esp. 40–41. See also Theodore W. Allen, *Invention of the White Race*, 24.

38. The reader may wish to sample some of the recent studies of whiteness, many of which attempt to bring whiteness into articulation. See, for examples, Richard Dyer's *White* and Allen's *Invention of the White Race*.

39. Allen, *Invention of the White Race*, 22.

40. This erasure of whiteness would be no less true here than in our more contemporary United States. Hence, especially the one-drop rules and their remnants in nineteenth- and twentieth-century legal and legislative state and national policies here in the United States.

41. It comes to be expected, then, as Kim F. Hall notes in her discussion of Ben Jonson's *Masque of Blackness*, that this first court masque commissioned by Queen Anne would be "both an elucidation of the nature of blackness and a celebration of empire. . . . [The] pride in the revival of ancient Britain is continually yoked to the glorification of whiteness." Hall, *Things of Darkness*, 133.

42. Antony's whiteness is a significant issue, as is exemplified by a 1987 production of Shakespeare's play that casts a black actor in the role of Antony. In its review the *Guardian* questions the authenticity of such casting. Loomba, who narrates the story in her study, notes that "generations of white Othellos are permitted while a single black Antony provokes an outrage" and goes on to conclude that "it is obvious that theatrical authenticity is a way of holding on to a lost empire." Loomba, *Gender*, 143–44. The English empire is very much a white space, and one may object to casting Antony as black for reasons quite at odds with those underlying the *Guardian* review: to cast Antony as black in a production with presumptions of "realistic" casting is to undercut, however unwittingly, the Roman loss that informs so much of Antony's anxiety, as well as Rome and Caesar's response to him.

43. Hall, *Things of Darkness*, 6–7. See Boose's argument about the Irish and not blacks as the group first to be shunted into discursive derogation. Although I don't think labeling the Irish as "first" quite works, since such derogation takes into its orbit a larger range of signification, the argument is a useful one for thinking about the racialization of the Irish and how even they become revisualized. Boose, "Racial Discourse," 36–37. I also recommend Ann Rosalind Jones, "Italians and Others," 101–19, and Jan Nederveen Pieterse, *White on Black*, esp. 212–15 of chapter entitled, "White Negroes." And although Walter S. H. Lim may be right that early modern England's two main colonial enterprises were Ireland and the New World (see his *The Arts of Empire*, 13), an African blackness would serve nevertheless as the quintessential and originary figure of English difference, an imaginary cultural measuring stick, as it were.

44. Writing of the origins of Africans, of Negroes, Africanus includes a separate section on "the signification of this word Barbar," whose primary origin, he writes, is "deriued of the verbe Barbara, which in their [Arabian] toong signifieth to murmur: because the African toong soundeth in the eares

of the Arabians, no otherwise than the voice of beasts." Leo Africanus, *History and Description of Africa*, 1:129.

45. Consider my reading in Chapter 1 of Stubbs's *Gaping Gulf*, in which he vividly associates national borders with racial ones.

46. For two recent studies concerning the relationship between Shakespeare and Ireland, see Christopher Highley, *Shakespeare, Spenser, and the Crisis in Ireland*, and Mark Thornton Burnett and Ramona Wray, eds., *Shakespeare and Ireland*. From the latter work, I especially recommend Andrew Hadfield, "'Hitherto She Ne're Could Fancy Him.'"

47. Richard Jobson, *Golden Trade*, 96. See also D(avid) B. Quinn's discussion of Jobson's rhetorical use of the Irish, *Elizabethans and the Irish*, 25–26.

48. Jobson, *Golden Trade*, 143–44.

49. *Ibid.*, 49–50.

50. Quinn, *Elizabethans and the Irish*, 27.

51. For examples, see Jan Nederveen Pieterse, *White on Black*; and Allen, *Invention of the White Race*.

52. Thomas Sowell, "The Economics of Slavery," 92, in his *Markets and Minorities*. All this shows an intricate history of race, racism, and economics, one continuously reifying, sustaining, and substantiating the needs of the others. Consider Hall's *Things of Darkness*, as well as her more current work on sugar: "Culinary Spaces."

53. Philip Sidney, *Prose Works*, 49–50.

54. See introduction to Spenser's *View of the State*, ed. Andrew Hadfield and Willy Maley; see also D(avid) B. Quinn, "'A Discourse of Ireland,'" esp. 166.

55. I will take my quotations from Grosart's edition of Spenser's 1596 text and not from James Ware's 1633 edition, which quite tellingly chastises (to recall Stephanie H. Jed) Spenser's text. Especially through a number of significant deletions, Ware's text becomes itself a wonderfully provocative reading of England's shifting rhetorical relationship to Ireland three decades after the completion of Spenser's original. Page numbers will be included in the body of the text, with reference to Spenser's original edition in parentheses and to Hadfield and Maley's edition of Ware's text in brackets. Also, I will sometimes include brief notes along with these page numbers.

56. References in my text to *History and Topography* are to the John J. O'Meara edition. Gerald of Wales summarizes the Irish in no uncertain terms:

> This people is, then, a barbarous people, literally barbarous. Judged according to modern ideas, they are uncultivated, not only in the external appearance of their dress, but also in their flowing hair and beards. All their habits are the habits of barbarians. Since conventions are formed from living together in society, and since they are so removed in these distant parts from the ordinary world of men, as if they were in another world

altogether and consequently cut off from well-behaved and law-abiding people, they know only of the barbarous habits in which they were born and brought up, and embrace them as another nature. Their natural qualities are excellent. But almost everything acquired is deplorable. (102–3)

For a more extensive critique of Gerald of Wales, see Robert Bartlett, *Gerald of Wales, 1146–1223*.

57. Spenser, *View of the State*, xvi; the reader should also see Highley, *Crisis in Ireland*, who argues that in the Renaissance the Irish were reconceptualized as "a race apart" (3); and Said, who argues that since Spenser's 1596 tract, "a whole tradition of British and European thought has considered the Irish to be a separate and inferior race, usually unregenerately barbarian, often delinquent and primitive," *Culture and Imperialism*, 236, but see also 222.

58. See also Hall, *Things of Darkness*, 145, for Spenser's emphasis on the adulteration of Spain by Africa.

59. Richard Brome, *The English Moore* (4.4.37). As I have shown and will continue to argue, the sentiment expressed here by Brome permeates the national and racial rhetoric of early modern England.

60. See Parker, *Shakespeare from the Margins*, 229–56.

61. See similar observations in Shuger, "Other White Barbarians," 503–4, and Bartlett, *Gerald of Wales*, chaps. 6–7. This gesture of borrowing indifferently from a nation's or people's history is all too familiar in early modern England's ethnographic accounts of Africa, not to say that this gesture is limited to England or to the early modern period.

62. Quinn has argued that "Irish wanderers and wandering customs upset Englishmen, mainly because they seemed to threaten the stability of life in town and village to which they were accustomed": *Elizabethans and the Irish*, 32.

63. Hughes and Larkin, *Tudor Royal Proclamations*, 3:134–36. Elizabeth's edict, "Ordering Arrest of Vagabonds, Deportation of Irishmen," calls specifically for the removal of any person residing in England but born in Ireland

except he be a householder known in some town where he liveth in the obedience of her majesty's laws, or be a menial servant with some nobleman, gentleman, or other honest householder, or do reside or be in commons in any house of court or chancery, as a student in the laws or a student in any universities, or else be sent out of Ireland by her majesty's deputy or some governors of the provinces there with commendation or about any service or suit recommended. (135)

A more complete grasp of this edict relies, I think, on considering it with respect to several other edicts, especially Elizabeth's 1596 and 1601 edicts calling for the deportation of Moors and Negroes and her 1563 edict regulating the persons permitted to "take" the queen's image.

64. Highley, *Crisis in Ireland*, 3–4.

65. Ware's edition omits most of this vituperative name-calling.

66. See Andrew Hadfield, *Spenser's Irish Experience*, 86.

67. Highley, *Crisis in Ireland*, 3; a number of recent critics have argued that Spenser saves his most invective remarks for the Old English. See, for example, Patricia Coughlan, ed., *Spenser and Ireland*; Hadfield, *Spenser's Irish Experience*, esp. 21–25, 111; and Highley, *Crisis in Ireland*, 3–133.

68. Moryson, *Itinerary*, 481. Moryson's discussion of Ireland runs throughout, but see esp. 481–86. Using rhetoric to link persons to animals and land is common too in classical and early modern Western narratives on Africa. See my discussion in Chapter 2 of Africans and bestiality.

69. Quinn, *Elizabethans and the Irish*, 2.

70. Boose, "Racial Discourse," esp. 45–47.

71. "Despise" instead of "dispose" in the Ware edition, 70.

72. Highley, *Crisis in Ireland*, 3–4.

73. Spenser seems to suspect and fear that cultural/racial identities are more continuous than discrete, with such cultural/racial fashioning moving ever so ominously toward the blackness of the African. This sense of not-so-chastised relations between the English (along with certain other Western persons) and Others is especially evident in Shakespeare's *Titus Andronicus* and, in a more associative fashion, in *The Merchant of Venice*. One of the best dramatic examples of such a cultural/racial continuum is Brome's *English Moore*, in which the gentile English woman Millicent is made to put on blackface by her Jewish husband. As the moral of the story goes, "Who could haue thought, / That subtle Iew, now cheated in his craft / Would haue disguised soe sweet a beauty soe?" (5.3.12–14). There is also the example of Queen Elizabeth I, who is said to refer to the French Alençon as her "little Moor." The underlying point seems to be that the English must be adamant about protecting their boundaries because the crossing of one boundary does eventually lead one to the blackness that is Africa. I've stressed a similar argument earlier in this book (see Chapter 1).

74. Anne Fogarty, "Colonization of Language," 79; see also Highley, *Crisis in Ireland*, 4.

75. Harrington, *Commonwealth of Oceana*, 227.

76. Highley, *Crisis in Ireland*, 111–12.

77. See Quinn, *Elizabethans and the Irish*, 79, where Quinn makes a similar observation, even though he sees these portrayals as far more "favorable" than the descriptions of the Irish found in written texts. Also see Quinn for more than twenty sixteenth-century illustrations of Irish persons, *Elizabethans and the Irish*, between 20 and 21.

78. Cf. Harrison, "Bodies of the Britons," where through a very nuanced

balancing act he attempts to prove the temperate masculinity of the English, 193–94.

79. Michael Neill, introduction to *Antony and Cleopatra*, by William Shakespeare, 94–95, 97.

80. Renato Rosaldo, *Culture and Truth*, chap. 3, esp. 71. Rosaldo argues too that "imperialist nostalgia occurs alongside a peculiar sense of mission, 'the white man's burden,' where civilized nations stand duty-bound to uplift so-called savage ones" (70).

81. In this respect my sense of nostalgia is similar to Susan Stewart's reading that the nostalgic in fact seeks "the absence that is the very generating mechanism of desire." As she clarifies later in the same project, "The nostalgic is enamored of distance, not of the referent itself." Stewart, *On Longing*, 23, 145.

82. Neill has observed that "Octavius's right to rule . . . is always implicitly linked to his inheritance of the heroic name of 'great Caesar'." Neill, introduction, 95.

83. Adelman, *Common Liar*, 132.

84. Harrison, "Bodies of the Britons," 193.

85. Antony's getting barbered, perhaps sacrificially barbered, can also be compared to Lavinia's sacrificial trimming in *Titus Andronicus* (see Chapter 1). The kind of barbering (grooming) Antony undergoes is less conspicuous but more suspect than the barbering undergone by Jonson's masqued gypsies in *The Gypsies Metamorphosed*, who assure their audience that their barbarism is only an ointment dyeing their faces, acquired "without spells, / By a mere barber, and no magic else" (lines 1389–90).

86. See Homi K. Bhabha, *Location*, 149.

87. In accord with several critics, James J. Greene reads Caesar's speech as a dilation of "the heroic ideal espoused by Caesar and nourished to perfection in an earlier time by the martial Antony," saying that "Caesar's nostalgic memory of an earlier, more heroic Antony captures succinctly the heroic, masculine ideal of the Romans." Greene, "Birth and Death of Androgyny," 27. I am arguing that there really is for Caesar no earlier more heroic Antony and that Caesar positions Antony against and not within a heroic Roman idealism.

88. Cf. Shuger, *Renaissance Bible*, 131; and Walter Burkert, *Homo Necans*, 16. See also Girard, *Violence and the Sacred*, 272–73, for the significance and workings of the "sacrificial preparation." The reader may wish to see Euripides' *Iphigenia in Aulis*, in which a stag takes Iphigenia's place at the moment of the sacrifice. Furthermore, both Aeschylus and Euripides compare Iphigenia to a sacrificial beast: in Aeschylus's *Agamemnon* she is lifted like "a goat for sacrifice" (line 234), and in *Iphigenia* the chorus says to Iphigenia, "You will be brought down from the hill caves / Like a heifer, red, white, unblemished, / And like a bloody victim / They will slash your throat" (lines 1084–87). For some other explicit comparisons of Iphigenia to a wild animal (a sacrificial beast), see

Aeschylus, *Agamemnon* (lines 1414–16), and Euripides, *Iphigenia in Tauris* (line 359). Shakespeare depicts Lucrece as "a white hind under the gripe's sharp claws, / [Pleading] in a wilderness where are no laws" (lines 543–44).

89. Nicole Loraux has observed in her reading of sacrificial virgins and stags that "the mountains made wild things out of every creature that lived in them." See her section "Heifer and Filly, Captured and Tamed," in *Tragic Ways*, 34–37, where she elaborates on the metaphorical and cultural connection between virgins and sacrificial beasts.

90. Rome (as well as Antony himself) implicates Antony further in this cannibalistic narrative. The hybridization of Antony is already fully evident when Antony first meets the Egyptian Cleopatra and "goes to the feast / And . . . pays his heart, for what his eyes eat only" (2.2.224–26), blurring the distinction between the eater and the eaten. A few scenes later Enobarbus speaks of Cleopatra as Antony's "Egyptian dish" (2.6.123), and later still, an enraged Antony reminds Cleopatra that he "found [her] as a morsel, cold upon / Dead Caesar's trencher" (3.13.116–17). Throughout the West cannibalism has functioned less as a sign of any empirical reality than as a way of signifying, that is, insisting on, racial and cultural difference. As David Kastan, Peter Stallybrass, and Nancy Vickers argue, cannibalism (along with polygamy) was one of the most "crucial points of colonial differentiation as [it was] constructed within the violent hierarchies of sixteenth-century travel narratives." Quoted in Carla Freccero, "Cannibalism, Homophobia, Women," 75. For more on the troping of cannibalism in the early modern period and in other eras as *the* marker between a civilized European West and the barbaric non-European West the reader may consult the following: Bernard W. Sheehan, *Savagism and Civility*, chap. 2; Peter Hulme, *Colonial Encounters*, 80–81; Jordan, *White over Black*, 28; Dorothy Hammond and Alta Jablow, *Myth of Africa*, 94; and Hadfield, *Spenser's Irish Experience*, esp. 66–67, 101–2, and 136–37.

91. See Plutarch's *Noble Lives* in Shakespeare, *Antony and Cleopatra*, in *A New Variorum Edition*, 407.

92. Highley, *Crisis in Ireland*, 142–43. According to Highley, starvation was again proposed in 1599 as one of the cornerstones of England's policy toward Ireland.

93. Spenser goes on to challenge the sympathetic responses the Irish received as a result of England's actions and also offers a defense of Gray, who had been blamed for the atrocities committed in Ireland (163–70 [102–6]).

94. Highley, the only other critic I am aware of who makes any comparison between the Irish famine and Caesar's Modena speech, argues that Caesar praises Antony's resilience. See Highley, *Crisis in Ireland*, for a more developed discussion of Shakespeare and the topos of famine, esp. 139–43.

95. See Clare Kinney, "The Queen's Two Bodies," 183. Also, see Girard on what he calls the "sacrificial crisis"—the need for some kind of ritual marker

of difference, especially between fraternal enemies: "It is not only in myths that brothers are simultaneously drawn together and driven apart by some-thing they both ardently desire and which they will not or cannot share—a throne, a woman or, in more general terms, a paternal heritage." Girard, *Violence and the Sacred*, esp. 61–65. In *Titus Andronicus* the reader may consider both the Gothic brothers, Chiron and Demetrius, who lust after Lavinia, and the Roman brothers, Bassianus and Saturninus, who lust after sovereignty.

Chapter 4

1. Said, *Orientalism*, 70–72 (emphases in text).
2. I wish to call attention to Homi K. Bhabha's argument that "fixity" plays an important role in the "ideological construction" of the Other in colonial discourse. Bhabha, *Location*, 66. And Said writes, Orientalism is performed by anyone who deals "with questions, objects, qualities, and regions deemed Oriental, [and who] will designate, name, point to, *fix* what he [*sic*] is talking or thinking about with a word or phrase, which then is considered either to have acquired, or more simply to be, reality." Said, *Orientalism*, 72. See also Frantz Fanon's comment: "The culture once living and open to the future, becomes closed, fixed in the colonial status, caught in the yolk of oppression. Both present and mummified, it testifies against its members." Quoted in Bhabha, *Location*, 78.
3. Bhabha, *Location*, 66.
4. Stewart, *On Longing*, 26–27.
5. Jack D'Amico, *Moor in English Renaissance*, 160.
6. I have in mind here Chris Tiffin and Alan Lawson, who have written that "colonialism conceptually depopulated countries either by acknowledging the native but relegating him or her to the category of the subhuman, or simply by looking through the native and denying his/her existence. . . . Only empty spaces can be settled, so the space had to be made empty by ignoring or dehumanizing the inhabitants." Tiffin and Lawson, *De-Scribing Empire*, 5.
7. Neill, introduction to *Antony and Cleopatra*, by William Shakespeare, 86.
8. I include the latter line here even though it is Cleopatra and not a Roman who makes this remark. Stephen Booth suggestively reads "amorous" here as an "exercise in syllabic shifting," arguing that it "approaches—but never quite reaches—play on 'blackamoor.'" Booth, "Shakespeare's Language," 14. Such a "shifting" encapsulates Cleopatra's racial character. The race of Shakespeare's Cleopatra has not been the subject of much critical or theatrical debate; indeed, her race has been largely made a nonissue in theatrical and critical circles. I find the silence around this issue very disturbing. I agree here with the always very astute Neill:

For it is a telling paradox of the play's stage history that, despite Shake-speare's clearly envisaging Cleopatra as a North African queen whose skin is either "tawny" or "black," there is no history of black Cleopatras as there has been, since the triumphs of Ira Aldridge in the mid-nineteenth century, a series of striking black Othellos. Instead the same Orientalism which laboured to transform Othello into a pale-skinned Arab of the highest caste has been entirely successful in presenting Cleopatra as an eastern exotic, whose race (when it is allowed to be an issue) is established by appeal to the historical "facts" of her Greek ancestry. Neill, introduction to *Antony and Cleopatra*, by William Shakespeare, 65.

As Neill also argues, casting *Antony and Cleopatra* with an all-black cast (as did the Talawa Theatre Company's 1991 production at the Bloomsbury Theatre in London) does not effectively draw out Rome's very material construction of Egyptian cultural and racial difference. Neill, introduction to *Antony and Cleopatra*, by William Shakespeare, 67. See also Errol Hill, *Shakespeare in Sable*, 7, on the subject of race and the staging of Shakespeare's Cleopatra. Some of the studies I have found most critically transformative and generous for thinking through the semiotics of Cleopatra's racial self are Janet Adelman's "Cleopatra's Blackness" (appendix C) in her *Common Liar*; Ania Loomba's *Gender*, esp. 75–78; and Kim F. Hall's *Things of Darkness*, 153–58, 182–87.

9. In a culturally rich discussion of the play, Loomba argues in a chapter entitled "Theatre and the Space of the Other" that "the issues of imperial expansion, political power and sexual domination are dramatically compressed into spatial and geographical shifts and metaphors." Loomba, *Gender*, 125. I discuss later in this chapter the very intimate relationship in Shakespeare's play between politicking and theatricalizing.

10. Some of the main texts informing and shaping the theoretical ideas especially in this section of this chapter are Christian Hansen, Catherine Needham, and Bill Nichols, "Discourses of Power"; Bhabha, "The Other Question" and "Of Mimicry and Man," both in his *Location*; Said, *Orientalism*; Hulme, *Colonial Encounters*; Tiffin and Lawson's introduction to *De-Scribing Empire*; Mary Louise Pratt, *Imperial Eyes*; and Stewart, *On Longing*.

11. This kind of narrative strategy, one in which one's subject disrupts or corrupts the coherence or stability of one's narrative, is found throughout Spenser's *View*, in which Irenius depicts Ireland as repeatedly diverting his narrative from its true course (see Chapter 3). Women of whatever race, like foreigners of whatever gender, are also prone to being made the object of this kind of narrative ploy. I am thinking especially of one early modern example and one nineteenth-century one. Robert Burton, in *Anatomy of Melancholy* (1621), struggles with his ability to narrate his scientific observation of the hysterical woman: "I will not swerve." Soon thereafter, however, he writes,

"But where am I? Into what subject have I rushed? What have I to do with Nuns, Maids, Virgins, Widows? I am a bachelor myself, and lead a Monastick life in a college. . . . I will check myself; though my subject necessarily require [*sic*] more, I will say no more." Burton, *Anatomy*, 355–56. The other example is from Freud, who in the preface to his *Studies in Hysteria* (1895) argues that any suggestion of prurience in his study is the fault of his subject, the hysterical woman, and not his narrative: "I must console myself with the reflection that the nature of the subject is evidently responsible for this, rather than any preference of my own." Freud, *Standard Edition*, 2:160–61. See also Freud, "Femininity," *Standard Edition*, 22:135; and "Aetiology," *Standard Edition*, 3:189.

12. Hansen, Needham, and Nichols, "Discourses of Power," 223–25. The authors map out "at least four [shared] structural qualities" of pornography and ethnography: (1) the rehearsal of distance but rarely of distantiation; (2) the move toward the containment of excess; (3) comprehending the quality of an image by capturing painstaking details, specificities, and techniques; and (4) dependence on narrative and expository realism to subjugate its subject.

13. Ibid., 210.

14. Norman N. Holland, *Psychoanalysis and Shakespeare*, 140.

15. Horace, "Ode 37." My translation is taken largely from the Loeb edition, *Odes and Epodes*, 98–99. In historical fact Cleopatra mysteriously withdrew from the Battle of Actium with her sixty Egyptian ships before Caesar declared victory. After his victory Caesar burned the remaining enemy's ships.

16. If the Roman way of sacrifice is a highly civilized way to die, providing the proof finally of *civitas*, then sacrificial death by being burned on a funeral pyre—sati or suttee—presumably signals its barbaric opposite. Dorothy M. Figueira observes, "While outraging Western sensibilities and exploiting Western curiosity about the grotesque and barbarian, the sati's existence satisfied European nostalgia for lost innocence. Figueira, "Sati in European Culture," 57. Figueira's essay will prove particularly useful for readers interested in a well-informed broad view of Europe's fascination with sati from the fifteenth through the eighteenth century.

17. Rosalie L. Colie, "The Significance of Style," 57–58.

18. See Lucy Hughes-Hallett, *Cleopatra*, 63.

19. Describing this mesmerizing, river-faring Cleopatra as a siren (which is also a culturally exotic—othered—figure) seems straightforward. And the label "cannibalistic" intends to make coherent several references in Enobarbus's description, especially those references that beg to portray her as almost literally devouring Antony. Cf. "When she first met Mark Antony, she purs'd up his heart upon the river of Cydnus" and "Pays his heart, / For what his eyes eat only" (2.2.186–87, 225–26). Also cf. 2.2.236–38. See my discussion of cannibalism in Chapter 3.

20. Laura Brown, "Amazons and Africans," 124. See also Emily C. Bartels,

who in a brief but perceptive reading of Enobarbus's speech argues, "Yet though his depiction is rich in detail, Cleopatra gets lost amidst it." Bartels, *Spectacles of Strangeness*, 7.

21. Alexander Leggatt, *Shakespeare's Political Drama*, 164. Leggatt also gives attention to the ways Enobarbus's speech seems to belie what we both think is its most mesmerizing subject. Although our readings share some basic insights into Enobarbus's character, where Leggatt sees Enobarbus as a realist, I see him as a more astute and unwavering Roman political maneuverer.

22. Tiffin and Lawson, *De-Scribing Empire*, 5.

23. Richard Hakluyt, *Principall Navigations*, 5:170–71.

24. Quinn, *Elizabethans and the Irish*, 58–59.

25. For some telling comparisons between Enobarbus and Plutarch see Plutarch on the barge scene and the story of the eight wild boars. Shakespeare, *Antony and Cleopatra*, in *A New Variorum Edition*, 412–13, 414. Shakespeare's Caesar should also be noted for his emulation of Plutarch (see my discussion in Chapter 3).

26. Herbert Blau, *Take Up the Bodies*, 289. Blau's "erotic" includes both politics and sex.

27. The always available link between Orientalizing and theatricalizing is emphatically evident throughout Said's *Orientalism*, where, for example, he writes, "The Orient . . . seems to be, not an unlimited extension beyond the familiar European world, but rather a closed field, a theatrical stage affixed to Europe." Said, *Orientalism*, 63. I would like to call attention here too to the Orient as being "a closed field . . . affixed to Europe" in the way that Orientalism confines and fixes the Orient—a point to which I will return. Said also says, "To save an event from oblivion is in the Orientalist's mind the equivalent of turning the Orient into a theater for his representations of the Orient." *Ibid.*, 86. See also 61, 71–72; and Bhabha, *Location*, 88–90. In these instances the theatrical assumes a role beyond the simple metaphorical.

28. See, for examples, Neill's introduction to the Oxford edition of the play.

29. Harrison, "Bodies of the Britons," 193.

30. Although the penis is measurable, the symbolic force of the penis, that is, the phallus, is not. The phallus is, of course, far more than a sexual entity and goes into the deep structures of Shakespeare's and our own phallocentric culture. As Ann Rosalind Jones writes, "'I am the unified, self-controlled center of the universe,' man (white, European and ruling class) has claimed. 'The rest of the world, which I define as the Other, has meaning only in relation to me, as man/father, possessor of the phallus.'" Jones, "Writing and the Body," 87.

31. A. Parker et al., introduction to *Nationalisms and Sexualities*, 1.

32. Richard Knolles, *Generall Historie of the Turkes*, (London: Printed by Adam Islip, 1603). Quoted in Vaughan, *"Othello": A Contextual History*, 24.

33. For a very good discussion of some of the cultural tropes associated with the overflowing Nile, see Adelman, *Common Liar*, 127–28.

34. One way to read Cleopatra's drama involving her slave Seleucus and the jewels and tokens she withholds from Caesar is as her attempt to expose Caesar to the materiality of his Egyptian quest. Caesar, a true competitor for Cleopatra, responds, "And believe / Caesar's no merchant, to make prize with you / Of things that merchants sold" (5.2.181–83). Cf. "Withhold not good from them to whom it is due, when it is in the power of thine hand to do it. . . . Surely he scorneth the scorners: but he giveth *grace* unto the lowly." Proverbs 3:27, 34 (emphasis added).

35. I can't help but think of M. G. Lewis's *The Monk* (1796), in which the sinister Matilda de Villanegas traps the saintly and unswerving Ambrosio by replacing his devotional picture of the Madonna with a portrait of herself dressed as the Madonna. After Ambrosio becomes enraptured with this new painting of the Virgin Mary, Matilda then makes her appearance and moves in for sexual and spiritual conquest.

36. Loomba argues that with her sacrificial death Cleopatra becomes "tamed" and replaces "the deadly Eastern inscrutability with a comprehensible version of the Madonna." Loomba, *Gender*, 129. For a good summary of some of the ways this moment has been read, see Miola, *Shakespeare's Rome*, 155.

37. For discussions of the relationship between Queen Elizabeth I and Shakespeare's Cleopatra, see Helen Morris, "Queen Elizabeth I 'Shadowed' in Cleopatra"; Keith Rinehart, "Shakespeare's Cleopatra and England's Eliza-beth"; Theodora A. Jankowski, "'As I Am Egypt's Queen'"; and Loomba, *Gender*, 76, 128. See also Mihoko Suzuki's study of the play, where she argues near the beginning of her short chapter on *Antony and Cleopatra* that Shake-speare "nostalgically represents Elizabeth . . . through Cleopatra" and then at the end of her chapter that "non-Western and nonwhite, [Cleopatra] is doubly Other as both woman and racially different." Suzuki, *Metamorphoses of Helen*, 259, 262. Suzuki, however, does not pursue a reading to help work through this apparent paradox.

38. Geoffrey Bullough, *Narrative and Dramatic Sources*, 5:216–17.

39. See Hughes-Hallett, *Cleopatra*, 83. For a more extended discussion of some of the cultural and iconographic associations between Isis and the Virgin Mary, see Joscelyn Godwin's *Mystery Religions in the Ancient World*, specifically the chapter "Isis and Serapis," 120–31. Of related interest here in thinking about empire and divinity is her chapter "The Imperial Cult," 56–63. For a rich multigenre study of Cleopatra in antiquity, as well as a few other choice moments, see Mary Hamer, *Signs of Cleopatra*, especially her discussion of Isis and the images of her as a mother nursing her child (11–13); Hamer also refers to the Virgin Mary.

40. James Melville's account is quoted at length in Rinehart, "Shakespeare's Cleopatra," 82–83.

41. Roy Strong, *Gloriana*, 21; also quoted in Erickson, "Representations," 517.

42. Erickson, "Representations," 517.

43. See discussions of these portraits in Erickson, "Representations," 517; and in Strong, *Gloriana*, 80–81, 88–89, 114. For an analysis and picture of the "Rainbow" portrait see Susan Frye, *Elizabeth I*, 102–3, even though she does not talk about color per se.

44. Kinney, "The Queen's Two Bodies," 185.

45. Judith Butler, *Gender Trouble*, 148 (her emphasis).

46. Hughes-Hallett, *Cleopatra*, 116.

47. For a comprehensive summary of Cleopatra as martyr, see Hughes-Hallett, *Cleopatra*, 113–31.

48. V. A. Kolve, "From Cleopatra to Alceste," esp. 130–31; also Hughes-Hallett, *Cleopatra*, 113–15, 121.

49. Kolve, "From Cleopatra to Alceste," 131. Whereas Kolve sees Cleopatra's death as only one of the poem's main subjects, I find her death *the* main subject of the poem.

50. Harold Clarke Goddard, *The Meaning of Shakespeare*, 2:199; and Steele Cammager, "Horace, *Carmina* 1.37," 86, respectively.

51. Lorraine Helms, "'High Roman Fashion,'" 559.

52. D'Amico, *Moor in English Renaissance*, 159.

53. Boose argues persuasively that the black woman threatens white patriarchy because she can give birth to the black children of white fathers: "The black man is representable. But within Europe's symbolic order of dominance and desire, the black woman destroys the system, essentially swallowing it up within the signification of her body." Boose, "Racial Discourse," 47–49. Perhaps I am arguing the other side of the same coin when I argue that dominant forms of signification seem to devour the black woman. Hall has written extensively on the enfolding of gender and race in early modern culture. See Hall, *Things of Darkness*.

54. See Margaret W. Ferguson, "Juggling the Categories of Race, Class, and Gender," 218–20. See also Hall's discussion of Ben Jonson's *Masque of Blackness* in *Things of Darkness*, esp. 133–36.

55. Hall, *Things of Darkness*, 67. Hall observes that "although the proverbial whitewashed Ethiope and the emblems depicting him usually refer to males, the figurative representation of this trope in poetry and drama is almost always gendered female" (66–67).

56. Aphra Behn, *Oroonoko*, 72. Oroonoko's own ambivalent racial identity seems to become decisively black at this point: "But when he found she was dead, and past all retrieve, never more to bless him with her Eyes, and soft

218 Notes to Pages 165–70

Language, his Grief swell'd up to rage; he tore, he raved, he roar'd like some Monster of the Wood, calling on the lov'd Name of Imoinda" (71–72). Oroonoko may be compared to Othello, who is said to become "a blacker devil" (5.2.129) once he kills the white, angelic Desdemona.

57. For a good discussion of racial identity in Behn's *Oroonoko*, see Ferguson, "Juggling the Catagories," 217–19. The phrase "at the least" is mine: I have put it in quotation marks to stress my conscious allusion to racial hierarchies: the three pertinent groups here would be ranked (in descending order) white, Native American, and then black.

58. Dion Boucicault, *The Octoroon*, 5.4.

59. Elizabeth Cary, *The Tragedy of Mariam* (1.2.190, 5.1.238, 5.1.195, 5.1.196, respectively). Barry Weller and Margaret W. Ferguson discuss Cleopatra as Mariam's antitype in their introduction to the play (41–42).

60. For a twentieth-century filmic attempt at a dismissive response to the threat of a white Cleopatra's imminent racial doom—a very loaded text, indeed—see Cecil B. DeMille's *Cleopatra* (1934), where the racial blackness of Egypt figures in a few frames of hard-laboring, seminude black male bodies. The film establishes the indisputability of Cleopatra's whiteness by having an ingenue happen upon a group of wise Roman matrons in a whispered conversation about Antony's ongoing affair in Egypt. They at first show surprise when the innocent young woman says she too has heard about Cleopatra. She betrays her innocence, however, provoking laughter when she answers their inquiry about what it is she knows about Cleopatra: "All kinds of things. Is she black?" For a more indulgent black racialization of a white Cleopatra see Joseph L. Mankiewicz's 1963 film, *Cleopatra*, starring Elizabeth Taylor, in which black bodies busy themselves around her person.

61. For the term *mori pudicam* see Jed, *Chaste Thinking*, 42.

62. Dympna Callaghan, "Re-reading," 171; Callaghan compares Cleopatra's and Mariam's references to themselves as milkmaids. In Cary's *The Tragedy of Mariam*, see 1.1.59–64.

63. Cf. Leonard Tennenhouse, *Power on Display*, 144.

64. See "The Suicide" chapter in Hughes-Hallett, *Cleopatra*, 113–31.

65. Mary D. Garrard, *Artemisia Gentileschi*, 210. Garrard's chapter "Lucretia and Cleopatra" has a commitment to a comparative analysis of Lucrece and Cleopatra and their importance to Gentileschi's artistic vision. Still, the main parts of the chapter offer a general and highly suggestive feminist critique of such self-sacrificing representations in Western art. See Garrard, *Artemisia Gentileschi*, 210–77.

66. Garrard, *Artemisia Gentileschi*, 211 (illustrations 174 and 175).

67. Hughes-Hallett, *Cleopatra*, 152; see also Kolve, "From Cleopatra to Alceste," esp. 151–52.

68. Garrard, *Artemisia Gentileschi*, 210; also 214. Garrard's reading also

echoes Iphigenia's story, her being turned into a scopic object for the Greek men as she submits her body to the sacrificial knife. For some evidence of such male voyeurism in earlier pictorial representations of self-sacrificing women, see Kolve, "From Cleopatra to Alceste," esp. 152.

69. L. T. Fitz's (Linda Woodbridge's) 1977 argument, about sexism and the critical reception of Shakespeare's Cleopatra, still holds more than a modicum of truth. Without challenging her essay, I am arguing that Shakespeare's boy tries to complicate the (hetero)sexism by exploding the negotiated fictions of the master's voyeurism. See Fitz, "Egyptian Queens and Male Reviewers." See also Lisa Jardine, *Still Harping on Daughters*, esp. chap. 1, "Female Roles and Elizabethan Eroticism," 9–36; and Jyotsna Singh, "Renaissance Antitheatricality." For a forthright reading of the male homoeroticism of boys in women's clothing on the early modern stage and in early modern drama, see Stephen Orgel, "Nobody's Perfect."

70. Neill, introduction. Neill also writes that Cleopatra's death "is the most self-consciously *performed*, the most elaborately gestural dying in all Shakespearian tragedy" (77–78 [emphasis in text]).

71. Phyllis Rackin argues what seems to be a more commonly held view, that "the speech threatens for the moment the audience's acceptance of the dramatic illusion." She concludes that "before the boy can evoke Cleopatra's greatness, he must remind us that he cannot truly represent it." Rackin, "Boy Cleopatra," 201, 207.

72. Bhabha, *Location*, 90–91. For a different but certainly related "theater of war," see Laura Levine, *Men in Women's Clothing*.

73. David Bergman, ed., *Camp Grounds*, 6. See also Bruce Rodgers, *Gay Talk*, s.v. *camp*: "*fr* [sic] theatrical 16th century England *camping* = young men wearing the costume of women in a play."

74. George Chauncey, *Gay New York*, 290.

75. Claire Sponsler, "Outlaw Masculinities," 340.

76. Ibid.

77. On the "high seriousness" of camp, see Bergman, *Camp Grounds*, 11. We may compare this camp to Bhabha's notion of mimicry as a threat to authenticity of colonial/imperial theatricalizations. See Bhabha, *Location*, 88–91.

78. Carol-Anne Tyler, "Boys Will Be Girls," 53.

79. Butler, *Gender Trouble*, 146.

80. Leggatt, *Shakespeare's Political Drama*, 183–84.

81. Gordon Williams, *A Dictionary of Sexual Language and Imagery in Shakespearean and Stuart Literature*, 1296–97. Williams has a long list of mid- to late-seventeenth-century examples. As Williams shows, the phrase "to put to the squeak" does carry connotations of sexual violence. Furthermore, it is important to note that several of Williams's examples make explicit or implicit reference not just to modest women but to virgins.

82. Cf. also *posture* and *posture girl* in Williams's *Dictionary of Sexual Language*.

83. See Patricia Parker's extended discussion of the term *preposterous* in *Shakespeare from the Margins*, 22–28.

84. Ibid., 27.

85. Not only here in Cleopatra's use of the word *posture* but throughout Shakespeare's play her character works to engage early modern theater's supporters and detractors, conversing with such detractors as Stephen Gosson, John Rainoldes, William Prynne, and Phillip Stubbes, as well as such defenders as Thomas Heywood, who in his *An Apology for Actors* (1612) would argue that the audience is never seduced by these gendered illusionists. However so, William Prynne (bolstered by Deuteronomy) would refer in *Histrio-Mastix* (1633) to transvestism as "that unnaturall sodimiticall sinne of uncleanesse" (208); and John Rainoldes would argue more forthrightly in *Th'Overthrow of Stage-Playes* (1599) that "a womans garment beeing put on a man doeth vehemently touch and moue him with the remembrance and imagination of a woman; and the imagination of a thing desirable doth stirr up the desire" (97; quoted in Lisa Jardine, "Boy Actors, Female Roles," 57). Rainoldes's pamphlet is heavily invested in critiquing gender, lust, and the misdirection of lust in the playhouses and on the stage. See also J. W. Binns, "Women or Transvestites"; Jonas A. Barish, *The Antitheatrical Prejudice*, 80–131; Michael Shapiro, *Gender in Play*, 37–47; and Levine, *Men in Women's Clothing*.

86. In Latin literature the "*threat* to penetrate another male . . . was used as a sign of superior virility and power," but carrying out that threat would identify one as a pathic homosexual. Richlin, *Priapus*, 221 (my emphasis). Richlin also cites Helen Benedict, "Men Get Raped, Too," *Soho News*, March 16, 1982, 12.

Afterword

1. The titles I use here are from the CNN Web site (<http://cnn.com>): "O. J. Simpson's Belongings on the Auction Block," Feb. 16, 1999 (accessed Feb. 25, 2000), <http://cnn.com/US/9902/16/simpson.auction.01/>; "Going, Going, Gone—Pieces of O. J. Simpson's Life Auctioned Off," Feb. 16, 1999 (accessed Feb. 25, 2000) <http://cnn.com/US/9902/16/simpson.auction.02/>. My use of O. J. Simpson here should not be read as a defense of him. Although Simpson's alleged crime and trial remain culturally fascinating for the way they drove national sentiment and interest, I do not intend by referencing them here to offer an opinion one way or the other about the killing of Nicole Brown Simpson and her friend Ronald Goldman in June 1994. The difference between Simpson's case and the Byrd and Shepard incidents diminishes, however, when we consider that in a very real way and to very real ends our society constructs blackness and gayness as crimes.

Bibliography

Acts of the Privy Council of England. New Series [1542–1628]. Ed. John Roche
   Dasent. 43 vols. London: H. M. Stationery Office, 1890–1949.
Adelman, Janet. *The Common Liar; An Essay on Antony and Cleopatra.* New
   Haven: Yale University Press, 1973.
———. *Suffocating Mothers: Fantasies of Maternal Origin in Shakespeare's Plays,
   "Hamlet" to "The Tempest."* New York: Routledge, 1992.
Aeschylus. *Agamemnon.* In *The Complete Greek Tragedies: Aeschylus I.* Trans.
   Richmond Lattimore. Ed. David Grene and Richmond Lattimore.
   Chicago: University of Chicago Press, 1953.
Africanus, Leo. *A Geographical Historie of Africa.* Trans. John Pory. 1600.
   Reprinted as *The History and Description of Africa and the Noteable
   Things Therein Contained.* Ed. Robert Brown. 3 vols. London: Bedford
   Press, 1896.
Aiken, George L. (1830–76). *Uncle Tom's Cabin: Or, Life Among the Lowly: A
   Domestic Drama in Six Acts.* New York: Samuel French, 1858.
Allen, Theodore W. *The Invention of the White Race.* London: Verso, 1994.
Althusser, Louis. "Ideology and Ideological State Apparatuses." In *Lenin and
   Philosophy and Other Essays,* trans. Ben Brewster. New York: Monthly
   Review Press, 1971.
Altman, Joel. "'Preposterous Conclusions': Eros, *Enargeia,* and the Composi-
   tions of *Othello.*" *Representations* 18 (1987): 129–57.
Andrews, Kenneth R. *Trade, Plunder, and Settlement: Maritime Enterprise and the
   Genesis of the British Empire, 1480–1630.* Cambridge: Cambridge
   University Press, 1984.
Atkins, John. *A Voyage to Guinea, Brasil and the West Indies.* London: C. Ward
   and R. Chandler, 1735.
Bal, Mieke. *Death and Dissymmetry: The Politics of Coherence in the Book of Judges.*
   Chicago: University of Chicago Press, 1988.
———. *Reading "Rembrandt": Beyond the Word-Image Opposition.* Northrop Frye
   Lectures in Literary Theory. Cambridge: Cambridge University Press,
   1991.

Baldwin, James. "Autobiographical Notes." In *James Baldwin: Collected Essays*,
    ed. Toni Morrison, 5–9. New York: Library of America, 1998.
Barish, Jonas A. *The Antitheatrical Prejudice*. Berkeley: University of California
    Press, 1981.
Barker, Simon. "Re-Loading the Canon: Shakespeare and the Study Guides."
    In *Shakespeare and National Culture*, ed. John J. Joughin, 42–57.
    Manchester: Manchester University Press, 1997.
Bartels, Emily. "Making More of the Moor: Aaron, Othello, and Renaissance
    Refashionings of Race." *Shakespeare Quarterly* 41 (1990): 433–54.
———. *Spectacles of Strangeness: Imperialism, Alienation, and Marlowe.*
    Philadelphia: University of Pennsylvania Press, 1993.
Barthelemy, Anthony. *Black Face, Maligned Race: The Representation of Blacks in
    English Drama from Shakespeare to Southerne*. Baton Rouge: Louisiana
    State University Press, 1987.
Barthes, Roland. *The Pleasure of the Text*. Trans. Richard Miller. New York: Hill
    and Wang, 1975.
Bartlett, Robert. *Gerald of Wales, 1146–1223*. Oxford: Clarendon Press, 1982.
Bataille, Georges. *Erotism: Death and Sensuality*. Trans. Mary Dalwood. 1962.
    Repr., San Francisco: City Lights Books, 1986.
Bate, W. Jackson. "The Crisis in English Studies." *Journal of Scholarly Publishing*
    14 (1983): 195–212.
Battenhouse, Roy W. *Shakespearean Tragedy, Its Art and Its Christian Premises*.
    Bloomington: Indiana University Press, 1969.
Beaumont, Francis, and John Fletcher. *The Works of Francis Beaumont and John
    Fletcher*. Cambridge English Classics, vols. 3 and 4, ed. A. R. Waller.
    Cambridge: Cambridge University Press, 1906.
Begley, Sharon, with Farai Chideya and Larry Wilson. "Out of Egypt: Seeking
    the Roots of Western Civilization on the Banks of the Nile."
    Newsweek, September 23, 1991, 49–50.
Behn, Aphra. *Oroonoko, or the Royal Slave*. New York: Norton, 1973.
Belsey, Catherine. *The Subject of Tragedy: Identity and Difference in Renaissance
    Drama*. London: Methuen, 1985.
Benedict, Helen. "Men Get Raped, Too." *Soho News*, March 16, 1982, 12.
Berger, John. *Ways of Seeing*. London: British Broadcasting Corporation, 1972.
    Repr., New York: Penguin, 1977.
Bergman, David, ed. *Camp Grounds: Style and Homosexuality*. Amherst: Univer-
    sity of Massachusetts Press, 1993.
Bernheimer, Charles, and Claire Kahane, eds. *In Dora's Case: Freud—Hysteria—
    Feminism*. New York: Columbia University Press, 1985.
Bhabha, Homi K. *The Location of Culture*. London: Routledge, 1994.
Binns, J. W. "Women or Transvestites on the Elizabethan Stage? An Oxford
    Controversy." *Sixteenth-Century Journal* 5 (1974): 95–120.

Blau, Herbert. *Take Up the Bodies: Theater at the Vanishing Point*. Urbana: University of Illinois Press, 1982.

Bloom, Harold. *Shakespeare: The Invention of the Human*. New York: Riverhead Books, 1998.

Bodin, Jean. *Method for the Easy Comprehension of History*. Trans. Beatrice Reynolds. New York: Columbia University Press, 1945.

Boone, Joseph A. "Vacation Cruises; or, The Homoerotics of Orientalism." *PMLA* 110 (1995): 89–107.

Boose, Lynda E. " 'The Getting of a Lawful Race': Racial Discourse in Early Modern England and the Unrepresentable Black Woman." In *Women, "Race," and Writing in the Early Modern Period*, ed. Margo Hendricks and Patricia Parker, 35–54. London: Routledge, 1994.

———. " 'Let it be hid': Renaissance Pornography, Iago, and Audience Response." In *Autour d'Othello*, ed. Richard Marienstras and Dominique Goy-Blanquet, 135–43. Amiens: Presses de l'UFR CLERC: Université Picardie, 1987.

———. "Othello's Handkerchief: 'The Recognizance and Pledge of Love.' " *English Literary Renaissance* 5 (1975): 360–74.

Booth, Stephen. "Shakespeare's Language and the Language of Shakespeare's Time." *Shakespeare Survey* 50 (1997): 1–17.

Boswell, John. *Christianity, Social Tolerance, and Homosexuality: Gay People in Western Europe from the Beginning of the Christian Era to the Fourteenth Century*. Chicago: University of Chicago Press, 1980.

Boucicault, Dion. *The Octoroon; or, Life in Louisiana*. 1861. Repr., Salem, N.H.: Ayer, 1987.

Bowers, A. Robin. "Emblem and Rape in Shakespeare's *Lucrece* and *Titus Andronicus*." *Studies in Iconography* 10 (1984–86): 79–96.

Bray, Alan. *Homosexuality in Renaissance England*. London: Gay Men's Press, 1982.

Bristol, Michael D. *Big-Time Shakespeare*. London: Routledge, 1996.

Brome, Richard. *The English Moore, or, The Mock-Marriage*. Ed. Sara Jayne Steen. Columbia: University of Missouri Press, 1983.

Brooks, Peter. "Freud's Masterplot." In *Literature and Psychoanalysis: The Question of Reading: Otherwise*, ed. Shoshana Felman, 280–300. Baltimore: Johns Hopkins University Press, 1987.

Brown, Laura. "Amazons and Africans: Gender, Race, and Empire in Daniel Defoe." In *Women, "Race," and Writing in the Early Modern Period*, ed. Margo Hendricks and Patricia Parker, 118–37. New York: Routledge, 1994.

Browne, Sir Thomas. *The Works of Sir Thomas Browne*. Vol. 2. Ed. Charles Sayle. Edinburgh: John Grant, 1927.

Bullough, Geoffrey. *Narrative and Dramatic Sources of Shakespeare*. Vol. 5. London: Routledge and Paul, 1957.

Bulwer, John. *Anthropometamorphosis: Man Transform'd: or, The Artificiall Changeling Historically Presented* . . . London: William Hunt, 1653.
Burkert, Walter. *Homo Necans: The Anthropology of Ancient Greek Sacrificial Ritual and Myth.* Trans. Peter Bing. Berkeley: University of California Press, 1983.
Burnett, Mark Thornton, and Ramona Wray, eds. *Shakespeare and Ireland: History, Politics, Culture.* London: Macmillan, 1997.
Burton, Robert. *The Anatomy of Melancholy.* Ed. Floyd Dell and Paul Jordan-Smith. New York: Farrar and Rinehart Inc., 1927.
Busch, Charles. *Vampire Lesbians of Sodom.* New York: Samuel French, 1985.
Butler, Judith P. *Bodies That Matter: On the Discursive Limits of "Sex".* New York: Routledge, 1993.
——. *Excitable Speech: A Politics of the Performative.* New York: Routledge, 1997.
——. *Gender Trouble: Feminism and the Subversion of Identity.* New York: Routledge, 1990.
Calderwood, James L. *Shakespearean Metadrama: The Argument of the Play in "Titus Andronicus," "Love's Labour's Lost," "Romeo and Juliet," "A Midsummer Night's Dream," and "Richard II."* Minneapolis: University of Minnesota Press, 1971.
Callaghan, Dympna. "Re-reading Elizabeth Cary's *The Tragedie of Mariam, Faire Queen of Jewry."* In *Women, "Race," and Writing in the Early Modern Period,* ed. Margo Hendricks and Patricia Parker, 163–77. New York: Routledge, 1994.
——. *Women and Gender in Renaissance Tragedy: A Study of "King Lear," "Othello," "The Duchess of Malfi," and "The White Devil."* Atlantic Highlands, N.J.: Humanities Press International, 1989.
Camden, William. *Britannia sive florentissimorum regnorum, Angliae, Scotia, Hiberniae* . . . *chorographica descriptio.* London, 1594 [1586].
——. *Britain, or a chorographicall description of the flourishing Kingdomes, England, Scotland, and Ireland.* Trans. Philemon Holland. London, 1610.
Camille, Michael. *The Gothic Idol: Ideology and Image-Making in Medieval Art.* New York: Cambridge University Press, 1989.
Cary, Elizabeth. *The Tragedy of Mariam, the Fair Queen of Jewry.* Ed. Barry Weller and Margaret Ferguson. Berkeley: University of California Press, 1994.
Cavell, Stanley. "Epistemology and Tragedy: A Reading of *Othello.*" In *William Shakespeare's "Othello."* Modern Critical Interpretations, ed. Harold Bloom, 7–21. New York: Chelsea House, 1987.
Charney, Maurice. *Shakespeare's Roman Plays: The Function of Imagery in the Drama.* Cambridge: Harvard University Press, 1961.
Chaucer, Geoffrey. *The Riverside Chaucer.* Boston: Houghton Mifflin, 1987.

Chauncey, George. *Gay New York: Gender, Urban Culture, and the Makings of the Gay Male World, 1890–1940.* New York: Basic Books, 1994.
Chew, Samuel. *The Crescent and the Rose: Islam and England During the Renaissance.* 1937. Repr., New York: Octagon Books, 1974.
Cicero. *Philippics.* Trans. Walter C. A. Ker. The Loeb Classical Library. 1926. Repr., Cambridge: Harvard University Press, 1995.
Clifford, James. "On Ethnographic Allegory." In *Writing Culture: The Poetics and Politics of Ethnography,* ed. James Clifford and George E. Marcus, 98–121. Berkeley: University of California Press, 1986.
———. *The Predicament of Culture: Twentieth-Century Ethnography, Literature, and Art.* Cambridge: Harvard University Press, 1988.
Clum, John M. *Acting Gay: Male Homosexuality in Modern Drama.* New York: Columbia University Press, 1992.
Colie, Rosalie L. "The Significance of Style." In *William Shakespeare's "Antony and Cleopatra."* Modern Critical Interpretations, ed. Harold Bloom, 57–85. New York: Chelsea House, 1988.
Commager, Steele. "Horace, *Carmina* 1.37." *Cleopatra.* Major Literary Characters, ed. Harold Bloom, 83–90. 1958. Repr., New York: Chelsea House, 1990.
Coughlan, Patricia, ed. *Spenser and Ireland: An Interdisciplinary Perspective.* University College, Cork: Cork University Press, 1989.
Cowhig, Ruth. "Blacks in English Renaissance Drama and the Role of Shakespeare's Othello." *The Black Presence in English Literature,* ed. David Dabydeen. Manchester: Manchester University Press, 1985.
Crooke, Helkiah. *A Description of the Body of Man. Together with the Controversie and Figures Thereto Belonging.* London: R. C. and John Clarke, 1651.
Crowne, John. *The Dramatic Works of John Crowne.* Ed. James Maidment and W. H. Logan. (1864). Repr., New York: Benjamin Blom, 1967.
Cunningham, Karen. "'Scars Can Witness': Trials by Ordeal and Lavinia's Body in *Titus Andronicus.*" In *Women and Violence in Literature: An Essay Collection,* ed. Katherine Anne Ackley, 139–62. New York: Garland, 1990.
D'Amico, Jack. *The Moor in English Renaissance Drama.* Tampa: University of South Florida Press, 1991.
Dekker, Thomas. *Lust's Dominion; or, The Lascivious Queen.* Vol. 4 of *The Dramatic Works of Thomas Dekker,* ed. Fredson Bowers, 115–230. Cambridge: Cambridge University Press, 1961.
Derrida, Jacques. "Living On/Border Lines." In *Deconstruction and Criticism,* ed. Harold Bloom et al., 75–176. New York: Seabury Press, 1979.
———. "Racism's Last Word." *Critical Inquiry* 12 (1985): 290–99.
Diehl, Huston. *Staging Reform, Reforming the Stage: Protestantism and Popular Theater in Early Modern England.* Ithaca, N.Y.: Cornell University Press, 1997.

Dollimore, Jonathan. *Radical Tragedy: Religion, Ideology, and Power in the Drama of Shakespeare and his Contemporaries*. Brighton, Sussex: Harvester Press, 1984.

———. *Sexual Dissidence: Augustine to Wilde, Freud to Foucault*. Oxford: Clarendon Press, 1991.

Donaldson, Ian. *The Rapes of Lucretia: A Myth and Its Transformations*. Oxford: Clarendon Press, 1982.

Doty, Alexander. *Making Things Perfectly Queer: Interpreting Mass Culture*. Minneapolis: University of Minnesota Press, 1993.

Douglas, Mary. *Purity and Danger: An Analysis of the Concepts of Pollution and Taboo*. London: Ark, 1995 [1966].

Dyer, Richard. *White*. New York: Routledge, 1997.

Eagleton, Terry. *Literary Theory: An Introduction*. Minneapolis: University of Minnesota Press, 1983.

Erickson, Peter. "Representations of Blacks and Blackness in the Renaissance." *Criticism* 35 (1993): 499–527.

Euripides. *Iphigenia in Aulis*. Vol. 4 of *Euripides*, ed. David Grene and Richmond Lattimore. Chicago: University of Chicago Press, 1958.

Ferguson, Margaret W. "Juggling the Categories of Race, Class, and Gender: Aphra Behn's *Oroonoko*." In *Women, "Race," and Writing in the Early Modern Period*, ed. Margo Hendricks and Patricia Parker, 209–24. New York: Routledge, 1994.

Fiedler, Leslie A. *The Stranger in Shakespeare*. New York: Stein and Day, 1972.

Figueira, Dorothy M. "Die Flambierte Frau: Sati in European Culture." In *Sati, the Blessing and the Curse: The Burning of Wives in India*, ed. John Stratton Hawley, 55–78. New York: Oxford University Press, 1994.

Fitz, L. T. (Linda Woodbridge). "Egyptian Queens and Male Reviewers: Sexist Attitudes in *Antony and Cleopatra* Criticism." *Shakespeare Quarterly* 28 (1977): 297–316.

Fogarty, Anne. "The Colonization of Language: Narrative Strategies in *A View of the Present State of Ireland* and *The Faerie Queene*, Book VI." In *Spenser and Ireland: An Interdisciplinary Perspective*, ed. Patricia Coughlan, 75–108. University College, Cork: Cork University Press, 1989.

Foucault, Michel. *Discipline and Punish: The Birth of the Prison*. Trans. Alan Sheridan. New York: Vintage Books, 1979.

———. *History of Sexuality: Volume 1: An Introduction*. Trans. Robert Hurley. New York: Vintage Books, 1980.

Fraser, Russell A., and Norman Rabkin, eds. *Drama of the English Renaissance*. 2 vols. New York: Macmillan, 1976.

Freccero, Carla. "Cannibalism, Homophobia, Women: Montaigne's 'Des Cannibales' and 'De l'amitié.'" In *Women, "Race," and Writing in the*

Early Modern Period, ed. Margo Hendricks and Patricia Parker, 73–83. London: Routledge, 1994.

Freud, Sigmund. *The Standard Edition of the Complete Psychological Works of Sigmund Freud*. 24 vols. Ed. James Strachey et al. London: Hogarth Press and the Institute of Psychoanalysis, 1953–74.

Frye, Susan. *Elizabeth I: The Competition for Representation*. New York: Oxford University Press, 1993.

Fryer, Peter. *Staying Power: The History of Black People in Britain*. London: Pluto Press, 1984.

Gallagher, Lowell. *Medusa's Gaze: Casuistry and Conscience in the Renaissance*. Stanford: Stanford University Press, 1991.

Garber, Marjorie. *Shakespeare's Ghost Writers: Literature as Uncanny Causality*. New York: Methuen, 1987.

Garrard, Mary D. *Artemisia Gentileschi: The Image of the Female Hero in Italian Baroque Art*. Princeton, N.J.: Princeton University Press, 1989.

The Geneva Bible: A Facsimile of the 1560 Edition. Intro. Lloyd E. Berry. Madison: University of Wisconsin Press, 1969.

Gerald of Wales. *History and Topography of Ireland*. Ed. J. O'Meara. 1951. Repr., New York: Penguin, 1982.

Gilbert, Sandra M., and Susan Gubar. "The Queen's Looking Glass: Female Creativity, Male Images of Women, and the Metaphor of Literary Paternity." In *The Madwoman in the Attic: The Woman Writer and the Nineteenth-Century Literary Imagination*. New Haven: Yale University Press, 1984.

Gilman, Sander L. *Difference and Pathology: Stereotypes of Sexuality, Race, and Madness*. Ithaca, N.Y.: Cornell University Press, 1985.

Girard, René. *Violence and the Sacred*. Trans. Patrick Gregory. Baltimore: Johns Hopkins University Press, 1977.

Goddard, Harold Clarke. *The Meaning of Shakespeare*. Vol. 2. Chicago: University of Chicago Press, 1951.

Godwin, Joscelyn. *Mystery Religions in the Ancient World*. San Francisco: Harper and Row, 1981.

Goffen, Rona. *Piety and Patronage in Renaissance Venice: Bellini, Titian, and the Franciscans*. New Haven: Yale University Press, 1986.

Goldberg, Jonathan, ed. and intro. *Queering the Renaissance*. Durham: Duke University Press, 1994.

Goodwin, Sarah Webster, and Elisabeth Bronfen. *Death and Representation*. Baltimore: Johns Hopkins University Press, 1993.

Gossett, Suzanne. "'Best Men Are Molded Out of Faults': Marrying the Rapist in Jacobean Drama." *English Literary Renaissance* 14 (1984): 305–27.

Goux, Jean-Joseph. "Vesta, or the Place of Being." *Representations* 1 (1983): 91–107.

Grady, Hugh. *The Modernist Shakespeare*. Oxford: Clarendon Press, 1991.

Greenblatt, Stephen. *Learning to Curse: Essays in Early Modern Culture*. New York: Routledge, 1990.

——— *Renaissance Self-Fashioning: From More to Shakespeare*. Chicago: University of Chicago Press, 1980.

Greene, James J. "Antony and Cleopatra: The Birth and Death of Androgyny." *University of Hartford Studies in Literature: A Journal of Interdisciplinary Criticism* 19 (1987): 24–44.

Griffin, Susan. *Pornography and Silence: Culture's Revenge Against Nature*. New York: Harper and Row, 1981.

Gubar, Susan. "'The Blank Page' and the Issues of Female Creativity." In *Writing and Sexual Difference*, ed. Elizabeth Abel. Chicago: University of Chicago Press, 1982.

Gwllory, John. *Cultural Capital: The Problem of Literary Canon Formation*. Chicago: University of Chicago Press, 1993.

Hadfield, Andrew. "'Hitherto She Ne're Could Fancy Him': Shakespeare's 'British' Plays and the Exclusion of Ireland." In *Shakespeare and Ireland: History, Politics, Culture*, ed. Mark Thornton Burnett and Ramona Wray, 47–67. London: Macmillan, 1997.

———. *Spenser's Irish Experience: "Wilde Fruit and Savage Soyl."* Oxford: Clarendon Press, 1997.

Hakluyt, Richard. *Hakluyt's Voyages; The Principall Navigations, Voyages, Traffiques and Discoveries of the English Nation Made by Sea or Over-land to the Remote and Farthest Distant Quarters of the Earth at Any Time Within the Compass of the 1600 Yeeres*. 8 vols. 1907. Repr., London: J. M. Dent and Sons, 1927.

Hall, Kim F. "Culinary Spaces; Colonial Spaces: The Gendering of Sugar in the Seventeenth Century." In *Feminist Readings of Early Modern Culture: Emerging Subjects*, ed. Valerie Traub, M. Lindsay Kaplan, and Dympna Callaghan, 168–90. Cambridge: Cambridge University Press, 1996.

———. *Things of Darkness: Economies of Race and Gender in Early Modern England*. Ithaca, N.Y.: Cornell University Press, 1995.

Halpern, Richard. *The Poetics of Primitive Accumulation: English Renaissance Culture and the Genealogy of Capital*. Ithaca, N.Y.: Cornell University Press, 1991.

Hamer, Mary. *Signs of Cleopatra: History, Politics, Representation*. London: Routledge, 1993.

Hamilton, Albert Charles. *The Structure of Allegory in "The Faerie Queen."* Oxford: Clarendon Press, 1961.

Hammond, Dorothy, and Alta Jablow. *The Myth of Africa*. New York: Library of Social Science, 1977.

Hansen, Christian, Catherine Needham, and Bill Nichols. "Pornography,
    Ethnography, and the Discourses of Power." In *Representing Reality:*
    Issues and Concepts in Documentary, by Bill Nichols, 201–28.
    Bloomington: Indiana University Press, 1991.
Hanson, Ellis. "Sodomy and Kingcraft in *Urania* and *Antony and Cleopatra*." In
    Homosexuality in Renaissance and Enlightenment England: Literary
    Representations in Historical Context. New York: Harrington Park, 1992.
Harley, J. B. "Meaning and Ambiguity in Tudor Cartography." In *English Map-*
    Making, 1400–1650, ed. Sara Tyacke, 22–45. London: British Library,
    1983.
Harrington, James. *"The Commonwealth of Oceana" and "A System of Politics."*
    Ed. J. G. A. Pocock. Cambridge: Cambridge University Press, 1992.
Harvey, William. *The Works of William Harvey*. The Sources of Science, no. 13.
    Trans. Robert Willis. New York: Johnson Reprint Corporation, 1965.
Helms, Lorraine. "'The High Roman Fashion': Sacrifice, Suicide, and the
    Shakespearean Stage." *PMLA* 107 (1992): 554–65.
Heminge, William. *The Fatal Contract*. *Medieval and Renaissance Texts*. Vol. 1, ed.
    Anne Hargrove. Medieval Institute Publications. Kalamazoo, Mich.:
    Western Michigan University, 1978.
Hendricks, Margo, and Patricia Parker, eds. *Women, "Race," and Writing in the*
    Early Modern Period. London: Routledge, 1994.
Highley, Christopher. *Shakespeare, Spenser, and the Crisis in Ireland*. Cambridge:
    Cambridge University Press, 1997.
Hill, Errol. *Shakespeare in Sable: A History of Black Shakespearean Actors*. Amherst:
    University of Massachusetts Press, 1984.
Hoff, Joan. "Why Is There No History of Pornography?" In *For Adult Users*
    Only: The Dilemma of Violent Pornography, ed. Susan Gubar and Joan
    Hoff, 17–46. Bloomington: Indiana University Press, 1989.
Holinshed, Raphael, William Harrison, et al. *Chronicles of England, Scotland, and*
    Ireland. Vol. 1. London: Richard Taylor and Co., 1807.
Holland, Norman N. *Psychoanalysis and Shakespeare*. New York: McGraw-Hill,
    1966.
Horace. The *Odes and Epodes*. Trans. C. E. Bennett. The Loeb Classical
    Library. Cambridge: Harvard University Press, 1952.
Horkheimer, Max, and Theodor W. Adorno. *Dialectic of Enlightenment*. Trans.
    John Cumming. 1972. Repr., New York: Continuum, 1991.
Hughes, Paul L., and James F. Larkin. *Tudor Royal Proclamations*. 3 vols. New
    Haven: Yale University Press, 1969.
Hughes-Hallett, Lucy. *Cleopatra: Histories, Dreams, and Distortions*. New York:
    HarperPerrenial, 1990.
Hulme, Peter. *Colonial Encounters: Europe and the Native Caribbean, 1492–1797*.
    London: Methuen, 1986.

Hume, Martin. *The Courtships of Queen Elizabeth: A History of the Various Negotiations for Her Marriage.* New York: Brentano's Publishers, 1926.

Hunter, G. K. *Dramatic Identities and Cultural Tradition: Studies in Shakespeare and His Contemporaries.* Liverpool: Liverpool University Press, 1978.

Jacobus, Mary. *Reading Woman: Essays in Feminist Criticism.* New York: Columbia University Press, 1986.

James I. *Basilicon Doron. The Political Works of James I.* Harvard Political Classics, ed. Charles Howard Mellwain, 3–52. Cambridge: Harvard University Press, 1918.

Jankowski, Theodora A. "'As I Am Egypt's Queen': Cleopatra, Elizabeth I, and the Female Body Politic." *Assays: Critical Approaches to Medieval and Renaissance Texts* 5 (1989): 91–110.

Jardine, Lisa. "Boy Actors, Female Roles, and Elizabethan Eroticism." In *Staging the Renaissance: Reinterpretations of Elizabethan and Jacobean Drama,* ed. David Scott Kastan and Peter Stallybrass, 57–67. New York: Routledge, 1991.

———. *Still Harping on Daughters: Women and Drama in the Age of Shakespeare.* Sussex: Harvester Press, 1983.

Jay, Nancy. *Throughout Your Generations Forever: Sacrifice, Religion, and Paternity.* Chicago: University of Chicago Press, 1992.

Jed, Stephanie H. *Chaste Thinking: The Rape of Lucretia and the Birth of Humanism.* Bloomington: Indiana University Press, 1989.

Jobson, Richard. *"The Golden Trade; or, A Discovery of the River Gambra" and "The Golden Trade of the Aethiopians" Set Down as They Were Collected in Travelling Part of the Yeares, 1620 and 1621.* London: Penguin, 1932.

Johnson, Rosalind. "African Presence in Shakespearean Drama: Parallels Between Othello and the Historical Leo Africanus." *Journal of African Civilization* 7 (1985): 276–87.

Jones, Ann Rosalind. "Italians and Others." *Renaissance Drama* (1987): 101–19.

———. "Writing and the Body." In *Feminist Criticism and Social Change: Sex, Class, and Race in Literature and Culture,* ed. Judith Newton and Deborah Rosenfelt, 86–104. New York: Methuen, 1985.

Jones, Ann Rosalind, and Peter Stallybrass. "Dismantling Irena: The Sexualizing of Ireland in Early Modern England." In *Nationalisms and Sexualities,* ed. Andrew Parker et al., 157–74. New York: Routledge, 1992.

Jones, Eldred D. *The Elizabethan Image of Africa.* Charlottesville: University Press of Virginia, 1971.

———. *Othello's Countrymen: The African Presence in English Renaissance Drama.* London: Oxford University Press, 1965.

Jonson, Ben. *Ben Jonson: The Complete Masques.* Ed. Stephen Orgel. New Haven: Yale University Press, 1969.

Joplin, Patricia Klindienst. "Ritual Work on Human Flesh: Livy's Lucretia and the Rape of the Body Politic." *Helios* 17 (1990): 51–70.

Jordan, Winthrop D. *White over Black: American Attitudes Toward the Negro, 1550–1812.* Chapel Hill: University of North Carolina Press, 1968.

Joshel, Sandra R. "The Body Female and the Body Politic: Livy's Lucretia and Verginia." In *Pornography and Representation in Greece and Rome,* ed. Amy Richlin, 112–30. New York: Oxford University Press, 1992.

Kahn, Coppélia. "*Lucrece:* The Sexual Politics of Subjectivity." In *Rape and Representation,* ed. Lynn A. Higgins and Brenda R. Silver, 141–59. New York: Columbia University Press, 1991.

———. *Roman Shakespeare: Warriors, Wounds, and Women.* New York: Routledge, 1997.

Kantorowicz, Ernst H. *The King's Two Bodies: A Study in Mediaeval Theology.* Princeton, N.J.: Princeton University Press, 1957.

Kaplan, Paul H. D. "The Earliest Images of Othello." *Shakespeare Quarterly* 39 (1988): 171–86.

Kastan, David Scott, and Peter Stallybrass. Introduction to *Staging the Renaissance: Reinterpretations of Elizabethan and Jacobean Drama,* ed. David Scott Kastan and Peter Stallybrass, 1–14. New York: Routledge, 1991.

Kendall, Gillian Murray. "'Lend Me Thy Hand': Metaphor and Mayhem in *Titus Andronicus.*" *Shakespeare Quarterly* 40 (1989): 299–316.

Kendrick, Walter M. *The Secret Museum: The History of Pornography in Literature.* New York: Viking, 1987.

Keuls, Eva C. *The Reign of the Phallus: Sexual Politics in Ancient Athens.* New York: Harper and Row, 1985.

King, Helen. "Bound to Bleed: Artemis and Greek Women." In *Images of Women in Antiquity,* ed. Averil Cameron and Amélie Kuhrt, 109–27. London: Croom Helm, 1983.

———. "Sacrificial Blood: The Role of the *Amnion* in Ancient Gynecology." *Helios,* n.s., 13 (1987): 117–26. (Special Issue: *Rescuing Creusa: New Methodological Approaches to Women in Antiquity,* ed. Marilyn Skinner.)

Kinney, Clare. "The Queen's Two Bodies and the Divided Emperor: Some Problems of Identity in *Antony and Cleopatra.*" In *The Renaissance Englishwoman in Print: Counterbalancing the Canon,* ed. Anne M. Haselkorn and Betty S. Travitsky, 177–86. Amherst: University of Massachusetts Press, 1990.

Knolles, Richard. *The Generall Historie of the Turkes.* London: Adam Islip, 1603.

Kolve, V. A. "From Cleopatra to Alceste: An Iconographic Study of *The Legend of Good Women.*" In *Signs and Symbols in Chaucer's Poetry,* ed. John P. Hermann and John J. Burke Jr., 130–78. University, Ala.: University of Alabama Press, 1981.

Kristeva, Julia. *Powers of Horror: An Essay on Abjection*. Trans. Leon S. Roudiez. New York: Columbia University Press, 1982.

Kyd, Thomas. *The Spanish Tragedy. The Revels Plays*. Ed. Philip Edwards. London: Methuen, 1959.

Lederer, Wolfgang. *Fear of Women*. New York: Grune and Stratton, 1968.

Leggatt, Alexander. *Shakespeare's Political Drama: The History Plays and the Roman Plays*. London: Routledge, 1988.

Levine, Laura. *Men in Women's Clothing: Anti-theatricality and Effeminization, 1579–1642*. Cambridge: Cambridge University Press, 1994.

Levith, Murray J. *Shakespeare's Italian Settings and Plays*. Basingstoke: Macmillan, 1989.

Lim, Walter S. H. *The Arts of Empire: The Poetics of Colonialism from Ralegh to Milton*. Newark: University of Delaware Press, 1998.

Little, Arthur L., Jr. "Absolute Bodies, Absolute Laws: Staging Punishment in *Measure for Measure*." In *Shakespearean Power and Punishment*, ed. Gillian Murray Kendall, 113–29. Madison, N.J.: Fairleigh Dickinson University Press, 1998.

———. "'An Essence That's Not Seen': The Primal Scene of Racism in *Othello*." *Shakespeare Quarterly* 44 (1993): 304–24.

———. "'Transshaped' Women: Virginity and Hysteria in *The Changeling*." In *Madness in Drama*, ed. James Redmond, 19–42. Cambridge: Cambridge University Press, 1993.

Livy. *The Early History of Rome: Books I-V of "The History of Rome from Its Foundation."* Trans. Aubrey de Sélincourt. 1960. Repr., London: Penguin, 1971.

———. *Livy*. Vol. 1. Trans. B. O. Foster. The Loeb Classical Library. Cambridge: Harvard University Press, 1952.

Loomba, Ania. *Gender, Race, Renaissance Drama*. New York: St. Martin's, 1989.

Loraux, Nicole. "Le corps etrangle." In *Le chatiment dans la cite*, ed. Y. Thomas, 195–218. Rome: Ecole Francaise de Rome, 1984.

———. *Tragic Ways of Killing a Woman*. Trans. Anthony Forster. Cambridge: Harvard University Press, 1987.

Lott, Eric. "White Like Me: Racial Cross-Dressing and the Construction of American Whiteness." In *Cultures of United States Imperialism*, ed. Amy Kaplan and Donald Pease, 474–95. Durham: Duke University Press, 1993.

Lukacher, Ned. *Primal Scenes: Literature, Philosophy, Psychoanalysis*. Ithaca, N.Y.: Cornell University Press, 1986.

Magnus, Pseudo-Albertus. *Women's Secrets: A Translation of Pseudo-Albertus Magnus's "De Secretis Mulierum" with Commentaries*. Ed. Helen Rodnite Lemay. Albany: State University of New York Press, 1992.

Maloof, Judy. *Over Her Dead Body: The Construction of Male Subjectivity in Onetti.* New York: P. Lang, 1995.

Marcus, Leah. "The Earl of Bridgewater's Legal Life: Notes Toward a Political Reading of *Comus.*" *Milton Quarterly* 21 (1987): 13–23.

———. "The Milieu of Milton's *Comus*: Judicial Reform at Ludlow and the Problem of Sexual Assaults." *Criticism* 25 (1983): 293–327.

Marrapodi, Michele, A. J. Hoenselaars, Marcello Cappuzzo, and L. Falzon Stantucci, eds. *Shakespeare's Italy: Functions of Italian Locations in Renaissance Drama.* Manchester: Manchester University Press, 1993.

Marsh, Terri. "Epilogue: The (Other) Maiden's Tale." In *Pornography and Representation in Greece and Rome,* ed. Amy Richlin, 269–84. New York: Oxford University Press, 1992.

McEachern, Claire. "*Henry V* and the Paradox of the Body Politic." *Shakespeare Quarterly* 45 (1994): 33–56.

McPherson, David C. *Shakespeare, Jonson, and the Myth of Venice.* Newark: University of Delaware Press, 1990.

Metzger, Lore. Introduction to *Oroonoko, or the Royal Slave,* by Aphra Behn. New York: Norton, 1973.

Middleton, Thomas. *The Ghost of Lucrece.* Ed. Joseph Quincy Adams. New York: Charles Scribner's Sons, 1937.

Miola, Robert S. *Shakespeare's Rome.* Cambridge: Cambridge University Press, 1983.

Montrose, Louis Adrian. "The Elizabethan Subject and the Spenserian Text." In *Literary Theory/Renaissance Texts,* ed. Patricia Parker and David Quint, 303–40. Baltimore: Johns Hopkins University Press, 1986.

——— "*A Midsummer Night's Dream* and the Shaping Fantasies of Elizabethan Culture: Gender, Power, Form." In *Rewriting the Renaissance: The Discourses of Sexual Difference in Early Modern Europe,* ed. Margaret W. Ferguson, Maureen Quilligan, and Nancy J. Vickers, 65–87. Chicago: University of Chicago Press, 1986.

Morris, Helen. "Queen Elizabeth I 'Shadowed' in Cleopatra." *Huntington Library Quarterly* 32 (1969): 271–78.

Morrison, Toni. *Playing in the Dark: Whiteness and the Literary Imagination.* New York: Vintage, 1993.

Moryson, Fynes. *Shakespeare's Europe: A Survey of the Condition of Europe at the End of the Sixteenth Century, Being Unpublished Chapters of Fynes Moryson's Itinerary (1617).* 2d ed. New York: Blom, 1967.

Mullany, Steven. "Civic Rites, City Sites: The Place of the Stage." In *Staging the Renaissance: Reinterpretations of Elizabethan and Jacobean Drama,* ed. David Scott Kastan and Peter Stallybrass, 17–26. New York: Routledge, 1991.

————— *The Place of the Stage: License, Play, and Power in Renaissance England.* Chicago: University of Chicago Press, 1988.

Myerowitz, Molly. "The Domestication of Desire: Ovid's *Parva Tabella* and the Theatre of Love." In *Pornography and Representation in Greece and Rome,* ed. Amy Richlin, 131–55. New York: Oxford University Press, 1992.

Naish, Camille. *Death Comes to the Maiden: Sex and Executions, 1431–1933.* New York: Routledge, 1991.

Nathan, Norman. "Othello's Marriage Is Consummated." *Cahiers Elisabethian* 34 (1988): 79–82.

Nead, Lynda. *The Female Nude: Art, Obscenity, and Sexuality.* London: Routledge, 1992.

Neely, Carol Thomas. *Broken Nuptials in Shakespeare's Plays.* New Haven: Yale University Press, 1985.

—————. "Women and Men in *Othello.*" In *Critical Essays on Shakespeare's "Othello,"* ed. Anthony Gerard Barthelemy, 68–90. New York: G. K. Hall, 1994.

Neill, Michael. "Changing Places in *Othello.*" *Shakespeare Survey* 37 (1984): 115–31.

—————. Introduction to *The Tragedy of Antony and Cleopatra,* by William Shakespeare, 1–130. Oxford: Clarendon Press, 1994.

—————. "Unproper Beds: Race, Adultery, and the Hideous in *Othello.*" *Shakespeare Quarterly* 40 (1989): 383–412.

Nelson, T. G. A., and Charles Haines. "Othello's Unconsummated Marriage." *Essays in Criticism* 33 (1983): 1–18.

Newman, Karen. "'And wash the Ethiop white': Femininity and the Monstrous in *Othello.*" In *Shakespeare Reproduced: The Text in History and Ideology,* ed. Jean E. Howard and Marion F. O'Connor, 141–62. New York: Methuen, 1987.

Nichols, Bill. *Representing Reality: Issues and Concepts in Documentary.* Bloomington: Indiana University Press, 1991.

North, Thomas. Extract from *Plutarch's Lives* (trans., 1579). In *Antony and Cleopatra,* by William Shakespeare. Ed. M. R. Ridley. 241–78. Cambridge: Harvard University Press, 1954.

—————. "*The Life of Marcus Antonius* and *The Comparison of Demetrius with Antonius* (trans., 1579)," from *Plutarch's Lives.* In *A New Variorum Edition of Shakespeare: "Antony and Cleopatra,"* ed. Marvin Spevack, 395–459. New York: Modern Language Association of America, 1990.

Olivier, Laurence. *On Acting.* New York: Simon and Schuster, 1986.

Orgel, Stephen. "Nobody's Perfect: Or Why Did the English Stage Take Boys for Women?" In *Displacing Homophobia: Gay Male Perspectives in*

Literature and Culture, ed. Ronald R. Butters, John M. Clum, and Michael Moon, 7–29. Durham: Duke University Press, 1989.

Orkin, Martin. "Civility and the English Colonial Enterprise: Notes on Shakespeare's *Othello*." *Theoria* 68 (1986): 1–14.

———. "Othello and the 'Plain Face' of Racism." *Shakespeare Quarterly* 38 (1986): 166–88.

Orkin, Martin, and Ania Loomba, eds. *Post-Colonial Shakespeares*. New York: Routledge, 1998.

Ortner, Sherry B. "Is Female to Male as Nature Is to Culture?" In *Woman, Culture, and Society*, ed. Michelle Zimbalist Rosaldo and Louise Lamphere, 67–87. Stanford: Stanford University Press, 1974.

Ovid. *Fasti*. Trans. James George Frazer. 2d ed. Revised by G. P. Goold. The Loeb Classical Library. Cambridge: Harvard University Press, 1989.

———. *Metamorphoses*. Trans. Arthur Golding (1567). Carbondale, Ill.: Southern Illinois University Press, 1961.

Oxford Latin Dictionary. Ed. P. G. W. Glare. Oxford: Clarendon Press, 1968.

Painter, William. *The Palace of Pleasure*. Vol. 1. Ed. Joseph Jacobs (1890). Anglistica and Americana: A Series of Reprints. Hildesheim: Georg Olms Verlagsbuchhandlung, 1968.

Paré, Ambroise. *On Monsters and Marvels*. Trans. Janis L. Pallister. Chicago: University of Chicago Press, 1982.

Parker, Andrew, Mary Russo, Doris Sommer, and Patricia Yaeger, eds. *Nationalisms and Sexualities*. New York: Routledge, 1992.

Parker, Patricia. "Fantasies of 'Race' and 'Gender': Africa, *Othello*, and Bringing to Light." In *Women, "Race," and Writing in the Early Modern Period*, ed. Margo Hendricks and Patricia Parker, 84–100. London: Routledge, 1994.

———. "Shakespeare and Rhetoric: 'Dilation' and 'Delation' in *Othello*." In *Shakespeare and the Question of Theory*, ed. Patricia Parker and Geoffrey Hartman, 54–74. New York: Methuen, 1985.

———. *Shakespeare from the Margins: Language, Culture, Context*. Chicago: University of Chicago Press, 1996.

Paster, Gail Kern. *The Body Embarrassed: Drama and the Disciplines of Shame in Early Modern England*. Ithaca, N.Y.: Cornell University Press, 1993.

———. "'In the Spirit of Men There Is No Blood': Blood as Trope of Gender in *Julius Caesar*." *Shakespeare Quarterly* 40 (1989): 284–98.

Pieterse, Jan Nederveen. *White on Black: Images of Africa and Blacks in Western Popular Culture*. New Haven: Yale University Press, 1992.

Pittenger, Elizabeth. "'To Serve the Queere': Nicholas Udall, Master of Revels." In *Queering the Renaissance*, ed. Jonathan Goldberg, 162–89. Durham: Duke University Press, 1994.

Pratt, Mary Louise. *Imperial Eyes: Travel Writing and Transculturation*. London: Routledge, 1992.

———. "Scratches on the Face of the Country; or, What Mr. Barrow Saw in the Land of the Bushmen." In *"Race," Writing, and Difference*, ed. Henry Louis Gates Jr., 138–62. Chicago: University of Chicago Press, 1986.

Prince, F. T., ed., Introduction to *The Poems*, by William Shakespeare, xi–xlvi. London: Methuen, 1960.

Prynne, William. *Histrio-Mastix*. 1633. Repr., with a preface by Arthur Freeman, New York: Garland, 1974.

Purchas, Samuel. *Hakluytus Posthumus, or Purchas His Pilgrimes: Contayning a History of the World in Sea Voyages and Lande Travells by Englishmen and Others*. Vol. 1. Glasgow: J MacLehose and Sons, 1905.

Quinn, D[avid] B. " 'A Discourse of Ireland' (circa 1599): A Sidelight on English Colonial Policy." *Proceedings of the Royal Irish Academy* 47, sec. C (1942): 151–66.

———. *The Elizabethans and the Irish*. Ithaca, N.Y.: Cornell University Press, 1966.

Rabinowitz, Nancy Sorkin. *Anxiety Veiled: Euripides and the Traffic in Women*. Ithaca, N.Y.: Cornell University Press, 1993.

Rackin, Phyllis. "Androgyny, Mimesis, and the Marriage of the Boy Heroine on the English Renaissance Stage." *PMLA* 102 (1987): 29–41.

———. "Shakespeare's Boy Cleopatra, the Decorum of Nature, and the Golden World of Poetry." *PMLA* 87 (1972): 201–12.

Rainoldes, John. *Th' Overthrow of Stage Plays*. Middleburgh, 1599.

Ralegh, Sir Walter. *The Discoverie of the Large, Rich and Bewtiful Empyre of Guiana*. Transcribed, annotated, and introduced by Neil L. Whitehead. Norman: University of Oklahoma Press, 1997.

Rambuss, Richard. *Closet Devotions*. Durham: Duke University Press, 1998.

Richlin, Amy. *The Garden of Priapus: Sexuality and Aggression in Roman Humor*. New Haven: Yale University Press, 1983.

———. Introduction to *Pornography and Representation in Greece and Rome*, ed. Amy Richlin, xi–xxiii. New York: Oxford University Press, 1992.

———. "Reading Ovid's Rapes." In *Pornography and Representation in Greece and Rome*, ed. Amy Richlin, 158–79. New York: Oxford University Press, 1992.

Ridley, M. R. Introduction to *Othello*, by William Shakespeare. London: Methuen, 1958.

Rinehart, Keith. "Shakespeare's Cleopatra and England's Elizabeth." *Shakespeare Quarterly* 23 (1972): 81–86.

Roach, Joseph R. *Cities of the Dead: Circum-Atlantic Performance*. New York: Columbia University Press, 1996.

Rodgers, Bruce. *Gay Talk: A Dictionary of Gay Slang*. New York: Putnam, 1979.

Roper, William. *The Lyfe of Thomas Moore, Knighte*. Ed. James Mason Cline. 1626. Repr., New York: Swallow Press, 1950.

Rosaldo, Renato. *Culture and Truth: The Remaking of Social Analysis*. Boston: Beacon Press, 1993.

Rosenberg, Marvin. *The Masks of Othello: The Search for the Identity of Othello, Iago, and Desdemona by Three Centuries of Actors and Critics*. Berkeley: University of California Press, 1961.

Rowe, Katherine A. "Dismembering and Forgetting in *Titus Andronicus*." *Shakespeare Quarterly* 45 (1994): 279–303.

Rudnytsky, Peter L. "The Purloined Handkerchief in *Othello*." In *The Psycho-analytic Study of Literature*, ed. Joseph Reppen and Maurice Charney. Hillsdale, N.J.: Analytic Press, 1985.

Ruggiero, Guido. *The Boundaries of Eros: Sex Crime and Sexuality in Renaissance Venice*. Studies in the History of Sexuality. New York: Oxford University Press, 1985.

Said, Edward. *Culture and Imperialism*. New York: Knopf, 1993.

———. *Orientalism*. New York: Vintage, 1979.

Salomon, Nanette. "Positioning Women in Visual Convention: The Case of Elizabeth I." In *Attending to Women in Early Modern England*, ed. Betty S. Travitsky and Adele F. Seeff, 64–95. Newark: University of Delaware Press, 1994.

Schulenberg, Jane T. "The Heroics of Virginity: Brides of Christ and Sacrificial Mutilation." In *Women in the Middle Ages and Renaissance*, ed. Mary Beth Rose, 29–72. Syracuse: Syracuse University Press, 1986.

Scobie, Edward. *Black Britannia: A History of Blacks in Britain*. Chicago: Johnson Publishing, 1972.

Scott, Mark W., ed. *Shakespearean Criticism*. Vol. 4. Detroit: Gale Research, 1987.

Sedgwick, Eve Kosofsky. *Between Men: English Literature and Male Homosocial Desire*. New York: Columbia University Press, 1985.

———. *Epistemology of the Closet*. Berkeley: University of California Press, 1990.

———. "Paranoid Reading and Reparative Reading; or, You're So Paranoid, You Probably Think This Introduction Is About You." In *Novel Gazing: Queer Readings in Fiction*, ed. Eve Kosofsky Sedgwick, 1–37. Durham: Duke University Press, 1997.

Shakespeare, William. *Antony and Cleopatra*. Ed. M. R. Ridley. Cambridge: Harvard University Press, 1954.

———. *Antony and Cleopatra*. In *A New Variorum Edition of Shakespeare*. Ed. Marvin Spevack. New York: Modern Language Association of America, 1991.

———. *The Merchant of Venice*. Ed. Kenneth Myrick. New York: New American Library, 1965.

———. *A Midsummer Night's Dream*. Ed. Wolfgang Clemen. The Signet
    Classic Shakespeare. New York: New American Library, 1963.
———. *Othello*. Ed. Alvin Kernan. New York: New American Library, 1963.
———. *Othello*. In *A New Variorum Edition of Shakespeare*. Ed. Horace Howard
    Furness. 1886. Repr., New York: Dover, 1963.
———. *Othello*. Ed. M. R. Ridley. The Arden Shakespeare. London: Methuen,
    1958.
———. *The Poems*. Ed. F. T. Price. The Arden Shakespeare. New York: Rout-
    ledge, 1961.
———. *Riverside Shakespeare*. Ed. G. Blakemore Evans. Boston: Houghton
    Mifflin, 1974.
———. *Titus Andronicus*. Ed. Eugene M. Waith. Oxford: Clarendon Press, 1984.
———. *The Tragedy of Antony and Cleopatra*. Ed. Michael Neill. Oxford:
    Clarendon Press, 1994.
*Shakespearean Criticism: Excerpts from the Criticism of William Shakespeare's Plays
    and Poetry, from the First Published Appraisals to Current Evaluations*. Vol.
    4, ed. Laurie Lanzen Harris. Detroit: Gale Research, 1984.
Shapiro, Barbara J. *Probability and Certainty in Seventeenth-Century England: A
    Study of the Relationships Between Natural Science, Religion, History, Law,
    and Literature*. Princeton, N.J.: Princeton University Press, 1983.
Shapiro, Michael. *Gender in Play on the Shakespearean Stage: Boy Heroines and
    Female Pages*. Ann Arbor: University of Michigan Press, 1997.
Sheehan, Bernard W. *Savagism and Civility: Indians and Englishmen in Colonial
    Virginia*. Cambridge: Cambridge University Press, 1980.
Shuger, Debora K. "Irishmen, Aristocrats, and Other White Barbarians."
    Renaissance Quarterly 51 (1997): 492–524.
———. *The Renaissance Bible: Scholarship, Sacrifice, and Subjectivity*. Berkeley:
    University of California Press, 1994.
Sidney, Philip. "A Discourse on Irish Affairs (A Fragment)." *The Prose Works of
    Philip Sidney*. Vol. 3, ed. Albert Feuillerat. Cambridge: Cambridge
    University Press, 1963.
Simone, Reno Thomas. *Shakespeare and "Lucrece": A Study of the Poem and Its
    Relation to the Plays*. Salzburg: University of Salzburg, 1974.
Singh, Jyotsna. "Renaissance Antitheatricality, Antifeminism, and Shakespeare's
    Antony and Cleopatra." *Renaissance Drama* 20 (1989): 99–121.
Sissa, Giulia. *Greek Virginity*. Trans. Arthur Goldhammer. Cambridge: Harvard
    University Press, 1990.
Smith, Bruce R. *Homosexual Desire in Shakespeare's England*. Chicago:
    University of Chicago Press, 1991.
Smith, Molly. "The Theater and the Scaffold: Death as Spectacle in *The Spanish
    Tragedy*." *Studies in English Literature, 1500–1900* 32 (1992): 217–32.

Snowden, Frank M., Jr. *Before Color Prejudice*. Cambridge: Harvard University Press, 1983.

Snyder, Susan, ed. *The Divine Weeks and Works of Guillaume de Saluste, Sieur Du Bartas*. New York: Oxford University Press, 1979.

Sowell, Thomas. *Markets and Minorities*. New York: Basic Books, 1981.

Spenser, Edmund. *The Faerie Queene*. Ed. Thomas P. Roche Jr. New Haven: Yale University Press, 1981.

———. *Spenser: Poetical Works*. Ed. J. C. Smith and E. de Sélincourt. 1912. Repr., New York: Oxford University Press, 1983.

———. *A View of the State of Ireland: From the First Printed Edition ([James Ware] 1633)*. Ed. Andrew Hadfield and Willy Maley. Oxford: Blackwell, 1997.

———. *A View*. Vol. 9 of *The Complete Works in Verse and Prose of Edmund Spenser*, ed. Alexander B. Grosart. N.p.: priv. circ., 1882–84.

Spivak, Gayatri Chakravorty. Translator's preface to *Of Grammatology*, by Jacques Derrida, ix–lxxxvii. Baltimore: Johns Hopkins University Press, 1976.

Splitter, Randolph. "Language, Sexual Conflict and 'Symbiosis Anxiety' in *Othello*." *Mosaic* 15 (1982): 17–26.

Sponsler, Claire. "Outlaw Masculinities: Drag, Blackface, and Late Medieval Laboring-Class Festivities." In *Becoming Male in the Middle Ages*, ed. Jeffrey Cohen and Bonnie Wheeler. The New Middle Ages. New York: Garland, 1997.

Sponsler, Claire, and Robert L. A. Clark. "Othered Bodies: Racial Cross-Dressing in the *Mistere de la Sainte Hostie* and the Croxton *Play of the Sacrament*." *Journal of Medieval and Early Modern Studies* 29 (1999): 61–87.

Spoto, Donald. *Laurence Olivier: A Biography*. New York: HarperCollins, 1992.

Stallybrass, Peter. "Patriarchal Territories: The Body Enclosed." In *Rewriting the Renaissance: The Discourses of Sexual Difference in Early Modern Europe*, ed. Margaret W. Ferguson, Maureen Quilligan, and Nancy J. Vickers, 123–42. Chicago: University of Chicago Press, 1986.

Stewart, Susan. *On Longing: Narratives of the Miniature, the Gigantic, the Souvenir, the Collection*. Baltimore: Johns Hopkins University Press, 1984.

Stimpson, Catherine R. "Shakespeare and the Soil of Rape." In *The Woman's Part*, ed. Carolyn Ruth Swift Lenz, Gayle Greene, and Carol Thomas Neely, 56–64. Urbana: University of Illinois Press, 1980.

Stoye, John. *English Travellers Abroad, 1604–1667: Their Influence in English Society and Politics*. Rev. ed. New Haven: Yale University Press, 1989.

Strong, Roy C. *Gloriana: The Portraits of Queen Elizabeth I*. New York: Thames and Hudson, 1987.

————. *Splendour at Court: Renaissance Spectacle and Illusion.* London: Weiden-
    feld and Nicholson, 1973.
Stubbs, John. *The Discovery of a Gaping Gulf whereinto England is like to be
    Swallowed by an other French Marriage.* Ed. Lloyd E. Berry. 1579. Repr.,
    Charlottesville: University Press of Virginia for the Folger Library,
    1968.
Suetonius. "Tiberius." *Suetonius.* Trans. J. C. Rolfe. Vol. 1. The Loeb Classical
    Library. 1914. Repr., London: William Heinemann, 1928.
Suzuki, Mihoko. *Metamorphoses of Helen: Authority, Difference, and the Epic.*
    Ithaca, N.Y.: Cornell University Press, 1989.
Sylvester, Beckford. "Natural Mutability and Human Responsibility: Form in
    Shakespeare's *Lucrece.*" *College English* 26 (1965): 505–11.
Tacitus. *The Annals.* Vols. 4–12. Trans. John Jackson. The Loeb Classical Library.
    Cambridge: Harvard University Press: 1951.
Tennenhouse, Leonard. *Power on Display: The Politics of Shakespeare's Genres.*
    New York: Methuen, 1986.
————. "Violence Done to Women on the Renaissance Stage." In *The Violence
    of Representation: Literature and the History of Violence,* ed. Nancy Arm-
    strong and Leonard Tennenhouse, 77–97. New York: Routledge, 1989.
Thomas, Keith Vivian. *Man and the Natural World: Changing Attitudes in England,
    1500–1800.* London: Allen Lane, 1983.
Tiffin, Chris, and Alan Lawson, eds. *De-scribing Empire: Post-colonialism and
    Textuality.* London: Routledge, 1994.
Todorov, Tzvetan. "'Race,' Writing, and Culture." In *"Race," Writing, and
    Difference,* ed. Henry Louis Gates Jr., 370–80. Chicago: University of
    Chicago Press, 1986.
Tokson, Elliot H. *The Popular Image of the Black Man in English Drama, 1550–
    1688.* Boston: G. K. Hall, 1982.
Torgovnick, Marianna. *Gone Primitive: Savage Intellects, Modern Lives.* Chicago:
    University of Chicago Press, 1990.
Tourneur, Cyril. *The Revenger's Tragedy. Drama in the English Renaissance.* Vol. 2,
    The Stuart Period, ed. Russell A. Fraser and Norman Rabkin, 21–54.
    New York: Macmillan, 1976.
Traub, Valerie. *Desire and Anxiety: Circulations of Sexuality in Shakespearean
    Drama.* London: Routledge, 1992.
Tricomi, Albert H. "The Aesthetics of Mutilation in *Titus Andronicus.*"
    Shakespeare Survey 27 (1974): 11–19.
————. *Reading Tudor-Stuart Texts Through Cultural Historicism.* Gainesville:
    University Press of Florida, 1996.
Tudela, Rabbi Benjamin of. *The Itinerary of Rabbi Benjamin of Tudela.* Vol. 1.
    Trans. and ed. A. Asher. New York: "Hakesheth" Publishing Co.,
    1942.

Tyler, Carol-Anne. "Boys Will Be Girls: The Politics of Gay Drag." In *Inside/ Out: Lesbian Theories, Gay Theories*, ed. Diana Fuss, 32–70. New York: Routledge, 1991.

Vaughan, Virginia Mason. *"Othello": A Contextual History*. Cambridge: Cambridge University Press, 1994.

Vickers, Brian. *Appropriating Shakespeare: Contemporary Critical Quarrels*. New Haven: Yale University Press, 1993.

Vickers, Nancy. " 'The Blazon of Sweet Beauty's Best': Shakespeare's *Lucrece*." In *Shakespeare and the Question of Theory*, ed. Patricia Parker and Geoffrey Hartman, 95–115. New York: Methuen, 1985.

———. "Diana Described: Scattered Women and Scattered Rhyme." In *Writing and Sexual Difference*, ed. Elizabeth Abel, 95–109. Brighton, Sussex: Harvester Press, 1982.

Vitkus, Daniel J. "Turning Turk in *Othello*: The Conversion and Damnation of the Moor." *Shakespeare Quarterly* 48 (1997): 145–76.

Waith, Eugene. "The History of Titus Andronicus." In *Titus Andronicus*, by William Shakespeare, ed. Eugene Waith. Oxford: Clarendon Press, 1984.

Waith, E. W. *The Herculean Hero in Marlow, Chapman, Shakespeare, and Dryden*. New York: Columbia University Press, 1962.

Walvin, James. *Black and White: The Negro in English Society, 1555–1945*. London: Penguin, 1973.

Warner, William Beatty. *Chance and the Text of Experience: Freud, Nietzsche, and Shakespeare's "Hamlet."* Ithaca, N.Y.: Cornell University Press, 1986.

Washington, Joseph R. *Anti-Blackness in English Religion, 1500–1800*. New York: E. Mellen Press, 1984.

Watney, Simon. *Practices of Freedom: Selected Writings on HIV/AIDS*. Durham: Duke University Press, 1994.

Webster's Third New International Dictionary of the English Language. Unabridged. Ed. Philip Babcock Grove et al. Springfield, Mass.: Merriam-Webster, 1986.

Wheelwright, Philip. *The Burning Fountain*. Rev. ed. Bloomington: Indiana University Press, 1968.

Whitehead, Neil L. Introduction to *The Discoverie of the Large, Rich and Bewtiful Empyre of Guiana*, by Sir Walter Ralegh. Norman: University of Oklahoma Press, 1997.

Williams, Gordon. *A Dictionary of Sexual Language and Imagery in Shakespearean and Stuart Literature*. London: Athlone Press, 1994.

Woodbridge, Linda. "Palisading the Body Politic." In *True Rites and Maimed Rites: Ritual and Anti-Ritual in Shakespeare and His Age*, ed. Linda Woodbridge and Edward Berry, 270–98. Urbana: University of Illinois Press, 1992.

———— *Women and the English Renaissance: Literature and the Nature of Womankind, 1540–1620.* Chicago: University of Chicago Press, 1984.

Woodbridge, Linda, and Edward Berry, eds. *True Rites and Maimed Rites: Ritual and Anti-Ritual in Shakespeare and His Age.* Urbana: University of Illinois Press, 1992.

Wynne-Davies, Marion. "'The Swallowing Womb': Consumed and Consuming Women in *Titus Andronicus*." In *The Matter of Difference: Materialist Feminist Criticism of Shakespeare*, ed. Valerie Wayne, 129–51. Ithaca, N.Y.: Cornell University Press, 1991.

Index

In this index, the word *passim* indicates scattered references to the index term within the page range specified; page numbers in *italics* indicate illustrative material.

Mummings, 173–74
Murder, 178; of Bassianus, 53; of Desde-
mona, 75, 85–87, 90–98, 101; of
Lavinia, 55–58. *See also* Self-sacrifice
Mythopoesis, 53–54
Mythos/mythology, 1, 4, 54; Dido and
Aeneas, 114–16; Lucrece, 29–30,
186n12, 187n14; origin myths,
76–78, 206–207n44; Phaeton, 76,
196n32

Nathan, Norman, 200n62
National-imperial culture, 1, 10–27
passim, 69, 86–87, 117, 126–41 *passim*,
156, 184n39, 192n86. *See also*
Imperialism
National Theatre (Old Vic), 94
Nation/empire, 34, 59
Natural order, 58, 120, 132–33, 136,
215n30
Natural selection, 152
Natural subjects, 16, 59
Nead, Lynda, 32–33, 38
Needham, Catherine, 147, 213n10,
214n12
Neely, Carol Thomas, 205n35
Negroes, 16–17. *See also* Africans
Neill, Michael, 195nn21,22, 196n25,
197n35; on *Antony and Cleopatra*,
134, 210n82, 212–13n8, 219n70; on
Othello, 79, 87, 201–202nn70,71
Nelson, T. G. A., 197–98n43, 200n62
New English, 23–24, 131–34, 135
New historicism, 5–7, 12, 18, 139,
182n20, 183n32, 184–85n42
Newman, Karen, 77, 195n22
New World, 6, 206n43
Nichols, Bill, 147, 213n10, 214n12
"Nigger" Shakespeare, 95
Nile, 216n33
Nostalgia, 23, 106, 117–18, 122, 126,
204n13, 210nn80,81. *See also*
Realpolitik nostalgia
Numbers, Book of, 66

Octavius (in *Antony and Cleopatra*), 162,
210n82
Old English, 23–24, 129–34 *passim*, 139,
192n86; 209n67
Old Vic (National Theatre), 94
Olivier, Sir Laurence, 94–95, 97, 98,
203n77
Orgel, Stephen, 219n69
Orientalism, 143, 154, 161, 170, 195–
96n23, 196n24, 212n2, 215n27
Origin myths, 76–78, 206–207n44
Orkin, Martin, 194n7, 197n38
Oroonoko, in *Oroonoko, or the Royal
Slave,* 165, 166, 217–18nn56,57
Orpheus, 54
Othello, 13, 21, 68–101 *passim*;
ambivalent racial identity of, 94–97,
100–1; black actors, 95–97, 184n33,
201–202n70, 203nn81,82; blackness
of, 22, 72–79 *passim*, 83–86, 93–98
passim, 106, 195n22, 198–99nn46,48,
202n74, 218n56; caricatures of,
95–97, *96, 97*, 165; and Desdemona,
5, 80–88, 199n50; and Iago, 82–85;
white actors as, 22, 78, 94–97,
202n74, 203nn81,82; "whitening"
of, 94–97
Othello, 1, 22, 68–101 *passim*, 123–24,
194n7, 199–200n56; "abuse" used
in, 88–90; Desdemona/Othello
relationship, 5, 79, 80–87, 200n62;
dream scenes, 82–83; handkerchief
scene, 80–81; homosexuality, 83–86
passim, 200nn57,58; illustrations for,
91, *92, 96, 97, 98,* 165, 202n71;
miscegenation, 59, 62–63, 72, 87, 93;
pre-texts, 75, 78, 79–80; primal
scene, 81–82, 86–87, 198–99nn46,
48,50; race, 75, 78–86, 197n35; rape/
murder scene, 75, 79, 85–87, 90–98,
101, 201–202nn70,71; symbolism of
bed and handkerchief, 79–82, 86,
101, 197nn39,43, 198n46; "thief"
scene, 88–90; as white sacrificial

Prejudice, 81
Preston, Mary, 78
Priapic appetite, 34
Primal scene, 81–82, 86–87,
198–99nn46,48,50
Primitivism, 126, 138, 152
Prince of Morocco (in *The Merchant of Venice*), 71–72, 196n27
Privy Council, deportation order, 73–74
"Prohibiting Portraits of the Queen,"
33–36, 187–88nn28,29, 192n85,
208n63
Protestantism, 68, 71, 131, 132
Prynne, William, 220n85
Psalms, Book of, 66, 158
Purchas, Samuel, 83
Purity: and imperialism, 69, 86–87, 132,
141–42; whiteness of, 162–67

Queer/queering, 119–22, 170, 172–76,
205n28
Quin, James, 185n2
Quinn, David, 152, 207nn47,54, 208n62,
209n77
Quintius, 51, 52–53

Rabinowitz, Nancy Sorkin, 9
Race/race narratives, 1–18 *passim*, 105,
190n50, 207n45, 209n73, 213n8; in
Antony and Cleopatra, 1, 5, 13, 87,
115, 116, 122–24; criminality of, 63,
190n50; disguising of, 60–61; in early
modern culture, 6, 7, 9, 126–27,
192n86, 208n59; and gender, 4, 12,
104, 163, 217–18n55,56,57; and
identity, 69–70, 163–67, 209n73; in
Othello, 72, 94–97, 100–101, 217–
18nn55,56,57; racial conversion, 24,
65, 163–79; racial difference, 5, 7, 23,
58, 60, 63; Shakespearean constructs
of, 14–15, 24, 27, 97–98, 100–101;
whiteness and purity, 59, 69, 122,
161, 162–67. *See also* Miscegenation,
Rape/rape narratives

"Racialist ideology," 195n21
Racism, 1, 4, 7, 11, 20, 75, 197n34,
205n37; function of, 18, 207n52;
language of, 76; in modern literary
criticism, 75; in *Othello*, 197n38
Rackin, Phyllis, 219n71
Radical realism, 144, 153
Rainoldes, John, 220n85
Raleigh, Sir Walter, 194n12
Rambuss, Richard, 185n42
Rape of Lucrece, The, 12, 31, 45–46, 63,
88, 107, 190n50, 201n70, 211n88
Rape of Lucrece (myth), 29–30,
186n12, 187n14
Rape/rape narratives, 1–5, 21–29, 48–
67 *passim*, 88, 101, 127–28; of culture,
11, 45, 58; and death, 27, 28, 87, 164,
185–86n4; in early modern culture,
28, 42, 58–59, 87, 148, 186nn7,8,10,
190n51; and homosexuality, 111, 118,
200n58; and marriage, 34, 53; and
miscegenation, 5, 44, 57, 59, 63, 65;
in *Othello*, 93–94, 148–49, 176; and
pollution, 60–62, 193n90; and
Priapic appetite, 34; racializing of, 4,
11, 45, 58–67, 90–94, 148, 177–78,
192–93n89; in *Titus Andronicus*, 48–
54, 62–67. *See also* Sacrifice/sacrifice
narratives
Rape-sacrifice, 9; of Lavinia, 25–27,
48–58, 62–67, 190–91n63; of
Lucrece, 29–57 *passim*, 89, 111–18
passim, 128, 164, 169–70, 188n35; in
Rome, 27, 48–57, 149, 185–86n4,
214n16
Rapists: black men as, 4, 5, 11, 22,
58–67, 87–93 *passim*, 101; Othello
as, 86–87, 90, 93, 101
Raptus (bride theft), 49–50, 86–101, 105
Ravenscroft, Edward, 57, 185n2
Realpolitik: metatheatrical space, 153–
57; murder, 178; nostalgia, 15–17, 71,
134–42
Redemption, 58–67

CPSIA information can be obtained
at www.ICGtesting.com
Printed in the USA
JSHW031047101222
34657JS00002B/147